Praise for James Reasoner

"Epic, well-researched historical fiction." —*Booklist*

"Reasoner spins a lively, suspenseful yarn." —*Publishers Weekly*

"A detailed work of historical fiction by a gifted writer."
—*The BookWatch*

"Climbs into the hearts and minds of the people who lived it and portrays vividly the volatile political situation as state after state seceded from the Union. . . . The reader can almost feel the heat of battle." —*Victoria (TX) Advocate*

"A tremendous Southern war story without the moonlight, magnolias, and plantations; a down-to-earth story of the common people. Don't miss it!" —*Valdosta (GA) Daily News*

"A ripping good read." —*The Civil War News*

JAMES REASONER

DRAW

THE GREATEST GUNFIGHTS OF THE
AMERICAN WEST

BERKLEY BOOKS, NEW YORK

IB

A Berkley Book
Published by The Berkley Publishing Group
A division of Penguin Group (USA) Inc.
375 Hudson Street, New York, New York 10014

This book is an original publication of The Berkley Publishing Group.

Copyright © 2003 by James Reasoner.
Title page photograph courtesy of Texas State Library and Archives Commission.
Cover design by Steve Ferlauto.
Text design by Tiffany Estreicher.

PRINTING HISTORY
Berkley trade paperback edition / December 2003

Library of Congress Cataloging-in-Publication Data

Reasoner, James.
    Draw : the greatest gunfights of the American West / James Reasoner. —
Berkley trade pbk. ed.
        p. cm.
    Includes bibliographical references.
    ISBN 978-0-425-19193-4
    1. Frontier and pioneer life—West (U.S.)—Anecdotes. 2. Outlaws—West
(U.S.)—Biography—Anecdotes. 3. Violence—West (U.S.)—History—19th
century—Anecdotes. 4. Firearms—West (U.S.)—History—19th century—
Anecdotes. 5. West (U.S.)—History—19th century—Anecdotes. 6. West
(U.S.)—Biography—Anecdotes. I. Title: Greatest gunfights of the American
West. II. Title.

F596.R3595   2003
364.1'092'278—dc22   2003060690
PRINTED IN THE UNITED STATES OF AMERICA

20   19   18   17   16   15   14   13

For Livia, Shayna, and Joanna

CONTENTS

INTRODUCTION

For more than two decades, I've been spinning yarns about the American West. Though many of these books and stories have what I hope is a solid historical background, in the final analysis, all of them are fiction. The stories in this volume, however, are true, as historically accurate as I could make them and flavored with what I think is reasonable speculation about the thoughts and emotions of the people involved in them. Because the people are at the heart of any story, historical or fiction.

I hope I've done right by the extraordinary people in these stories. That was my aim.

Thanks to Kimberly Lionetti, a fine editor who has been involved with this project from the beginning. And special thanks to fellow author L. J. Washburn, who did the lion's share of the research and truly made everything come together . . . and who, in real life, happens to be my beautiful wife Livia. Appreciation is also due to the many fine writers and historians who have come before me and done such a wonderful job of chronicling the history of the Old West. This book would not exist except for the trails they blazed.

More than anything else, I've always considered myself a storyteller. I hope you, the reader, enjoy these yarns. I think they're good'uns.

James Reasoner

PART ONE

MAN TO MAN

Go get your gun. We'll fight it out.

—*Warren Earp*

LUKE SHORT'S WHITE ELEPHANT SHOOT-OUT

On the evening of February 7, 1887, Luke Short paused just inside the doorway of the White Elephant Saloon, an establishment he owned in partnership with several other men. The White Elephant was one of the finest saloons, restaurants, and gambling halls in Fort Worth, Texas. Located at 310 West Main Street, it had a listing in the city directory that boasted of its menu featuring fresh fish, oysters, and wild game. The saloon area offered only the best wines, liquors, and cigars. It was dominated by a forty-foot-long mahogany bar, an ornate back-bar with an arched mirror, and cut-glass chandeliers that spread a warm yellow glow over the opulent scene. In the rear of the room was a wide, carpeted staircase that led up to Luke Short's pride and joy: the second-floor gaming rooms that he ruled like a veritable king. In fact, since his arrival in Fort Worth a little over three years earlier in 1883, he had become known as "the king of the gamblers." Chuck-a-luck Johnny Gallagher had told him up in Dodge City that he ought to try his luck in Fort Worth, and the move had worked out well for Short.

The prospect of giving all this up was enough to make a man pause and think it over. Short had made up his mind, though, and he was not going back on the decision now. He walked on into the White Elephant. He was small in stature, a nattily dressed man with a neatly trimmed mustache. He raised a hand in greeting to Jake Johnson, one of his partners in the enterprise. Short had made up his mind to sell his interest in the place to Johnson.

Short and Johnson moved to the stairs. Short's gaze flicked around the room. Though he had checked the saloon's occupants when he first entered, the sort of habit that kept a man alive on the frontier, he examined them again just to be sure no enemies were lurking nearby.

There was no sign of the man Short was looking for, former Marshal Timothy Courtright.

The two gamblers went upstairs and stepped into a small office to conclude their deal. Short took the bill of sale, rested it on the desk, plucked a pen from its holder, signed his name, and then dated the document: February 7, 1887.

The transaction was finished.

LUKE Short was born in either Mississippi or Arkansas—the record is unclear on that—in 1854, one of seven children born to J. W. and Hettie Short. The family moved to Texas in 1856, when Luke was a toddler two years of age, and settled on Elm Creek in Grayson County, seventy miles northeast of Fort Worth. Luke had not left the state again until he was a young man working as a cowboy on the cattle drives across Indian Territory to the railhead in Kansas. Cowboying had not suited him, so after a while, he stayed in Kansas and tried his luck at gambling.

For the first time in his life, Luke Short had found what he was meant to do.

Gamblers were a restless bunch, drifting around the frontier

Luke Short . . . This dapper gambler and gunman was widely known and respected on the frontier . . . and feared by those who crossed him.

(Courtesy of National Archives and Records Administration)

94129

The so-called Dodge City Peace Commission. Standing, left to right: W. H. Harris, Luke Short, Bat Masterson. Seated, left to right: Charley Bassett, Wyatt Earp, Frank McLain, Neal Brown. In June of 1881 this illustrious group, most of them former lawmen, gathered in Dodge City because of friction between Luke Short and the city's mayor. What could have been a violent confrontation never came about, probably because no one wanted to face this bunch of famous gunmen.

(Courtesy of National Archives and Records Administration)

towns, their only true friends the men who followed the same
siren song. Short made friends: Wyatt Earp and Doc Holliday,
who were usually together but not always, and the former buffalo
hunter and scout Bat Masterson. "The Dodge City Gang," the
four of them were called when they were dealing in Tombstone,
Arizona Territory, because they had come there from Dodge.
Short's stay in Tombstone was marred by a run-in with a man
named Charlie Storms, who'd gotten liquored up and come looking for Short, intending to gun him down for some slight offense.
That had worked out badly for Charlie, who was so drunk when
he reached for his gun that he might as well have been moving in
slow motion. Short emptied his Colt .45 into Charlie's body
before the man got off a shot.

Short moved back to Dodge not long after that and went to
work dealing faro at the Long Branch Saloon. He was so successful that he bought an interest in the saloon, then found himself in
the middle of a conflict with the owners of the rival Alamo
Saloon. The owners of the Alamo aligned themselves with the so-
called "reform" political movement, which was really out to
reform things by shutting down competing businesses. Fearing
the tense situation would deteriorate into violence, Short put out
the word, and his friends answered. Not long after that, Wyatt,
Bat, Doc, and several other gun-toting acquaintances rode into
Dodge, and Short formed them into what he jokingly called the
Dodge City Peace Commission.

The name may have been a joke, but the result of the commission's formation was that peace did indeed descend on Dodge
City once more. Nobody wanted to go up against that bunch.
The whole affair left a sour taste in Short's mouth, however. He
had never cared for the sort of political infighting that brought on
what came to be known as the Dodge City War. He only wanted
to be left alone to run his gambling rooms and make a living in
the manner he most enjoyed. So when Chuck-a-luck Johnny told
him that Fort Worth was wide open, Luke Short went back home

to Texas, taking with him his wife Marie, an unusually beautiful woman whom he had married in Tombstone.

Their house in Fort Worth was at Sixth and Pecan, a good eight-block walk from the White Elephant. Luke Short was careful to keep his family life separate from his career as a gambler and saloon owner.

At the southern end of downtown Fort Worth was the area known as Hell's Half Acre, a section of rowdy saloons, cribs, and gambling dens near the railroad tracks and the Texas & Pacific depot. The White Elephant was not one of those dives. It was uptown, which meant it was fancier, quieter, more genteel. Still, in the winter of 1887, it was not unusual to see Timothy Courtright in the place. Courtright was a tall, lean man who habitually wore a dark suit and vest, a tan hat, a white shirt, and a string tie. The gunbelt strapped around his hips sported two holsters. Twin Colts rode butt-forward in the holsters. Courtright had a mustache and long, fair hair that waved around his ears and fell over the back of his neck.

Timothy Isaiah "Longhair Jim" Courtright was a mere shadow of the man he had been a decade earlier, but there was still an air of menace about him. People who had been around Fort Worth when Courtright served three terms as city marshal, from 1876 to 1879, swore that there was no one faster or more accurate with his guns. The past few years had sullied his reputation somewhat, but still, no one wanted to cross him.

During Courtright's visit to the White Elephant on February 7, Jake Johnson informed him that he had just bought Luke Short's interest in the business. There had been trouble between Courtright and Short, and perhaps Johnson was trying to head off any further friction. However, it was possible that this could backfire. Courtright considered Johnson a friend, and perhaps it was because of that, and because of Johnson's part-ownership of the White Elephant, that he had not pressed his feud with Luke Short.

Perhaps now Courtright would consider Short fair game.

Courtright had always been a drinker, even when he was serving as city marshal. The fact that he wore a badge never stopped him from drinking and gambling and shooting pool. But he did a good job of keeping Hell's Half Acre under control. His reputation as a gunman made even the toughest man leery of crossing him.

But the times were different now, and Luke Short was an uncommon man with steady nerves and a cool head. Those were the qualities that had made Short a success as a gambler and kept him alive in times of trouble. But if it came to a showdown with Courtright, could Short match the former marshal's speed? No one knew.

A decade earlier, Courtright had ruled Fort Worth, wearing the city marshal's badge and keeping the peace—but not with such a tight grip that the money ever stopped flowing. He arrested the troublemakers, but only after they had spent all they had to spend in the saloons and cribs and gambling dens, and everyone was happy. The city fathers, with their air of respectability tainted by greed; the saloon owners; the madams; the slick-fingered dealers; the soiled doves . . . everyone got their cut, including the marshal and his deputies, who augmented their meager salaries with a hefty percentage of the fines they created with their arrests. The money Courtright made in this manner, along with the wages his wife Betty drew from her employment at Ella Blackwell's Shooting Gallery, enabled them to live in style.

Then, suddenly, it was all over. He finished third in a five-man race in the annual election for city marshal. Just like that, he was turned out of the office he had so enjoyed filling.

Gambling and drinking were the only other things he was good at. He tried to make a living running a keno game, but it was hard. So was living in Fort Worth with all its reminders of his past glories. He'd decided it was time for a change of scenery and headed west. He worked as a guard for a mining company in Lake Valley, New Mexico, then fell in with an old friend who was also fast on the draw, Jim McIntire. Both of them went to work for a wealthy, powerful rancher, John Logan, who happened to have been Courtright's commanding officer when a much younger Tim was serving as a scout in the Union Army during the Civil War.

Logan hired Courtright and McIntire for their gun skills, not for their abilities as cowboys. Squatters and rustlers were moving into the area, and it was their job to clean out those elements. They did that job a little too well to suit the New Mexican authorities, gunning down a couple of stubborn sodbusters on May 4, 1883.

It was back to Texas for Courtright and McIntire, one jump ahead of the law.

Courtright returned to Fort Worth, figuring he would be safe there in his old haunts. Thinking that he could cash in on his law-enforcement experience, he opened the Commercial Detective Agency. It was none too successful, but it kept him in bullets and whiskey.

Then the New Mexico authorities had gotten the cooperation of the Texas Rangers in capturing Courtright. They tricked him, coming up to him in the Cattle Exchange Saloon in Hell's Half Acre on October 18, 1884, and asking him to look at some photographs for them. The photographs were pictures of outlaws, the Rangers said, and they wanted to know if Courtright had seen any of them around Fort Worth.

Courtright had gone with the lawmen to the Ginocchio Hotel, where he'd found drawn guns waiting for him instead of photographs of miscreants. The more sensible part of him had prevailed, and he had allowed them to take him into custody without putting up a fight. Word got around quickly that Longhair Jim had been arrested. Courtright still had friends in Fort Worth, a lot of them, in fact. A mob gathered outside the hotel, and the authorities had been forced to slip Courtright out the back way and hustle him into a carriage, then make a run for it to the city jail at the other end of town. The effort was successful, and Courtright had to suffer the galling humiliation of being locked up in the same hoosegow that he had filled with prisoners nearly every night.

The law had him, but not for long. A man of Courtright's reputation and standing in the community did not eat off a tray brought into the jail. Accompanied by guards, he went across the street to the Merchant's Restaurant for his meals. His friends soon took advantage of that arrangement to concoct an escape plan. One evening when Courtright sat down to supper at his usual table, there were two pistols hidden underneath it, hanging on nails and just waiting for his supple hands to grasp them.

Courtright's guards found themselves staring down the barrels of those weapons. They were not foolish enough to try to stop him as he backed out of the restaurant, leaped onto a waiting horse, and raced away.

If the story had stopped there, Courtright might have ridden off into legend. People would have talked for years about the daring escape. But after a couple of years, he had gotten homesick. He missed Betty, too. A fugitive from the law could not very well drag his wife around with him. Eventually, Courtright had decided that he had to turn himself in and take his chances with the New Mexico courts.

Several years had passed since the shooting of the homesteaders. Witnesses had died or moved on in that time. The territory's case pretty much collapsed, and in the spring of 1886, Courtright was back in Fort Worth, cleared of all charges by a New Mexico jury. He was free to do whatever he wanted. He reopened the detective agency and started visiting the gambling halls again. Longhair Jim Courtright was home.

But things had changed. Fort Worth had a new king of the gamblers.

His name was Luke Short.

ACTUALLY, Courtright and Short were not strangers to each other. They got along well enough so that Short even loaned Courtright some money when Courtright was on his way to New Mexico Territory to stand trial for the killings.

But it was only a matter of time before friction developed. Courtright was a denizen of the southern end of town, Hell's Half Acre. Short was firmly ensconced uptown. Perhaps if they had stayed separated by a dozen or so blocks, nothing would have happened. But the White Elephant was just too tempting a target for the scheme that Courtright developed soon after his return to Fort Worth.

Courtright did what he had to in order to make a living. He signed on with the Missouri, Kansas, and Texas Railway—better known as the KATY Railroad—as a strikebreaker when a labor dispute threatened to shut down rail traffic. Riding in the cab of one of the KATY's engines as a guard, Courtright foiled an attempt by strikers to stop the train several miles south of town. He did that by drawing both guns and blazing away at the strikers, who returned the fire with rifles. One of Courtright's fellow guards was killed in the shooting, but Courtright wounded one of the strikers and drove off the rest with his accurate shots. Despite the fact that only one death resulted from the clash, it was soon being called the Fort Worth Massacre, and Courtright was notorious for his part in it.

Such notoriety certainly did not hurt when he began enlisting businesses in Hell's Half Acre as clients for his detective agency. He did not do any detecting for them, however. The setup was nothing more than an early-day protection racket, with Courtright collecting fees that were actually bribes. It was a lucrative operation.

And if there was money to be made that way downtown, reasoned Courtright, there would be even more money uptown. The place to start, he decided, was the White Elephant Saloon.

However, Short adamantly refused Courtright's thinly veiled hints. Courtright suggested that Short hire him as a special officer to keep the peace in the White Elephant. Short told Courtright in no uncertain terms that he would sooner pay Courtright to stay away from the saloon than have him spend time there, and he was not going to do that, either. The abrupt dismissal infuriated Courtright.

Since then, Courtright had done everything in his power to cause trouble for Luke Short, using his influence with the city fathers to threaten indictments and the closing of the White Elephant. Short had responded calmly that he would pay any legal fines and fight any trumped-up arrests in the courts. Courtright might not have known it, but Short had dug in his heels. He was not going to be moved.

But the increasing friction and the growing hostility on the part of Fort Worth's legal establishment worried Short. Once again he was facing a situation like the one that had developed in Dodge City. The Peace Commission had helped straighten out that mess. Maybe the trouble in Fort Worth could be dealt with on a smaller scale. This time Short sent for only one of his old friends, Bat Masterson.

Even with Bat in town to back any play he might want to make, Short had already begun to think that perhaps his stubbornness was not the way to play out this hand. He still was not willing to buy off Courtright, but perhaps if he left town for a while, the problem would solve itself. The way Courtright was drinking these days, his health could not hold up for long. Once Courtright's own demons had caught up with him, Short could come back to Fort Worth and resume his life there. Or, if things were going well wherever he went after leaving town, he could just stay where he was and enjoy his life with his wife and children. Either way, the problem would be solved without any violence.

So he made his proposal to Jake Johnson, and Johnson agreed.

As of February 7, 1887, Luke Short no longer owned any part of the White Elephant Saloon and Restaurant.

Unknown to Short, on that same evening, after stopping at the White Elephant, Timothy Courtright wandered into a Hell's Half Acre dive and began drinking his way through a bottle. At one point, as he peered into the amber depths of the glass of whiskey he held in his hand, one of the other patrons heard him say, "I've lived past my time."

———————

LUKE Short might not own any part of the White Elephant anymore, but the next evening, February 8, 1887, he returned there anyway. Perhaps old habits were hard to break. It was a cold night. He went in, hung up his hat and overcoat, and went upstairs to the gambling room.

Jake Johnson was there, and so was Bat Masterson. The mustachioed Masterson, as dapperly dressed as Short himself, greeted his old friend. They had a drink and watched the play at the gaming tables for a while; then Short went downstairs to have his boots shined.

He walked into the saloon, where a bootblack stand was located. As he sat there and had his boots shined and buffed, an acquaintance came up to him and told him that Longhair Jim Courtright was looking for him.

Johnson had told Short about informing Courtright of their business deal. Short had hoped that would end things, that Courtright would realize he intended to move on. Evidently that was not the case.

Short had no desire to talk to Courtright, and said as much to the man who had brought him the message. He returned upstairs when the bootblack was finished. He had never been one to go looking for trouble.

Short did not say anything to Jake Johnson or Bat Masterson about Courtright looking for him, but a short time later, one of

Longhair Jim Courtright, lawman, detective, and gunman, wearing the tin star that had been stripped from him by the time of his fatal confrontation with Luke Short.

(Courtesy of Denver Public Library, Western History Collection)

the waiters from the restaurant hurried upstairs to the gambling room. He came over to Short and Johnson and told them that Marshal Courtright was downstairs causing quite a commotion and insisting that he wanted to see Luke Short.

Johnson had been playing billiards. He volunteered to go downstairs and see if he could get Courtright to leave without causing any more trouble. Short agreed.

Johnson tossed the stick onto the pool table and followed the waiter to the stairs. He found Courtright waiting in the restaurant's foyer. Courtright demanded to see Short, and when Johnson asked what about, Courtright suggested that they talk about it outside. They stepped out into the cold night.

Immediately, Johnson spotted a man standing nearby, and recognized him as Charley Bull, Courtright's partner in the Commercial Detective Agency. Bull stood there quietly, lounging against a street lamp, and did not seem to mean anyone any harm.

Courtright and Johnson talked for a few moments, Courtright

insisting that he just wanted to put things right between him and Short. Courtright seemed more sober than usual, and his notoriously quick temper gave every indication of being under control. Johnson decided that perhaps a conversation between Short and Courtright would bring a peaceful end to the hostilities between them. He told Courtright that he would go in and speak to Short, without promising that Short would agree to see Courtright.

Johnson went back into the White Elephant and climbed the stairs to the second floor. When he told Short what Courtright had said, Short refused to go downstairs and speak with Courtright, preferring to let things lie the way they were.

For a few more minutes, Johnson tried with no luck to convince Short to go downstairs and talk to Courtright. Suddenly, the decision was taken out of their hands, as Courtright himself appeared at the top of the stairs leading to the White Elephant's gaming rooms, angrily saying that he had gotten tired of waiting.

Short was tired, too, tired of the whole business. If Courtright had just stayed where he belonged, down in Hell's Half Acre, the problem never would have developed. Short glanced around. Bat Masterson was playing keno, and Short did not want to disturb him.

Short asked Courtright what he wanted, and Courtright invited Short to come discuss the matter with him in the street. Short and Johnson both recognized Courtright's invitation for what it really was: Courtright was calling Short out. He wanted to settle the trouble with gunplay. And there was no way Short could decline without being branded a coward. The story would be all over Fort Worth by the next day.

Short agreed to talk with Courtright. Courtright's eyes lit up. He was in his element now. Soon he would be facing an enemy over the barrel of his gun.

The three men walked down the stairs together. Short got his hat, but left his overcoat hanging up. Before they went out, Johnson asked if Charley Bull was still outside. Courtright replied that Bull had no part in what was going on.

Short's former partner had just done him the favor of warning him that Charley Bull could be skulking around somewhere outside, ready to ambush him. It was more likely, though, that Courtright's pride would force him to face Short alone.

Their breath fogged in the air as they stepped onto the boardwalk in front of the White Elephant. Courtright drifted down the street, and Short had no choice but to follow. Johnson hung back, watching.

Courtright paused in front of the open door to Ella Blackwell's Shooting Gallery. Short glanced through the door, perhaps wondering if Betty Courtright was working in there tonight.

Courtright turned to face him. The two men stood about four feet apart. Courtright said angrily that it was time they settled the problems between them.

Short calmly replied that there was nothing to settle. He hooked his thumbs in the armholes of his vest, an unthreatening stance if ever there was one. Despite that, Courtright accused Short of wanting to kill him.

Short replied that he was not even carrying a gun. That was a lie. A short-barreled .45 was resting in the specially made, leather-lined vest pocket where Luke Short usually carried it. Short moved his hands down to the bottom of the vest, as if to raise it so that Courtright could see that he did not have a weapon tucked behind his belt or holstered on his hip.

The movement of Short's hands was all the excuse Courtright needed. He shouted, "Don't you pull a gun on me!" and his right hand stabbed toward the reversed butt of the six-shooter he wore on that side.

After that, it was all instinct and cool nerve for Luke Short. His right hand was already moving. It dipped into the vest pocket and came up with the .45. Courtright's gun had already cleared the holster.

Short's first shot was fast, from the hip. The bullet caught Courtright somewhere in the body. Courtright staggered back a step, his revolver still unfired in his hand. Short lifted his arm, extending the gun toward the former marshal as he triggered four more times. The light on the boardwalk was bad, but the muzzle flashes lit up the night and showed Courtright being rocked back by each of the slugs as they drove into him. While the echoes of the shots were still rolling along Main Street like thunder, Courtright fell backward through the door of the shooting gallery. Longhair Jim, the famous gunman, had not gotten off a single shot.

Men rushed past Short to gape at the fallen Courtright. A voice asked him if he had done this. Short looked over to see an acquaintance, Bony Tucker, one of Fort Worth's city policemen. Without saying anything, Short handed over the still-smoking pistol to Tucker.

Tarrant County Sheriff B. H. Shipp came up on Short's other side and told him that he was under arrest and would be taken to the city jail. Short nodded and spoke for the first time since the shooting, claiming that it was self-defense and that Courtright had reached for his gun first. Short went along peacefully with the lawman as behind them in the doorway of the shooting gallery, Longhair Jim Courtright breathed his last.

One way or another, the feud was over.

——————

WHAT came to be known as the Shoot-out at the White Elephant, even though it actually took place a few yards down the street in front of Ella Blackwell's Shooting Gallery, was the last Old West gunfight in Fort Worth, Texas. Timothy Isaiah "Longhair Jim" Courtright was buried in Pioneer's Rest Cemetery the next day,

February 9, 1887, in the biggest, fanciest funeral Fort Worth had ever seen. Courtright had come down in the world since his glory days as town marshal, but he still had plenty of friends.

Some of those friends gave thought to invading the city jail and lynching Luke Short. The presence of a well-armed Bat Masterson standing guard over Short soon put an end to that idea. The mob might be angry, but they had sense enough not to want to go up against Bat.

A few days later, after hearing testimony from the few witnesses who had actually seen the fight, among them Jake Johnson, the Tarrant County Grand Jury refused to indict Luke Short, instead returning a verdict of justifiable homicide. One bit of evidence to come out of the hearing was that Short's first shot had hit the cylinder of Courtright's revolver, jamming it so that it would not fire, as well as almost completely severing his thumb from his hand before it passed on into his body. Either of those things might have doomed Courtright; together they sealed his fate.

Luke Short died six and a half years later, on September 8, 1893, succumbing to the lingering effects of buckshot wounds he had suffered in a gunfight with another business rival, Charlie Wright. He is buried in Oakwood Cemetery, on a hill overlooking the Trinity River, across from the bluff on which Fort Worth was built.

Not too far away, having been moved there years later from Pioneer's Rest, is the grave of Timothy Courtright.

END OF AN EARP

One day, one incident, one fight can make a legend. Just being in the presence of history often is enough to make a person a historic figure in his own right. On the other hand, not being in the right place at the right time . . . well, that just about ruins it.

Take the case of Warren Earp.

The youngest of six brothers, Warren was born in Iowa in 1855. His brothers, from oldest to youngest, were Newton (a half brother born to the first wife of Nicholas Earp, the family patriarch), James, Virgil, Wyatt, and Morgan. The family moved to Colton, California, in 1863. Warren grew up there and watched his brothers leave home one by one (Newton, James, and Virgil had already enlisted in the Union Army and taken part in the Civil War). Warren remained in Colton, where his father was at various times both a judge and a saloon-keeper. Warren tended bar in the saloon and listened to the stories that spread as his brothers grew more and more famous as frontier lawmen. He must have been at least a little jealous. What young man wouldn't be if he was bombarded constantly by tales of the colorful, exciting adventures his older brothers were experiencing? They had even tamed the wild cowtown of Dodge City, Kansas!

So when Warren heard that James, Virgil, Wyatt, and Morgan had moved to the silver-mining boomtown of Tombstone, Arizona Territory, he wasted no time getting there himself. Surely, adventure was on the horizon at last for him.

Virgil, the most solid and dependable of the badge-toting brothers, gave Warren not only a place to stay but a job as well. A veteran lawman by this time, Virgil was working as both a deputy U.S. marshal and Tombstone's chief of police. Warren had a room in Virgil's house and worked for him as a jailer, though sometimes he was also allowed to ride with the posses that Virgil raised whenever some crime was committed and there were lawbreakers to pursue.

Some of those lawbreakers were rustlers from the infamous "cowboy" faction that became the mortal enemies of the Earps and their friends, including Doc Holliday. During one early clash with the "cowboys," Warren was a member of the posse and sustained a leg wound that was serious enough to send him back to California to recuperate at the family home.

The gun battle in which Warren was injured took place in July 1881. On October 26, 1881, the hostility between the Earps and the "cowboys" exploded into what is probably the most famous gunfight in the history of the Old West: the Gunfight at the O.K. Corral. Many volumes have been written about this epic shootout, but if they mention Warren Earp, they do so only in passing, for one simple reason. He wasn't there. He was sitting in California recovering from his wound while Wyatt, Virgil, Morgan, and Doc Holliday were shooting it out with the Clantons and McLaurys.

It is impossible to know whether or not Warren would have taken part in the gunfight if he had been in Tombstone. It seems probable that he would have, considering that he had ridden in posses with his brothers on previous occasions and was regarded as a fierce fighter at this stage of his life. But speculation aside, Warren Earp did not return to Tombstone until early in 1882. He came back then because his brother Virgil had been ambushed and seriously wounded while walking across Allen Street, one of Tombstone's main thoroughfares. The blame for the shooting was laid on several of the "cowboys," and the motive was clear: revenge for the deaths of their friends and relatives in the already famous gunfight.

The most serious wound cost Virgil the use of his left arm. Warren stayed with Virgil and his wife Allie to help out with caring for his brother. Also, it seemed inevitable that more violence would occur, and Warren, now recovered from his own wound with only a slight limp to show for it, wanted to be on hand in case of trouble.

The "cowboys" were not through exacting their vengeance. In March of 1882, while Wyatt and Morgan were playing pool in a billiard parlor on Allen Street, gunmen opened fire through the glass in the rear door. One of the shots passed through Morgan's body, mortally wounding him. The assassins fled into the night, leaving Wyatt and his friends to carry Morgan's bloody body into another room of the billiard parlor. Warren rushed to the place when he heard that Morgan had been shot, and arrived before his brother died, but there was nothing anyone could do to help. After lingering for a little less than an hour, Morgan died.

Morgan's murder started Wyatt, Warren, Doc Holliday, and several of their friends on a vendetta that would come to be known as the Arizona War. Warren, who was known as the Tiger because of the ferocious way he threw himself into a fight, was on hand when enemies tried to ambush the train that was carrying Morgan's body back to California, along with Virgil and Allie. Wyatt killed Frank Stilwell in this clash, shotgunning him as Stilwell and other members of the "cowboy" faction were about to open fire on the railroad car where Virgil and Allie were sitting.

Wyatt and Warren were the only Earps still capable of fight-ing, but they had the assistance of Doc and several other gun-handy companions as they set out to track down the rest of the men responsible for Morgan's killing. The Earps were now fugi-tives from the law they had served in the past; arrest warrants were issued for them, charging them with the killing of Frank Stilwell. Cochise County Sheriff Johnny Behan attempted to serve those warrants as the group left Tombstone on their vengeance ride, but when Wyatt and Warren refused to stop and be arrested, Behan didn't press the issue; wisely, no doubt, under the circumstances, since he didn't have a posse at his back.

Over the next few days, three members of the "cowboys" died at the hands of the Earps and their friends. Florentino Cruz, who may have been holding the horses so that the men who bush-whacked Morgan could make a fast getaway, met his fate in the Dragoon Mountains. He was killed at a woodcutting camp owned by Pete Spence, another member of the "cowboy" faction and one of the men suspected in Virgil's ambush. At Iron Springs, the pursued tried to turn the tables on their pursuers, as several men including Johnny Barnes and Curly Bill Brocious tried to set up an ambush of the Earps and their companions. Instead, Brocious and Barnes wound up dying in the fierce exchange of gunshots.

Though many members of the "cowboys" were still at large, the killings of Stilwell, Cruz, Brocious, and Barnes proved to be too much to be tolerated in the territory's sharply divided, emo-tionally charged political atmosphere. In the eyes of many, Wyatt and Warren had crossed the line into outlawry, and even some of those who had supported them in the past decided that they had to be brought in. The slaughter had to stop. A large party of law-men started on their trail.

The Earps still had friends, though, and when word reached them of the posse that had been sent out to apprehend them, Wyatt and Warren realized that, like it or not, their vendetta was over. The group split up, with Wyatt, Warren, and Doc Holliday heading for Colorado while the others scattered to the four winds. None of them would ever be brought to trial for their actions. Indeed, if not for the political pressures being brought to bear, most authorities likely would have admitted that the Earps' vengeance had been justified.

There was talk of extraditing Wyatt and Warren from Colorado to Arizona. There was talk of a pardon from the territorial governor. In the end, not much was done either way. Wyatt and Warren decided to go back to California. That was the closest thing to a home that they had now. Doc Holliday opted to stay behind in Colorado, where he would meet his own fate.

Wyatt, always restless, never stayed in one place for long. He packed up and left California. Warren remained in Colton. As a young man, hearing the stories of his illustrious brothers, he had longed to be with them, to be one of the gallant, gunfighting Earp brothers. He had gotten that wish, taking part in all of their Arizona adventures except the most notorious one, the shoot-out in the vacant lot next to Fly's Photo Gallery, just down the street from the O.K. Corral. Now Morgan was dead, Virgil was a near-cripple, Wyatt was gone off to the Yukon, and Warren's career as a peace officer had ended with him being a wanted outlaw. Nothing had worked out quite the way he expected and hoped that it would.

Finding it difficult to hold a job, Warren retreated into a life of drinking, gambling, and fighting. He spent most of his time in various saloons. Quick to take offense, he heard insults in almost everything anyone had to say to him, and he retaliated with whatever means was at hand—guns, knives, fists, once even a broken bottle. The local law seems to have given Warren the benefit of the doubt in these scrapes, probably because the Earp family was still well respected in Colton, especially Warren's father Nicholas, the former judge. Often, the only arrests made were of those unfortunates who had provoked Warren's wrath.

Virgil, despite his almost useless left arm, was elected city marshal of Colton, and evidently prevailed upon Warren to settle down for a while. Warren still spent most of his time in saloons, but now he was working again as a bartender, as he had done before leaving Colton for Tombstone the first time. From 1885 until 1893, he was able to stay out of trouble, but then his temper got the best of him yet again and he was arrested for stabbing a man during an altercation. The victim recovered from the attack and Warren was found not guilty when tried for the offense. But Warren had worn out his welcome in California anyway. He left Colton and headed for Arizona Territory once more, despite the fact that technically he was still wanted for murder there.

If he intended to lie low and not call attention to himself once he got to Arizona, he did a bad job of it. His first stop was Yuma, where he quarreled with a man over the affections of a woman and threatened to kill his rival. Evidently in need of funds, Warren modified his threat and suggested that if the man paid him off, his life would be safe. This led, not surprisingly, to charges of extortion. Warren had to pay a fine, but served no jail time in return for a promise that he would get out of Yuma.

By 1894, Warren was in the town of Willcox, where he was hired as a range detective by a local rancher, Colonel Henry Clay Hooker. Hooker owned not one but two successful ranches, and hired Warren to track down rustlers, fence cutters, and the like. Warren also worked part of the time driving a freight wagon.

But his unstable nature never left him at peace for very long. He quarreled with a local cowhand named Johnny Boyett, again over a woman. On July 4, 1900, Warren challenged Boyett to a gunfight, but the cowboy declined. Warren allowed Boyett to walk out of the saloon where the confrontation took place, but that wasn't the end of the matter.

Two days later, in another Willcox saloon, Warren and Boyett ran into each other again. "Go get your gun," Warren immediately told the cowboy, who was unarmed. "We'll fight it out." Boyett tried to defuse the situation, insisting that he didn't want any trouble. Warren continued prodding him, making the accusation at one point that Boyett had been hired by an unnamed person to kill him.

Boyett finally stalked out of the place, and Warren left the saloon as well, going into an adjoining restaurant. A few minutes later, Boyett returned to the saloon carrying not one pistol, but two. Warren had finally goaded Boyett to the point where the cowboy was willing to fight, even though his opponent would be one of the famous Earp brothers.

Hearing the commotion, Warren stepped into the doorway between the saloon and the restaurant. Boyett saw him, jerked up both guns, and triggered a shot from each. Both slugs missed, chewing splinters from the wall instead. Boyett, in the grip of rage, charged after Warren. His guns went off again, probably by accident, but the bullets went into the floor.

Moving quickly, Warren left the restaurant by the front door and circled back around to the saloon's side entrance. He came up behind Boyett, who whirled around to face him. Despite Warren Earp's flaws, he did not lack for courage, and he demonstrated that quality now. While he had been the one to challenge Boyett to a gunfight, Warren actually was unarmed. With his coat and vest open to show that he wasn't carrying a gun, he walked slowly toward Boyett, perhaps hoping to either calm him down or to get close enough to grapple with him and take away his guns.

Whatever Warren had in mind, it didn't work. Boyett fired one more shot, striking Warren in the heart. Warren stumbled, driven back slightly by the impact of the bullet, and then pitched forward on his face. In all likelihood, he was dead when he hit the floor.

Johnny Boyett was never indicted for the killing of Warren Earp, who was buried in Willcox. Boyett disappeared soon after the incident, and rumors circulated that Wyatt and Virgil had killed him to avenge the death of their brother, just as Wyatt and Warren had gone after the men responsible for Morgan's murder.

That seems highly unlikely, however, since Wyatt was in Alaska at the time and could hardly have undertaken such a long journey without anyone being aware of it. It's certainly possible, though, that Boyett, fearing the vengeance of the Earps, deemed it wise to move on and drop out of sight.

All his life, Warren Earp lived in the shadow of his famous older brothers. If not for the leg wound that sent him home to California to recuperate, in all probability he would have walked down the streets of Tombstone on that famous day, along with Wyatt, Virgil, Morgan, and Doc. He shared all the dangers with them before and after the Gunfight at the O.K. Corral, but by missing that one event, he became an afterthought, a footnote, to those who chronicled the bloody saga of Tombstone.

But he was still an Earp, through and through, and he died trying to live up to the name.

DOC'S LAST GUNFIGHT

In 1884, Leadville, Colorado, was quite a boomtown. Nine years earlier, in 1875, a miner named Will Stevens found silver in nearby California Gulch. Though Stevens tried to keep his discovery a secret, eventually the news got out and prospectors flocked to Leadville. Quite a few years earlier, in 1860, gold had been found in California Gulch as well, prompting a brief boom, but the gold ran out two years later, and when it was gone, so was most of the bustling activity that had filled Leadville. The town led a sleepy existence until the bonanza turned up by Stevens. After that Leadville's population exploded, not just with miners but also merchants, saloon-keepers, gamblers, prostitutes, and all the others who dedicated themselves to removing whatever profits the miners made from their pockets.

The Monarch Saloon was one of Leadville's finest. Like most such establishments, it had a faro bank and a professional gambler who ran it. On a hot August night, this gambler—tall, with graying hair, a mustache, and a gaunt, almost haggard face—was seated at a table when the batwing doors at the saloon's front entrance were slapped open. A man with a gun in his fist and an angry expression on his face stalked into the room and roared out a curse as he spotted his quarry. "Holliday!" he shouted.

And with a sigh, the gambler reached for his gun. Violence had come calling one final time on Doc Holliday.

———————

JOHN Henry Holliday, like so many of the legendary figures in the history of the Old West, began life as a Southerner. He was born in Georgia in 1851. There seems to be some question about whether, as a young man, he actually studied dentistry at a college in Baltimore or merely learned how to pull teeth by watching others do it. At any rate, he called himself a doctor of dentistry and set up a practice in Atlanta in 1872. Sickly, plagued by coughing fits, Holliday consulted a doctor and was diagnosed with consumption, as tuberculosis was known in those days. There was no cure for the condition. The doctor's only advice was for Holliday to seek out a warmer, drier climate. That might prolong his life.

The young dentist had another reason for leaving Georgia. As did most Southerners of the era, he had a dislike for the black former slaves who had been freed by the Civil War. When Holliday found three such men swimming in what he considered his own private swimming hole, he pulled a pistol and fired at them. Some say that Holliday only fired warning shots over the heads of the men to chase them out of the water; others claim he wounded or killed them. Whichever story is true, the incident, along with his medical condition, gave Holliday ample cause to leave Georgia and head west, to Texas.

Arriving in Dallas, he set up another dental practice, but was none too successful at it. He had other skills, though, especially with cards. He became a gambler to augment his income from dentistry, and took to it so well that soon gambling was his profession and dentistry was just a sideline.

Holliday was good with a gun, too, and inevitably he got mixed up in a shooting scrape over a game of cards. Nobody was killed, but Holliday found it prudent to move on west to the town of Jacksboro. The Army had a post there, Fort Richardson, and not surprisingly, many of the soldiers liked to visit the town's saloons when they got the chance. Here Holliday killed his first man (if, in fact, he didn't kill any of those freed slaves back in Georgia). A soldier accused him of cheating, the table was turned over, men dove for cover, and guns banged, leaving the trooper dead on the floor.

Though such corpse-and-cartridge affairs were seldom seen as cause for prosecution, Holliday thought it wise to move on since the Army was involved. He drifted around Texas and Colorado for a while, deadening himself against the pain of his illness with copious quantities of whiskey. The Who-hit-John was no cure-all, but it made a hell of an anesthetic if a man drank enough of it.

In Fort Griffin, Texas, Holliday made two acquaintances who would have a big impact on the rest of his life: a buffalo hunter named Wyatt Earp and a prostitute known variously as Katherine Elder, Katie Elder, and Big Nose Kate Fisher. When Holliday killed a man with a knife during an argument over cards, Kate saved him from being lynched by setting fire to a barn and then spiriting Holliday out of Fort Griffin during the resulting commotion.

Arriving in Dodge City, Kansas, with Kate, Holliday set up another dental practice in Room 24 of the Dodge House, offering a money-back guarantee if the customer was not satisfied. Wyatt Earp was in Dodge, too, working as a deputy city marshal and also gambling, something that cemented his friendship with the young dentist, who by now was known to most simply as Doc Holliday. During a confrontation with a gang of trigger-happy Texas cowboys who were after his scalp, Earp was saved by the timely arrival of Holliday, who covered the cowboys with Earp's shotgun while the lawman pistol-whipped the ringleader of the gang and hauled him off to jail. This was, as far as we know, the first time Doc Holliday backed Wyatt Earp's play in a gun fracas.

It would not be the last.

RESTLESS by nature, saddled with a troublesome illness, unable to sustain a romance with Big Nose Kate, who left him and came back to him several times, Holliday continued to drift around the West. For a time he sold his gun in the bloody railroad war between the Santa Fe Railroad and the Denver & Rio Grande. He gambled and drank, drank and gambled, an existence punctuated by sporadic bursts of violence. Several dead men in Colorado and New Mexico were linked to Doc Holliday.

When Holliday heard that Wyatt Earp and his brothers had gone to Tombstone, a silver-mining boomtown in Arizona Territory, he followed them there, taking Kate with him. Settling down to life as a gambler in Tombstone, Holliday watched as the conflict between the Earps and the so-called "cowboy" element led by Ike Clanton escalated. By now, although he was still quite skilled with a six-gun, Holliday's weapon of choice was a shotgun, and that was what he carried on the afternoon of October 26, 1881, when he walked down the streets of Tombstone alongside Wyatt, Virgil, and Morgan Earp on their way to confront Ike and Billy Clanton, Frank and Tom McLaury, and Billy Claiborne. They met, of course, in front of Fly's Photograph Gallery, near the O.K. Corral, and the ensuing gunfight insured Doc Holliday's place in the annals of the Old West.

The famous shoot-out wasn't the end of it, though. In retaliation for what had happened, both Virgil and Morgan Earp were shot from ambush. Virgil survived, though he was badly wounded, but Morgan was killed. Wyatt took it upon himself to avenge the wounding of one brother and the murder of another, and Holliday pitched in to help him. The exact details are still fuzzy, even after all these years, but when it was all over, several more men were dead and there were warrants out for the arrest of Wyatt Earp and John Henry "Doc" Holliday. Both of them left Arizona Territory and headed for Colorado.

There the two old friends went their separate ways, Wyatt heading for Gunnison while Holliday settled down in Pueblo, south of Denver. Holliday's consumption was worse than ever, and he didn't even attempt to hang out his shingle as a dentist, relying solely on gambling for his living now. He became a fixture at a saloon called the Cominque Club. He was accepted in Pueblo, despite his notorious reputation.

A trip to Denver to watch a horse race landed Holliday in more trouble. A man came up behind him on the street, jammed a couple of guns in his back, and declared that he was under arrest. The man marched Holliday at gunpoint to the local authorities and identified himself as Perry Mallan, a deputy sheriff from Los Angeles, California. He claimed that he was arresting Holliday in order to have him extradited back to Arizona, to face trial for crimes allegedly committed there.

In reality, Mallan wasn't a peace officer at all, but rather a small-time confidence man and extortionist who had crossed paths with Holliday before and had a grudge against him. Mallan's scheme to cause trouble for Holliday fell apart when Bat Masterson, who was serving as the sheriff of Las Animas County at the time, stepped in and used his influence to hold things up until Mallan could be identified as a criminal. By now, the authorities in Arizona had been notified that Holliday was in custody in Denver and attempted to have him extradited, but Masterson blocked that maneuver as well. Masterson and Holliday were never close, but Bat was good friends with Wyatt Earp and helped Holliday for that reason.

Getting sicker all the time, coughing up blood almost constantly from his ravaged lungs, Holliday moved on to Deadwood, Dakota Territory, when he was released by the Colorado authorities. Trouble followed him, as usual, and he had to shoot a man

A young and handsome Doc Holliday,
before consumption wasted his frame
and slowed his gun hand.

(Courtesy of Old West Photos)

there. Turning south again, he returned to Colorado, this time to
Leadville. A silver boom was going on there. The pickings would
probably be good for a skillful cardplayer. . . .

BIG Nose Kate was long gone, having left him for good—despite
the fact that she claimed to her dying day to be the legal widow of
Doc Holliday, a claim with no evidence to support it. With his
health worsening, Holliday took over the faro bank in the
Monarch Saloon. Finding himself short of funds, he borrowed
five dollars from one of the saloon's bartenders, Billy Allen.
Somehow, after that Holliday was never flush enough to pay back
the loan. Allen grew angry over the matter and kept pressing Holliday for the money. In time, he became so frustrated that he
threatened Holliday with violence if Holliday didn't pony up the
dough. Allen must not have been thinking. He was threatening
not just any gambler, but rather Doc Holliday, friend of Wyatt
Earp, veteran of the already famous Gunfight at the O.K. Corral,
reputed to be the killer of at least thirty men.

Calmly Holliday advised Allen not to start anything unless he had a gun in each hand.

Allen's anger—over a five-dollar loan!—boiled over until he couldn't stand it anymore. He armed himself, went to the Monarch, and slammed into the saloon, no doubt knowing that he would find Holliday there. When Allen burst into the place, yelling and waving a gun around, Holliday knew he had no choice but to defend himself. By this time, Holliday's speed on the draw was probably only a vestige of what it once had been, but he was still fast enough. He drew, the gun seeming to flicker into his hand, and fired in one smooth motion. The first shot missed. Allen still hadn't fired, but surely he would soon. Holliday cocked his single-action .45 revolver and pulled the trigger again. This time the slug smashed through Allen's upper arm, knocking him off his feet as he dropped the pistol he had been brandishing.

There was an uproar in the saloon by now. Holliday turned to one of the shocked bystanders, one of Leadville's leading citizens by the name of Bradbury. With the courtliness that was part of his Southern heritage, Holliday turned over his gun to Bradbury and drawled a request that Bradbury not allow anyone to shoot him in the back.

The local law arrived to arrest Holliday. Allen was only wounded, but the West was becoming more civilized, even boomtowns such as Leadville. Not even the famous Doc Holliday could go around shooting up the citizens without answering for it in a court of law. However, when the trial took place, there were more than enough witnesses to clear Holliday. He had fired in self-defense, and that was reflected by the verdict of not guilty.

That was the last gunfight for Holliday, the last violent incident in a bloody, colorful career as gambler, gunman, and participant in at least one of the West's best-known shoot-outs. Following his acquittal at Leadville, Holliday moved to Glenwood Springs, Colorado, where several hot springs and health spas were located. He registered at the Glenwood Springs Hotel (which was actually a sanitarium) and took frequent baths in the springs in the hope that the hot, mineral-laden water would help his condition. The tuberculosis was too far advanced for anything to help it, and on November 8, 1887, he fell into a coma. He never came out of it, dying later that same day at the age of thirty-six.

Before he lost consciousness, Holliday was heard to mutter, "This is funny." No one knows for certain what he was talking about. It could be that he was commenting on the fact he was about to die in bed, instead of on his feet in some smoke-filled saloon or on sun-drenched frontier street, gun in hand as he faced his enemies.

THE LONG BRANCH
SALOON'S SPECTACULAR
FRAY

Western author and historian William MacLeod Raine tells the story of the drunken cowboy who boarded a train in Kansas, in the days when the railroad was pushing its way across that frontier state. When asked by the conductor for his ticket, the cowboy, deep in his cups, pulled out some coins and said, "I want to go to hell."

"Get off at Dodge," the conductor replied without hesitation. "One dollar, please."

Hell was a pretty good description of Dodge City most of the time in those days. Originally called Buffalo City, it was a tiny settlement five miles west of the military post known as Fort Dodge. Founded by Charlie Rath and Robert Wright, who dealt in buffalo meat and hides, Buffalo City existed to serve the hordes of hunters who descended on the Great Plains in the late 1860s to begin the slaughter of the vast herds of shaggy, hump-backed beasts. Whiskey peddlers rolled in with their wagons full of barrels of rotgut, followed by the gamblers and soiled doves who made it their mission to take whatever remained of the money

the buffalo hunters earned after the whiskey peddlers were
through with them.

The town's growth exploded in the summer of 1872, when
the tracks of the Atchison, Topeka & Santa Fe Railroad reached
the little settlement. It might have remained Buffalo City if the
Postmaster General hadn't objected. Kansas already had one
town called Buffalo and another called Buffalo Station. Buffalo
City would have been one Buffalo too many, in the judgment of
the Postmaster General. So, in honor of nearby Fort Dodge, Buffalo City became Dodge City, and so it would remain long after
the fort was gone.

The town continued to grow. By the late 1870s, Front Street,
which flanked both sides of the Santa Fe tracks, had dozens of
saloons along its length. One of the best was the Long Branch. A
rather narrow room, deeper than it was wide, the Long Branch
was dominated by its long, fancy hardwood bar, with a mirrored
back-bar topped by a set of longhorns on the wall behind it, as
well as a large painting depicting an Indian fight. The rear section
of the room was filled with a scattering of tables, overlooked by a
moose head with an impressive span of antlers mounted on the
rear wall. The whole scene was lit by an oil chandelier that hung
in the center of the room and several other hanging oil lamps
positioned along the walls.

Like all saloons, the Long Branch had its regular customers,
men who could be found there nearly every night. Two such reg-
ulars were Levi Richardson, who owned a freight line headquartered in Dodge City, and Frank Loving, better known as
"Cock-eyed Frank," who made his living as a gambler. Both men,
as patrons of the Long Branch, were well acquainted with each
other, and they had something else in common: Both of them
were interested in the same woman, one of Dodge City's dance-
hall girls whose name has not come down to posterity.

So there was already bad blood between the two men on the
evening of April 5, 1879. Richardson was in the Long Branch,

drinking. There is no way of knowing if he thought he might run into Frank Loving, nor what Richardson planned to do if he did see Cock-eyed Frank. But Loving wasn't in the saloon, so after a while, Richardson tossed off the last of the whiskey in his glass, thumped the empty down on the bar, and turned toward the door. He had almost reached it when fate sent Frank Loving striding into the Long Branch from the boardwalk outside.

The two men must have eyed each other narrowly as Loving walked past Richardson and headed for the back of the room. After hesitating a second, Richardson swung around and followed the gambler. Loving sat down, but instead of taking a chair, he perched a hip on one of the tables. Richardson did likewise, choosing the same table in what seemed like a deliberate attempt to goad Loving. A couple of unfriendly words passed between the two men, and then Loving stood up.

Facing Richardson, the gambler said, "If you have anything to say about me, why don't you come and say it to my face like a gentleman, and not to my back, you damn son of a bitch."

Furious, Richardson stood up, too, and sneered. "You're not man enough to fight," he said to Loving.

Pale-faced, the gambler snapped, "You try me and see."

It was a challenge that could not be ignored, not in this time and place.

Richardson didn't lose any time reaching under his coat for a gun. He was a businessman, not a shootist, but his revolver came out quickly. At the same time, Loving was slapping leather, too. Both men were caught up in the emotions of the moment, with rage and adrenaline pumping wildly through their veins. They thrust their guns at each other, standing so close that the barrels of the weapons almost touched.

Richardson got off the first two shots, but despite the close range, he missed and the bullets flew harmlessly past Loving. The gambler pulled the trigger, but the hammer of his gun just snapped on a bullet that misfired. Loving darted toward the billiard table as Richardson fired twice more and missed both times.

Roaring in anger, Richardson came after Loving. The gambler tried to fire again, and this time the gun in his hand belched flame and lead. He squeezed off two more rounds, forcing Richardson to abandon the pursuit and duck for cover behind a cast-iron, pot-bellied stove. Richardson triggered a fifth shot.

Loving went down, but he had only slipped. He wasn't hit. As he fell, one of the shocked bystanders, William Duffey, reached over and plucked the gun out of Richardson's hand. Duffey was convinced that Loving was wounded, and he didn't want Richardson shooting the gambler while he was down.

Chaos filled the Long Branch by now. Not only was the roar of the shots deafening, but also the men in the saloon added to the din by shouting curses and questions. City Marshal Charley Bassett burst through the front door of the Long Branch and bellowed for everybody to cease fire and shut up. Bassett had been in a nearby saloon when the shooting broke out, and had come to the Long Branch at a dead run.

Frank Loving stood up after slipping and falling. With all the confusion around him, he never noticed that William Duffey had disarmed Richardson. Seeing his enemy still trying to hide behind the stove, Loving kept shooting. In a situation like this, following the golden rule of "shoot first and figure it out later" could keep a man alive. Loving's aim had finally settled down. All three of the shots he fired after he stood up found their target, ripping through Levi Richardson's torso. Richardson gasped in pain and surprise and sagged backward, bloodstains already blooming on his clothes. Duffey, still holding Richardson's pistol, caught him before he could fall to the floor and steered him onto one of the tables, where Richardson lay down and gasped out his last breaths. He died as the hubbub in the saloon settled down at last.

Charley Bassett bulled up beside Loving and wrenched the pistol out of his hand. Somebody yelled to fetch the doctor for

Richardson, but it was too late. This gunfight had claimed its only victim, and there was nothing anybody could do for the freighter now.

Cock-eyed Frank Loving was brought before a coroner's jury without any delay. This worthy body of frontiersmen listened to the evidence and then quickly reached the inevitable conclusion: Levi Richardson had been killed by Frank Loving in self-defense. The fact that Richardson's gun had five empty shells in it was all the evidence the jury needed to reach its verdict. There was nothing remarkable about it.

What was remarkable was that between them, Richardson and Loving had fired eleven shots in the close confines of the Long Branch Saloon. Three bullets had struck Richardson. The other eight slugs had gone into the walls of the saloon and done no harm except to paint and plaster. Considering how crowded the place was and how wildly the two men had been firing, it was surprising, even amazing, that no one else had been struck by any of the lead that was flying around.

Frank Loving's career as a gunman following the fight with Richardson was short and not so sweet. Only three years later, in 1882, he was killed in a gunfight with Jack Allen at Trinidad, Colorado. Loving must have used up most of his luck avoiding the bullets fired by Richardson in the Long Branch. When he went up against Allen, his luck ran out completely.

But in Dodge City, they still talked about how two rivals for a girl had shot up the Long Branch in an argument over her. Not much in the way of immortality, but for Levi Richardson and Cock-eyed Frank Loving, it would have to do.

SHOOT-OUT AT THE TUTTLE DANCE HALL

For Newton, Kansas, 1871 was the town's day in the sun, so to speak. In previous years, the huge cattle drives that came up the trails from Texas converged on Abilene, fifty miles north, because that was the closest railhead where the drovers could sell their herds. But in 1871, the tracks of the Atchison, Topeka & Santa Fe Railroad reached Newton, and that became the new destination for the tens of thousands of rangy longhorns—and the wild Texas cowboys who brought them there.

In every cowtown, inevitably trouble broke out between the local citizens and the cowboys who were anxious to blow off steam after long, hard weeks on the trail. Newton was no different. The railroad tracks ran east and west and cut the town in half. North of the tracks was where the respectable people lived. South of the tracks was the area known as Hide Park; a misspelling, perhaps, inspired by London's Hyde Park. There were many Englishmen in the Old West, and some of them were even known to frequent red-light districts. At any rate, the saloons, dance halls, brothels, and gambling dens of Hide Park were where the Texans congregated when they came to Newton.

On August 11, 1871, a special election was held in Newton. On the ballot was the question of whether the county should issue bonds to help finance the construction of the Wichita & Southwestern Railroad, which would connect Newton with the burgeoning town of Wichita. Elections of all sorts were nearly always contentious affairs in the Old West, so the Newton town council decided to appoint several special policemen to help keep order in case trouble broke out. The problem with that idea was that some of the men appointed to quell trouble were the sort that were much more likely to cause it.

One of the special policemen was Mike McCluskie, a burly local man who had worked in Newton as a night watchman. Another was a Texan named Billy Bailey (though some said his real name was Wilson), a cowboy who had come up the trail through Indian Territory and made up his mind to stay in Newton and try to make his living as a gambler.

On the night of the election, instead of hanging around where the ballots were being counted, McCluskie and Bailey decided to head south of the tracks to a saloon in Hide Park instead. Trailing after them in the shadows came a young man known as Riley. Little more than a boy, Riley was wracked by consumption and everyone in Newton assumed that his days were numbered. For all of his rough manner, McCluskie had taken pity on Riley and befriended him, causing the youngster to look on him with something akin to hero worship. Like a dog, Riley trailed after McCluskie everywhere the bigger, older man went.

On this night, as McCluskie and Bailey played cards in some Hide Park dive, an argument broke out between them. No one knows the exact cause. A disagreement over the game, maybe, or perhaps an old grudge that had grown out of the fact that Bailey was a Texan and McCluskie, like most of the citizens of Newton, resented and disliked the Texans even though they depended on the cowboys and the trail herds for most of their income. For whatever reason, McCluskie and Bailey stepped out into the street to settle things. Some historians say that such man-to-man showdowns never took place in the Old West, but in this case it seems fairly evident that such a shoot-out did take place. Guns were drawn, shots rang out, and McCluskie walked away from the confrontation while Bailey lay dead behind him in the street.

No doubt the young consumptive called Riley watched what happened that night, and McCluskie must have grown even larger in his estimation.

Like all the Texans in Newton, Bailey had friends from the Lone Star State. Word of his death got around quickly, and rumors began to fly in the saloons. One of Bailey's friends, a cowboy named Hugh Anderson, was especially incensed about Bailey's death. Anderson vowed to settle the score for Bailey.

McCluskie, though a troublemaker, was no fool. He decided to follow the better part of valor and rode out of Newton, intending to stay away until the furor over Bailey's death died down. McCluskie either underestimated how upset Anderson and his Texas pards were, or else he just couldn't stay away from the fleshpots of Hide Park. Eight days after the shooting, on August 19, 1871, McCluskie was back in Newton. He went to Perry Tuttle's Dance Hall to have a drink and cut a rug with the soiled doves who worked there. At one time, McCluskie had worked for the railroad, and Tuttle's was frequented by railroaders who were still friendly with McCluskie. As usual, Riley lurked in a corner of the place, looking on in admiration of his hero.

Someone who had seen McCluskie in the dance hall must have gone running to find Hugh Anderson, because suddenly the doors of the hall were thrust open and Anderson strode in, followed by several of his friends. The Texans didn't waste time or breath on words. They had guns in their hands, and they started shooting as soon as they were in the dance hall. Colt flame bloomed in the smoky air, which became even more clouded with powder smoke. A slug tore through McCluskie's neck and knocked him off his feet. Though seriously wounded, McCluskie managed to get up and drag his revolver from its holster. He threw lead back at Anderson, hitting the cowboy in the thigh and knocking him down. But Anderson's friends were still shooting, and McCluskie was hit twice more. This time when he fell to the sawdust-littered floor, he didn't get up.

There must have been a pause then, a few seconds of shocked hush. But the respite from gunplay lasted only a heartbeat, because Riley, seeing McCluskie fatally wounded, slipped behind the Texans and locked the doors of the dance hall. His hand went under his coat and came out holding a pistol. No one in Newton had ever seen Riley with a gun before. Certainly no one had ever taken him for a pistoleer. He was just a scrawny kid on his last legs, dying of the consumption.

But on this night, Riley dealt out death as it was seldom seen, even on the frontier.

The gun in his hand crashed out shot after shot. Some of the Texans died without a sound as Riley's bullets ripped through them and pitched them to the floor. Others lived long enough to cry out in pain and surprise. Even though they were under attack and were being mowed down by Riley's unexpected assault, some of the cowboys managed to put up a fight. Unfortunately for the bystanders in the dance hall, the Texans' shots went wild. A railroader named Patrick Lee was hit in the groin and fatally wounded. Other men were less seriously injured.

To those who found themselves in the smoke-filled, hellish place that the dance hall had become in little more than the blink of an eye, the shoot-out must have seemed to last for a long time. In reality, less than a minute passed from the first shot to the last. Hugh Anderson, who had fired that first shot, was one of the luckiest men in the place. When McCluskie shot him in the thigh, he went down and stayed down, so the bullets that filled the air passed harmlessly over his head. Six of his companions were not so fortunate. They were all dead. Counting McCluskie and the bystanders who had been killed, the death toll in the dance hall stood at either nine or ten. The exact number was in dispute then and still is.

One man who had not been hit, as far as anyone knows, was Riley. When the smoke cleared, the youngster had disappeared. No one knew where he had gone, but he was never seen again in Newton, or anywhere else that history has recorded. His fate is unknown, but not the fact that on a hot August night in Newton, he proved himself to be one of the deadliest gunfighters in the West.

———◆———

THERE are a couple of postscripts to this story. Enough witnesses survived to point the finger of blame at Hugh Anderson for starting the shooting. He was arrested by the local law and charged with manslaughter. Before his trial could come up, however, his father arrived in Newton, having received word down in Texas of what had happened. The elder Anderson had hurried up to Kansas to see what he could do for his son. Somehow, he persuaded the authorities to let him take Hugh back to Texas to recover from his wound. It is unclear whether the charges were dropped against Anderson, but he never stood trial for what happened in the Tuttle dance hall.

Fate had something else in store for Hugh Anderson. The cycle of vengeance had one more revolution to make. Almost two years later, in June 1873, Anderson was working as a bartender at Harding's Trading Post in Medicine Lodge, Kansas, southwest of Newton. After recovering from the wound suffered in the dance-hall shoot-out, Anderson had drifted back to Kansas instead of staying home in Texas. Quite probably he had not forgotten the bloody events of that night, but it must have come as a surprise to him when he received word that Mike McCluskie's brother

Art was in Medicine Lodge and planned to avenge his brother's death.

To give credit where credit is due, Anderson didn't attempt to run. Perhaps he sensed that flight would be futile, that Art McCluskie would continue to pursue him to the ends of the earth if necessary to settle the score.

At Anderson's request, Harding, the owner of the trading post and a respected man in Medicine Lodge, arranged a showdown between the two men. While many of the townspeople looked on, Anderson and McCluskie met in the street in front of the trading post in another of those man-to-man gunfights that supposedly never took place. Harding had set this up as more of a formal duel. Anderson and McCluskie stood facing away from each other, each man with a gun in his hand, with twenty paces separating them. Harding gave the signal that the fight was to commence. Anderson and McCluskie spun around and blazed away at each other.

McCluskie scored first, drilling Anderson through the arm—but not his gun arm. Anderson fell to his knees, knocked off his feet by the shot, but he had the will and the presence of mind to fire again. His slug ripped away McCluskie's jaw.

Driven by rage and stubbornness, McCluskie overcame the agony of his wound and ran forward, closing the distance between him and Anderson. He eared back the hammer of his gun, ready to fire again as soon as he judged himself close enough. Anderson beat him to the punch, squeezing off two shots before McCluskie could pull the trigger. One slug caught McCluskie in the shoulder, while the other smashed into his midsection. McCluskie toppled forward, evidently fatally wounded.

His fall brought him closer to Anderson, though, and he managed to fire his gun again. This time the bullet tore into Anderson's belly. Anderson doubled over in the street.

McCluskie wasn't finished. Perhaps knowing that he was

done for, he wanted to be sure that Anderson went to hell first. He dropped his gun and drew his knife. As the onlookers gasped in horror, McCluskie began to drag his blood-soaked form through the dust of the street toward the Texan.

Some of the citizens called out to Harding to put a stop to this ghastly business. The trading post owner shook his head, declaring that Anderson and McCluskie had wanted a fight to the finish. That was exactly what they were getting.

McCluskie had almost reached Anderson by now. He pushed himself up and lifted the knife above his head, the blade poised for the death stroke. But before he could strike, Anderson, who had been lying on his face, rolled onto his side. Unknown to McCluskie or any of the bystanders, he had pulled his own knife from its sheath. With the last of his strength, he drove it upward, burying the blade in McCluskie's neck. Blood gushed from the wound and flooded the street around the two men. As McCluskie collapsed, dying, he brought his knife down and stabbed it deep into Anderson's side. That finished off the Texan. The two mortal enemies died there, practically in each other's arms, as the dirt street soaked up the spilled blood.

In modern parlance, what went around had come around, and the blood debt was settled. The only loose end was the young, disease-ridden gunman named Riley, and history has never been able to tie that one up. At this late date, it seems doubtful that it ever will.

6

LEVY, THE UNDERRATED GUNFIGHTER

One of the most enduring images of the Old West is the gunfight, the showdown in the middle of the street where two men face each other, slap leather, and blaze away. Some modern writers state categorically that such a thing never happened. Never, ever, not once.

Yet there are contemporary accounts of such gunfights occurring. Not at the rate they did and still do in Western fiction, of course. But if the middle-of-the-street showdown is a myth, then as with most myths, there is a kernel of truth to it.

Consider the case of Jim Levy, virtually unknown today but said by some who knew him to be one of the most deadly gunfighters in the West.

Born in Ireland of Jewish parents in 1842, Levy traveled to America sometime in the next three decades. The circumstances of his emigration are unknown. Perhaps his family came across the Atlantic to escape the great potato famine in Ireland and brought young Jim with them, or maybe he made the crossing at a later date on his own. What we do know is that in 1871 he was in Pioche, Nevada, working as a miner in the area's silver mines.

Pioche, while not a boomtown like some of the other mining camps, was a busy place. The mines produced relatively high-grade ore and attracted quite a few men to the area. Many of them, naturally, were pretty rough characters. Two such men were Mike Casey and Thomas Gosson. After arguing over something (exactly what is not known), the two men yanked out their guns and started shooting. Gosson was hit and knew that the wound was a mortal one. He had accumulated a pretty good stake from his efforts in the mines, so before life slipped away from him, he declared in the presence of witnesses that anyone who killed Mike Casey could claim five thousand dollars from his (Gosson's) estate.

With a bounty like that on his head, Casey was a marked man. It's unrecorded whether Jim Levy was the first one to go after him in an attempt to collect the blood money, but Levy was definitely the one who succeeded. He came up against Casey in the street in front of Pioche's general store and fired a shot that put Casey on the ground. Casey wasn't dead, though, only wounded, and in order for Levy to collect the bounty, the miner had to die. Levy walked up to the fallen man, but instead of putting another bullet in Casey's body, he bent over and began whaling Casey on the head with his gun. This is no way to treat a pistol—or a wounded man, for that matter—and some of the bystanders who considered themselves Casey's friends took exception to the brutal way Levy had chosen to finish him off. One of them pulled out a revolver and let fly at Levy, hitting him in the jaw.

The wound must have been severe enough to keep Levy from gunning down the man who had just shot him, because there is no record of such a killing. The shot came too late to save Mike Casey, however. His skull was bashed in already.

Levy remained in Pioche for a while, recovering from his injury. Those who knew him said that the shoot-out with Casey prompted a change in Levy, made him harder and more cold-blooded. There were more fights while he was in Nevada and at least one more killing, that of a man named Thomas Ryan. Ryan might have been the man who shot Levy in the jaw. Such an idea is pure speculation, but it seems logical that Levy would not have wanted the man who wounded him to get away with it. The fact that Levy was put on trial for the killing but acquitted is a possible indication that the jury considered the shooting justified.

Following the trial, Levy drifted to Virginia City, Nevada, and took up the pasteboards. Life as a gambler suited him, but when the word flew out of the Black Hills that gold had been discovered in Dakota Territory, Levy found himself unable to resist the siren song of the precious yellow metal. Along with thousands of other gold-seekers from all over the country, he lit a shuck for the Black Hills.

Levy didn't make it all the way to Dakota. He stopped in Cheyenne, Wyoming, which had become a jumping-off point for the prospectors heading to the Black Hills. In this bustling frontier community, Levy took up gambling again and probably made a pretty good living at it. Certainly there was no shortage of suckers for him to fleece, assuming that he even needed to cheat in order to clean out most of them.

Not surprisingly, though, some of the sore losers believed that Levy was shading his luck a little more than was proper and decorous. One such loser was Charlie Harrison, an Easterner who was a professional gambler himself. Harrison also had a reputation as a gunman, and was rumored to have killed several men in fair fights. He was said to be fast on the draw, mighty fast.

Jim Levy didn't care about that. When he and Harrison argued over cards and Harrison started flinging out insults directed at Levy's being both Irish and Jewish, Levy challenged him to back up his words with lead. Harrison was only too happy to oblige, and the two enemies arranged to confront each other on the street in front of Frenchy's Saloon.

The details of how far apart the two men stood and who went for his gun first are lost to history. It seems likely, though, that this was exactly the sort of gunfight that later was popularized in novels and films. Both men drew and fired, with Harrison getting off the first shot. The first several shots, in fact, because while Harrison was burning powder as fast as he could, Levy stood calmly in the street, ignored the bullets flying around him, and drew a bead on his adversary. When the gun in Levy's hand finally roared and bucked, Harrison was thrown backward by the slug slamming into him. The gambler from the East was fast, all right, but his aim was wild, wild as hell, and his speed hadn't bought him a thing except a few ounces of lead.

With his gun trained on Harrison, Levy walked over to his wounded enemy and stood above him. Unlike the incident in Pioche where he had bludgeoned Mike Casey to death, this time Levy used his gun for its more accustomed purpose and pumped another bullet into Harrison's body. The witnesses in Cheyenne didn't like this, either, but none of them took any potshots at Levy. His reputation as an icy-nerved killer had accompanied him to Wyoming from Nevada, and this gunfight with Charlie Harrison only increased Levy's standing as a gunman to step aside from.

This brief battle in front of Frenchy's Saloon took place on March 9, 1877. Harrison, shot twice by Levy, lingered until March 22 before dying of his wounds. Levy faced no legal charges in the killing. When word of what had happened spread, more famous pistoleers such as Wyatt Earp and Bat Masterson said that the showdown between Levy and Harrison was a perfect example of the fact that it was better for a shooter to be accurate than fast.

Apparently Levy was infected with the same wanderlust that defined many Westerners. From Cheyenne he moved on to Leadville, Colorado, and then to Tombstone, Arizona Territory. Both towns are well known for the gunplay that occurred in them, but Levy seems to have avoided trouble somehow during his sojourns in those famous frontier communities. Given his contentious nature, though, and his reliance on a gun to settle arguments, it was inevitable that sooner or later he would find himself involved in violence again.

It happened in Tucson. The Fashion Saloon was one of the town's most popular watering holes, so it's natural that Levy would ply his trade as a gambler there. He got in some sort of sharp disagreement with the man who ran the Fashion's faro bank, a fellow gambler named John Murphy. Hot words were exchanged, and someone—probably Levy—suggested that the two of them face each other in the street to settle things. The time for the showdown was to be the next morning, giving each man the opportunity for one more night's sleep on this earth before entering into an eternal rest.

Levy had to be feeling pretty good about his chances. After all, he had been in two such gunfights and had emerged alive and victorious from both of them. And he was a dangerous man. Wyatt Earp and Bat Masterson had said so, hadn't they?

Maybe John Murphy had heard what Wyatt and Bat had to say about Jim Levy. Or maybe he was just a practical man above all else. That night, a little after midnight on June 5, 1882, Murphy and two friends, Dave Gibson and Bill Moyer, were walking down the street in Tucson when they noticed Levy lounging in the doorway of the Palace Hotel. One of the trio pulled a gun and fired at Levy, and the other two joined in immediately.

Not expecting trouble until the next morning, Levy was taken by surprise when the guns began blasting. Slugs chewed splinters from the doorjamb just above his hat. It was then that the usually cool-headed Levy made a mistake and panicked. He thought someone inside the hotel was shooting at him, so he lunged across the boardwalk and out into the street. This made him an even better target for Murphy, Gibson, and Moyer. The three of them blasted him to pieces. Levy never had a chance.

That was true in more ways than one. Murphy and his companions probably planned to say that they had acted in self-defense, fearing that Levy was about to shoot at them. Given Levy's reputation as a killer, that tactic probably would have stood an excellent chance of working. The only thing wrong with it was that when people poured out of the hotel, drawn by the fusillade of shots, they searched Levy's bloody body and found that he didn't have a gun on him. Levy, the notorious gunfighter, had been unarmed when Murphy and the others opened up on him.

Even in the Old West, where the law was enforced rather capriciously, that was enough to prompt an arrest. Murphy, Moyer, and Gibson were thrown in the hoosegow and charged with murder. They never stood trial on those charges, however. While waiting for the case to come up in court, the three men managed to break out of jail. A posse pursued them but failed to catch them, so Levy's killers eluded justice. Where they went and what happened to them later has never been discovered. Their fate is just one of many unanswered questions in the history of the West.

And Jim Levy, feared far and wide as a gunman in his day, is almost as unknown today as the men who killed him.

THE CAPTURE OF
"BLACKFACE CHARLEY"
BRYANT

In 1892, Hennessey, Oklahoma Territory, was a small, quiet settlement northwest of Guthrie, the territorial capital. One of the few two-story buildings in town was the Rock Island Hotel, run by a former rancher, Ben Thorne, and his sister Jean. The hotel was a rather run-down, squalid place, but on this June day, the man who lay in bed in one of the second-floor rooms didn't care how fancy his surroundings were. He was sick, and all he wanted was a place to rest. Whatever disease he had, he was sure he had caught it from some soiled dove. There was a doctor over in the town of Mulhall who was supposed to have had some success at curing such conditions, so the man in the hotel room had set out to see him. He'd made it only as far as Hennessey, though, before weariness made him halt and take a room at the hotel. His sister lived here in Hennessey; he knew the town, knew the folks who lived here. It would be safe enough for him to rest for a few days before traveling on, he decided. As he lay in bed, he fingered the black mark on his left cheek, the result of a powder burn when a gun had gone off practically in his face during a saloon fight. It was the middle of the day, and he had asked for his lunch to be brought up to him. He expected it soon.

What Blackface Charley Bryant didn't know was that Jean Thorne was already on her way upstairs with a tray. And close behind her on the stairs was a man with a gun in his hand. . . .

———————✦———————

CHARLEY Bryant wasn't always an outlaw. He started out as a cowboy, a puncher who rode for Oscar Halsell's HX Bar ranch on the Cimarron River. Quite a few of Halsell's riders were reckless young men who drifted easily to the wrong side of the law, including Bill Doolin. (For more on Doolin, see "The Doolin Bunch vs. the U.S. Marshals," elsewhere in this volume.) In 1891, Bryant, Doolin, and several other Oklahoma cowboys fell in with three brothers from Kansas, Bob, Grat, and Emmett Dalton, who were just beginning their career as outlaws. Though some say that the Daltons were involved in several robberies in California with their brother Bill prior to this, it is more likely that their first real criminal act was the holdup of the Santa Fe express train at Wharton on May 9, 1891.

This robbery was planned by Bob Dalton, with the strategy used to carry it out influenced heavily by similar jobs pulled by the James Gang and the Younger brothers. The Guthrie-Wichita Express barreled northward, stopping only if it was signaled to do so at one of the small towns on its route. The Santa Fe timetable, which was adhered to as closely as possible by the engineers, called for the train to pass through Wharton at 10:13 P.M.

Shortly before that time, several members of the gang rode up to the station, but only two of them went inside with bandannas pulled up over their faces and guns in their hands. One of these men was definitely Charley Bryant; it seems likely the other was Bob Dalton, who would have wanted to see firsthand that his carefully orchestrated plan was carried out correctly. Only one man was on duty in the station at this time of night. He looked up to see himself covered by two masked desperadoes and did the only thing he could: He raised his hands and cooperated.

The outlaws ordered the station agent to set the signals so that the express train would stop. As soon as the man had done so, the bandits pushed him into a chair and bound his hands behind him. They didn't consider him a threat any longer, and the train would soon be there.

When the engineer saw the signals at Wharton, he hit the brakes and brought his locomotive hissing and lurching to a halt. Almost before the train stopped, one of the Dalton gang had leaped into the cab and shoved a gun in the engineer's face. Farther back, at the express car, the messenger opened the door to see why the train had stopped. He must have known that was a mistake as soon as he found himself staring down the barrels of several rifles. The messenger raised his hands and backed away from the door, giving the outlaws room to climb in.

Equally as puzzled as the express messenger, the train's conductor hopped down from the caboose and started forward along the line of stopped cars. Out in the darkness, a rifle barked and the slug kicked up cinders from the roadbed at the conductor's feet. A voice called out for him to elevate and stand where he was. Again, the conductor had no choice but to obey. The outlaws had gotten the drop on him just as surely as they had the station agent and the express messenger.

Inside the express car, the two holdup men forced the messenger to stuff a grain sack full of money from the safe. When that was done, to the tune of about fifteen hundred dollars, the outlaws turned to climb down from the car onto the platform.

That was when Charley Bryant, one of the two bandits in the express car, looked through the window of the depot and saw that the man they had tied up had gotten loose somehow. He was hunched over his telegraph key, no doubt tapping out a warning about the holdup. Without hesitating, Bryant brought his rifle to his shoulder and fired. The station window shattered as the bullet punched through it and slammed into the agent, knocking him away from the telegraph and onto the floor. The wound was a fatal one.

Bryant and his companion leaped on their horses, which were being held by other members of the gang, and raced off into the darkness, taking their loot with them and leaving a dead man behind them. The beginning of several outlaw careers had been christened in blood.

Early the next morning, the Daltons and the other outlaws, including Charley Bryant, stole a small herd of horses. They came across the animals while they were putting distance between themselves and the scene of the train holdup at Wharton, and the smart thing to do would have been to leave the horses alone and keep dusting along the trail. Being outlaws, they did the greedy but dumb thing instead. The stolen horses slowed them down, and worse still, the theft brought out another group of pursuers. This posse, made up of cowboys and ranchers, was chasing horse thieves, not train robbers, and had no idea that the men they sought were the same ones responsible for the holdup and murder at Wharton.

That evening, along a stream aptly named Skeleton Creek, the posse caught up to the unsuspecting outlaws, and several shots were fired before the gang abandoned the stolen horses and took off for the tall and uncut. Again they left a dead man behind, a posse member named Starmer.

With two killings to their credit in less than twenty-four hours, the newly formed Dalton Gang may have decided that the smart thing to do would be to lie low for a while. In this case, the period of inactivity involving the gang lasted some thirteen months. Maybe they were debating whether to continue their career of outlawry, or maybe they were just waiting for the right time to resume their crimes.

Some members of the gang—Bill Doolin, Dick Powers, and

Dick Broadwell—returned to the HX Bar ranch and went back to work as cowboys. The Dalton brothers lay especially low, because the express messenger had identified Bob Dalton as one of the masked men who had held him up, prompting the press to start printing sensational stories about the so-called Dalton Gang. The other bandit was unknown to the messenger, but he had a large dark smudge on his left cheek. This was the man who had fired the fatal shot at the station agent, and his description was circulated to lawmen throughout Oklahoma Territory.

Months passed, and although the train robbery at Wharton was not forgotten, the furor over it had died down considerably. The Santa Fe Railroad offered a thousand-dollar reward for information leading to the arrest and conviction of the desperadoes, along with another thousand for the capture of the man who had killed the station agent.

By August of 1892, Charley Bryant had fallen ill, most likely from syphilis. In seeking medical help, he found out about a doctor in the town of Mulhall who might be able to cure him. Bryant set out to see him, but stopped in the town of Hennessey, hoping to regain some of his strength.

Bryant was known in Hennessey, mostly because his sister Daisy lived there. Daisy was said to be quite attractive, as well as quite well endowed, and she was a particular favorite of Bob Dalton. With this connection to the Daltons and the fact that Bryant sported a black mark on his cheek, it should come as no surprise that someone finally suspected he might have had something to do with the robbery at Wharton and the killing of the station agent. It's more surprising that no one seems to have tumbled to it until Deputy U.S. Marshal Ed Short did so.

Short was assigned to the marshal's office in Guthrie, but worked out of the Hennessey area. When he decided that he wanted to lay hands on Bryant, he went first to the 3 Circle Z ranch, where Bryant had worked recently as a cowhand. Bryant wasn't there, of course, but from the way Short went hurrying

back to Hennessey, it seems likely someone on the 3 Circle Z
told him where to find the man he was looking for.

Short probably questioned Ben and Jean Thorne and found
out that Bryant was upstairs. When Jean Thorne started up the
stairs with a lunch tray for Bryant, Short was right behind her.
Jean rapped on the door of Bryant's room, identified herself, and
was told by the ill outlaw to come in. Short threw the door open
instead and leveled his pistol at Bryant. A gun lay on the table
beside the bed, but Bryant didn't reach for it. Short had the drop
on him, and to make a grab for the gun would be to commit suicide.

When Bryant was dressed, Short snapped a pair of manacles
on him. Short couldn't be sure how many friends Bryant had in
Hennessey, or how likely those friends might be to try to help
him escape once they heard that he had been captured by the
law. The smart thing to do, Short decided, was to get out of town
as quickly as possible. He wanted to get Bryant to Guthrie and
lock him up there, but the next train heading in that direction
wouldn't pass through Hennessey until the next day. Short figured out an alternate plan. When the northbound, a Rock Island
Line train, came through that evening, heading for Wichita, Short
and Bryant would board it. Bryant could spend the night in
Wichita's sturdy jail, and then Short could take him back to
Guthrie on the Santa Fe train the next day.

The plan might well have worked if Short had been a little
more careful.

Timing their departure from the hotel so that they wouldn't
have to wait long at the station, Short hustled his prisoner onto
the train without any trouble. Instead of taking Bryant into one of
the passenger cars, Short installed him in the baggage car. The
baggage clerk could help him keep an eye on the prisoner during
the run up to Wichita, Short reasoned.

This Rock Island train was a local, not an express like the one
the Dalton Gang had robbed at Wharton. It stopped at every sta-

tion, regardless of whether or not the signals were up. After several such stops, the train rolled into a small settlement called Waukomis. Ever since being captured, Bryant had been the very picture of dejection. He sat with his head down, his manacled hands clasped between his knees. His illness may well have had something to do with his attitude, too. Here he was, sick as a dog just because he had gone to bed with the wrong woman, and now he was facing prison—or worse, a noose.

It must have seemed to him that he had nothing to lose. . . .

When the train stopped at Waukomis, Ed Short pulled his pistol and handed it over to the baggage clerk, asking him to watch Bryant while he stepped out onto the platform for a breath of air. Short kept his rifle with him, tucked under his arm.

The clerk agreed to Short's request, but he had paperwork to do and after a few minutes grew distracted as he sat at his desk. He stuck the deputy's pistol in one of the cubbyholes used for sorting mail so that he might concentrate better on what he was doing.

It's impossible to know whether Bryant had been watching for just such an opportunity or if he just happened to see a chance for a break. But in the next moment, acting with surprising speed, Bryant lunged across the car and got both of his manacled hands on the gun that the clerk had so carelessly laid aside. Shocked and scared, the clerk threw up his hands and backed away, not even trying to keep Bryant from reaching the door.

When Bryant, now armed, leaped out onto the platform, Ed Short was only a few yards away. Bryant didn't hesitate. He blazed away at the man who had arrested him and clapped him in irons.

Bryant's first shot smashed into Short, inflicting a mortal wound. Short didn't die instantly, though. He was able to turn and bring up his rifle. It cracked twice even as Short was sagging to his knees. The bullets tore through Bryant and knocked him backward. He tumbled down the platform steps. Short, his life slipping away as blood pooled around him, dropped the rifle and crawled forward to reach down and clutch Bryant's legs. Bryant wasn't going to get away. That determined thought may well have been going through Ed Short's mind as he drew his last breath.

The deputy was right. Blackface Charley Bryant was dead. The man who fired the first fatal shot in the Dalton Gang's reign of banditry had been brought to justice.

PART TWO

GANGS

Don't shoot. I am unarmed and helpless. I am the man you are looking for. I am Sam Bass.

—Sam Bass

1

BATTLE FOR THE COUNTY SEAT

In the Old West, as today, there were many things that could lead to violence. Some of them were so mundane it seems odd that men were willing to fight and die for them.

Such as outright war between communities over which one would serve as the county seat . . .

In Kansas in the late 1880s, as new counties were being organized in the western part of the state, the towns in those counties were fierce rivals in the race to be named as the county seat. Some economic benefits could accrue from being the center of county government, as any business deals struck by the county would usually favor the town that served as its seat. However, for the most part it seemed to be bragging rights that prompted the rivalries. Some towns went so far as to hire bands of gunmen to "protect their interests." That protection usually involved intimidating voters—at the point of a gun, if necessary—into voting for one town over another in the elections that were held to determine the location of the county seat. And when the election was over, the losing town sometimes resorted to hiring their own gun-men to "appeal" the results. It was a bloody time on the prairies of western Kansas.

One of the most violent such clashes, and one involving some names that would become well-known in the history of the West, occurred in Gray County, west of Dodge City, where the commu-nities of Cimarron and Ingalls both vied to be named the location of the county seat. An election to settle the issue was held in 1887, and Cimarron emerged victorious. The citizens of Ingalls insisted the election had not been fair and that fraudulent votes had been cast by railroad workers who had no right to cast ballots in the contest. They went to court and filed a suit to overturn the results of the election.

The court case dragged on for a year, and eventually went all the way to the Kansas Supreme Court. Finally, the court decided in favor of the plaintiffs from Ingalls. The election results were ruled invalid, and the Supreme Court declared that henceforth, Ingalls would be the county seat of Gray County.

Naturally, this decision didn't go down well with the inhabi-tants of Cimarron. While the court case had been making its tor-turous way through the various levels of Kansas jurisprudence, another election had been held, this one for the office of county clerk. Newt Watson, the candidate from Ingalls, won, and when the Supreme Court declared that Ingalls was the new county seat, Watson sent a message to Cimarron demanding that the county seal and all the county records be turned over to him. The local officials in Cimarron refused, and the stage was set for a violent confrontation.

George Bolds, a surveyor who was one of the leaders of the faction from Ingalls, was something of a firebrand as well. He sug-gested that Ingalls hire a group of men to go to Cimarron and retrieve the seal and the records. Such things were not without precedent. There had been similar trouble between the towns of Leoti and Coronado, up in Wichita County, and several people had been killed. One of the men involved in that clash was a young peace officer from Dodge City named Bill Tilghman. Bolds suggested that Watson and the other county officials from Ingalls get in touch with Tilghman and hire him to take charge of the effort to recover the seal and the records from Cimarron. Tilghman accepted the offer.

Bill Tilghman was a former buffalo hunter, a tall, strapping young man who was an expert shot with both pistol and rifle. He had hunted in Kansas and down in the Texas Panhandle and had seen his share of trouble, fighting off Indians on several occasions and nearly freezing to death when a sudden winter storm hit. At Adobe Walls, the scene of a famous battle between buffalo hunters and Indians in the Texas Panhandle, Tilghman met another young hunter named Bat Masterson and formed a friendship that lasted the rest of his life. Tilghman, Masterson, and Neal Brown formed a partnership and hunted buffalo together until the herds dwindled to the point that it was no longer profitable. Masterson and Brown went to Dodge City, where they were known already, and became lawmen. Masterson was elected sheriff of Ford County and Brown was a deputy city marshal, serving under Jim Masterson, Bat's brother.

Tilghman drifted over to Dodge City, too, and may have served as one of Bat Masterson's deputies; the record is unclear on that. What is known is that after trying his hand at ranching and running a saloon, Bill Tilghman became the marshal of Dodge City in 1884. He was well respected, even feared, and the formerly wild and woolly Dodge City settled down considerably while he was in office. The cattle trade fell off in 1886, following a huge blizzard, and things became too quiet in Dodge to suit Tilghman. He decided not to run for re-election and went back to ranching.

But although he was far from the sort of flamboyant glory-seeker that, say, Wild Bill Hickok was, law enforcement was in Tilghman's blood by now. The desire to see that the law was car-

William Tilghman, in a photo taken later in his life . . . one of the most famous scouts, buffalo hunters, and lawmen in the history of the West, whose career spanned the early days of the frontier up to the Oklahoma oil boom of the twentieth century.

(Courtesy of Denver Public Library, Western History Collection)

ried out fully and fairly may be what led to his involvement in the County Seat Wars. The money to be made and the excitement to be had probably were factors as well.

Once he had accepted a fee of one thousand dollars from the citizens of Ingalls, Tilghman began to make his plans for the raid on Cimarron's courthouse. He couldn't carry out such a daring, dangerous scheme by himself, of course. He recruited several men to help him, including Neal Brown and Jim Masterson, like Tilghman former lawmen from Dodge City. Some say Wyatt Earp was also a member of Tilghman's party, but that seems open to debate. What is certain is that George Bolds, the hot-tempered young surveyor, was part of the group.

Tilghman decided to hit the courthouse early on the morning of January 2, 1889. Not only was it the day after a holiday, but it was also a Sunday. The churchgoers would be getting ready for services; the folks who had been celebrating the holiday and carousing the night before would still be sleeping off their celebration. That was Tilghman's theory, anyway. He hoped he and his men could get into Cimarron, get the records and the county seal from the courthouse, and be out of town before anyone knew what was going on.

It didn't quite work out that way.

The men drove into Cimarron in a wagon and stopped in front of the courthouse. They carried rifles and pistols and wore badges, having been sworn in as deputies by Tilghman, who had been appointed temporary sheriff of Gray County by Newt Watson so as to give this expedition some official standing. It was a clear, cold winter morning, and not many people should have been stirring. Tilghman and his companions hopped down from the wagon, went into the unlocked county clerk's office, and started carrying out bundles of files and documents.

How the ruckus got started is unknown. Someone in Cimarron may have spotted the raiders at the courthouse and figured out what was going on, or news of Tilghman's plan could have leaked some other way. At any rate, gunshots suddenly shattered the peacefulness of this Sunday morning as Cimarron residents opened fire on Tilghman's party from surrounding buildings.

Tilghman, George Bolds, and several other deputies were outside by the wagon when the shooting started. A bullet burned Tilghman's leg, wounding him but not severely. A man named Ed Brooks was hit in the belly, a more serious wound. George Bolds suffered three wounds in a matter of seconds as one bullet ripped through his leg and two more smashed into his body. He was bleeding like a stuck pig as a couple of his companions helped him into the wagon. The deputy at the reins, Charlie Reicheldeffer, was wounded as well, but managed to stay on the driver's seat and hang on to the leathers.

Tilghman had brought his old buffalo gun with him. The heavy carbine boomed again and again, Tilghman reloading between each shot with the practiced ease of a veteran buffalo hunter. The massive slugs tore through the buildings where the bushwhackers were holed up, and caused them to duck for cover, giving Tilghman's party the chance to get the wounded men into the wagon. Reicheldeffer flapped the reins and shouted to his team, and the horses took off, racing out of Cimarron with the wagon bouncing behind them. Tilghman kept up a covering fire from the back of the wagon.

The problem was that not all of the men had gotten out of the courthouse after the shooting started. Four of them were still inside: Jim Masterson, Newt Watson, Fred Singer, and Billy Allensworth. Too much lead was flying through the air for them to risk making a dash to the wagon before it rolled away. When Tilghman and the others were gone, the citizens of Cimarron turned their attention to the courthouse instead. The four men were trapped there, and no doubt the townspeople intended to make an example of them and teach the folks over in Ingalls a lesson. Tarring and feathering would be the least the men in the courthouse could expect if they were taken prisoner by the enraged inhabitants of Cimarron. There might even be a lynching. . . .

Masterson and the others raced up the stairs to the second floor of the courthouse, knowing that it would be better to fight from the high ground. They trained their guns on the staircase, and sure enough, as soon as the attackers worked up enough courage, they rushed into the courthouse and started up the stairs, shouting curses as they came.

Masterson, Watson, Singer, and Allensworth opened fire, throwing a deadly hail of lead down the stairs. Defiant shouts quickly became yelps of pain and fear as the townspeople retreated from that barrage. Several of them had been wounded, and they had failed to do any damage to the defenders on the second floor of the courthouse.

Jim Masterson, though never as famous as his brother, was

cool-headed in a fight and a solid, dependable lawman. He probably exerted a calming influence on his three companions. As long as their ammunition lasted, they could hold off the attacks on the courthouse. The only real worry was that the attackers might set the place on fire. Masterson and his friends wouldn't be able to deal with that.

The people from Cimarron weren't ready to go that far—yet. Instead they carried a ladder around to the rear of the courthouse and propped it against the wall, hoping they could swarm up it through an open window and catch the defenders from behind. Masterson's keen hearing warned him, however, and he rushed to the window where the top of the ladder rested. Putting a booted foot against the top rung, he shoved as hard as he could, and was rewarded by frightened yells from the men already on the ladder as it toppled backward. A few shots sent the men on the ground scurrying away. They wouldn't try that tactic again.

Masterson rejoined the others and waited to see what the enemy would come up with next. They didn't have long to wait. Faint sounds told them that the attackers were in the first-floor room underneath them. That was the only warning they had before guns roared and bullets began to punch through the wooden floor.

Hurriedly, the defenders climbed on top of desks and filing cabinets in the office where they had taken refuge. One of the men even hopped on top of a steel safe. The extra protection shielded them from the slugs smacking through the floor, but didn't do anything to lessen the nerve-wracking din. No one knows for sure how long this part of the assault lasted, but it must have seemed longer than it really was to the men who crouched there on top of the furniture as hundreds of bullets heated the air only inches away from them.

Meanwhile, on the prairie west of Cimarron, the wagon carrying Bill Tilghman and his companions still raced toward Ingalls with a party of gunmen from Cimarron chasing after them. Every time the pursuers threatened to close in, Tilghman's buffalo rifle drove them back. Several men were hit, and finally, as Ingalls came into view in the distance, the men from Cimarron turned back. The presence of a heavily armed group of men riding out from Ingalls to meet Tilghman probably played a large part in the decision.

The wagon bed was full of blood, most of it having leaked out of George Bolds's bullet-ventilated body. There was so much blood it soaked into some of the records taken from the county clerk's office in the Cimarron courthouse. But Bolds was clinging stubbornly to life. When the wagon reached Ingalls, he was hustled to the nearest doctor's office, along with the other wounded men. Tilghman's bullet scratch was minor, and he was more concerned with getting word to Dodge City about what had happened than he was with getting that wound patched up. Tilghman had been forced to leave four men behind, including his good friend Jim Masterson, and his uncertainty about their fate had to be eating away at him.

In Cimarron, the standoff between the men on the second floor of the courthouse and the townspeople besieging them might have gone on for a long time, but after several hours the key in the Cimarron telegraph office began to click. As the clerk listened to the dots and dashes and took down the message, his eyes must have widened in surprise. Cimarron was in for real trouble. The clerk probably ripped the message off his pad and ran down the street toward the courthouse as fast as he could.

The telegram was from Bat Masterson, and its message was simple: His brother Jim and the others would be allowed to leave town safely, or Bat would descend on Cimarron with enough gun-tough men in tow to wipe the place off the map.

The stubborn pride that had prompted this bloody battle had its limits. The men of Cimarron were proud, but they weren't fools. They let Jim Masterson and the others go.

No one in Tilghman's group died from his wounds, not even

George Bolds. There was only one fatality on Cimarron's side, a man named J. W. English. Trouble might have flared up again between the two towns, but the governor of Kansas, John A. Martin, sent in the state militia to keep the peace. Ingalls remained the county seat for a time, but eventually it was moved back to Cimarron. . . .

Without any bloodshed this time.

THE LAST DALTON RAID

ust moments after nine o'clock in the morning of October 5, 1892, five men rode into the town of Coffeyville, Kansas, not far from the Kansas-Oklahoma border. Though the streets of the settlement were unpaved, Coffeyville was a bustling, growing community. It already sported two banks in the center of town, on adjoining sides of a large plaza. The First National was in a block of buildings to the east, facing Union Street, while the Condon Bank stood by itself to the west, facing south into the plaza. As the banking center for this prosperous region of successful ranches and farms, Coffeyville's two financial institutions often had a large amount of cash in their vaults. Such was the case this morning.

And that was why the five men riding into town had the banks as their destinations. The Dalton Gang had come to Coffeyville to do something no band of outlaws had ever accomplished before, not even the James Gang and the Youngers. They were going to rob both banks at the same time. . . .

In the Old West, many men rode at various times in their lives on both sides of the law. The Dalton brothers were prime examples of this. Born in Missouri into a large family of ten boys and five girls (two of whom died in infancy), Bob, Grat, and Emmett Dalton would become well known first as lawmen, then as outlaws. Before that, though, they were cowboys, riding for ranches in Indian Territory, where they would meet many of the men who later joined forces with them to rob trains and banks.

The first Dalton brother to pack a badge was the oldest, Frank. He went to work for the Indian Police, and became known as a competent manhunter responsible for capturing several whiskey runners who were bringing liquor into the Nations and illegally selling it to the Indians. Frank's activities on behalf of the law brought him to the attention of Judge Isaac Parker, who presided over the federal court in Fort Smith, Arkansas, that had jurisdiction over Indian Territory. When Parker offered Frank Dalton a position as a deputy United States marshal, Frank accepted and continued the same work of hunting down whiskey runners and rustlers and horse thieves.

In 1887, during a violent confrontation between Frank and another deputy and several whiskey smugglers, Frank was shot and badly wounded. One of the whiskey runners managed to jam the muzzle of his Winchester in Frank's mouth and blow his head off before the other deputy killed him.

Bob, Grat, and Emmett had idolized their older brother. Bob was already working as an Indian Policeman, and Frank's death in the line of duty prompted the other two to join the Indian Police as well. They weren't as devoted to the concepts of law and order as Frank had been, however, and the brothers soon found themselves giving in to the temptation to use their official positions to line their own pockets. They took bribes from whiskey smugglers and from white settlers who wanted to be allowed into Indian Territory to grab land. Also, when a pretty female cousin whom Bob had his eye on took up with another man, Bob shot and killed the man, then claimed that the victim had been a criminal and was trying to escape.

Some say the Daltons came by their lawless ways naturally, since their mother was a second cousin to the infamous Younger brothers, who had ridden with Jesse James. It's no secret that growing up in Missouri and Kansas, the Daltons heard plenty of glamorous, exciting stories about their notorious relatives. Bob especially was quite impressed with Jesse James, and may have thought at an early age that someday he would emulate Jesse's exploits.

Despite their bending of the law as Indian Policemen, the Daltons had good enough reputations to be hired as deputy U.S. marshals, as their brother Frank had been before them. This gave them even more opportunities for graft and corruption. As lawmen, they had ridden all over the territory. They knew all the best hiding places, and they soon became experts at stealing horses and hiding them until they could be slipped across the border and sold. It was during this time as well that they came across an isolated cave formed by a limestone ledge jutting out over the Cimarron River. This came to be known as Dalton's Cave, and was used frequently by the gang as a hideout during their train-robbing days.

The brothers' time as lawmen came to an end when they arrested a young Indian accused of robbing a store. Shooting first and asking questions later, the Daltons filled the boy full of lead with no provocation. Miraculously, the boy survived his wounds, but the damage to the reputation of the three Dalton brothers, which was already shady at best, was too much to be accepted by Judge Parker. They were relieved of their badges and fired as deputy marshals.

Without the shield that their positions had given them, their horse-stealing activities came to light, and all three brothers decided that it might be best for them to leave Indian Territory before a lynch mob came after them. They drifted west to New Mexico, where they robbed a crooked card dealer. That got them in hot water, so for the first time, the Dalton brothers split up. Emmett went back to Indian Territory, while Bob and Grat headed farther west to visit their brother Bill in California.

Much speculation has centered around Bob and Grat Dalton's trip to California. Bill Dalton had become involved in politics out there, and the smart thing for him to do would have been to send his brothers packing. Instead, he honored family ties and welcomed them. However, it wasn't long before word got around that Bob and Grat were desperadoes on the run, and when several train robberies occurred in the area, the Daltons, including Bill, got the blame. Bill Dalton's political career was over before it had much of a chance to get started.

Historians still disagree about what really happened while the Daltons were in California. Some accept the story that they carried out the train robberies of which they were accused, while others completely discount the idea. Supposedly, Bob and Grat were arrested and tried for the crimes, but somehow Bob was found innocent while Grat was convicted. According to this version, Bob headed back to Indian Territory and Grat escaped from the law while he was being taken to prison. This yarn has it that Grat got out of his handcuffs while he was on a train carrying him to the penitentiary, and made a daring leap from the moving train into the San Joaquin River. Other writers of Old West history claim that none of this happened and that Bob and Grat were never even put on trial for the California robberies. At this late date, the full truth of the matter may never come to light, but evidence seems to indicate that Bob and Grat did not take part in any train robberies while they were in California. Just the rumors, however, were enough to ruin Bill Dalton's political hopes. Though he returned to Oklahoma later, he never rode as a member of his brothers' gang, joining up instead with Bill Doolin's Oklahombres. (See "The Doolin Bunch vs. the U.S. Marshals" elsewhere in this volume.)

Back in Oklahoma, Bob Dalton, who was the undisputed leader among the brothers despite not being the oldest (that was Grat), put together the group that would become known far and wide as the Dalton Gang. It included himself, his brothers Grat and Emmett, Bill Doolin, Bill Powers, Dick Broadwell, Bitter Creek Newcomb, and Blackface Charley Bryant. Bob was ready to move up from horse stealing to something bigger and better: train robbery. The gang's first job was to hold up the Santa Fe express at Wharton. (See "The Capture of 'Blackface Charley' Bryant" elsewhere in this volume.)

Though the robbery at Wharton was a success, the gang didn't strike again for over a year. In the summer of 1892, they resumed their activities, pulling off several train robberies, including holdups at Red Rock and Adair. All of these crimes followed the pattern established in the gang's first holdup at Wharton. They rode in just before a train was due, took over the station, and cut the telegraph wires into the place, sometimes taking other prisoners in the town as well. Then the station agent was forced at gunpoint to set the signal lights so that the train would stop. When it did, the outlaws swarmed aboard, some of them holding guns on the conductor, engineer, and fireman, while others forced the express messenger to open the safe in the express car. Bob Dalton always threatened to dynamite the safe if the messenger didn't cooperate, but he never had to follow through on that threat. The messengers did the sensible thing and let the bandits get away with the loot.

At the robbery in Adair, however, trouble broke out because the Daltons didn't know that the money shipment on the train was accompanied by several armed guards. There was a brief but

fierce battle between outlaws and guards, during which two innocent bystanders, both of them doctors, were wounded, one fatally.
The shots that killed one doctor and wounded the other were
fired by the guards, not by the Dalton Gang, and that tragic death
was the only thing accomplished by the fusillade. The outlaws
got the money they were after and rode away without a scratch.

Despite the gang's success at robbing trains, Bob Dalton had
his sights set higher. He still wanted to do something that would
lift him and his brothers to the same level as Frank and Jesse
James and the Younger brothers (forgetting, perhaps, that by now
Jesse and one of the Youngers, John, were dead, and the other
three Youngers were in prison; Frank James was the only one of
that earlier gang still breathing free air). The plan that Bob came
up with was daring. No one had ever robbed two banks at the
same time before. But Bob decided that was exactly what the
Dalton Gang would do. As targets, he picked the First National
Bank of Coffeyville, Kansas, along with the Condon Bank practically next door. The Daltons had lived in Coffeyville for quite a
while when they were younger, and they knew the town very
well.

But the town knew them, too. . . .

———◆———

ONCE Bob Dalton had decided what he wanted to do, he had to
sell the others on the idea. Grat and Emmett, being his brothers,
were easy to convince. Bill Powers and Dick Broadwell also
agreed to go along on the raid after thinking it over. Bill Doolin
was more hesitant, but finally said that if the others were going,
he would, too. The six men rode to the vicinity of Coffeyville and
spent the night of October 4, 1892, camped nearby on Onion
Creek. Early on the morning of October 5, they mounted up and
rode toward the settlement.

Six men started out, but only five got there. Along the way,
Bill Doolin's horse went lame. No one could expect a man to

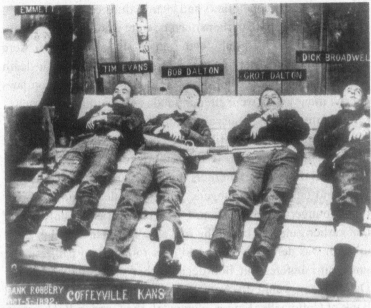

The bodies of the Dalton brothers, along with two members of their gang, after their ill-fated attempted bank robbery at Coffeyville, Kansas, October 5, 1892. The badly wounded Emmett Dalton, at upper left, survived his injuries and lived for many years afterward, becoming a bestselling author with his account of the gang's activities, *When the Daltons Rode*.

(Courtesy of Denver Public Library, Western History Collection)

make a getaway, guns blazing, on a lame horse, so he turned around, saying that he would dab a loop on a likely looking mount they had passed in a field a ways back. He would catch up with the others later, he said.

Whether or not this is actually the way it happened is open to debate. Maybe Bill Doolin's horse really did come up lame. Maybe he was just trying to save face and had decided to back out of what he considered an unwise plan. What is known for sure is that Doolin was not in Coffeyville on that fateful morning.

The three Daltons and their two companions rode on into town, and once again chance played a vital part in what was to come. Bob had planned to leave their horses in front of the Condon Bank where they would be handy once the robberies were concluded. However, the street in front of the bank was torn up due to some repairs going on, and there was no place to tie the horses. They were forced to lead the animals down an alley west of the Condon Bank, where they fastened the reins to an iron post.

Again the historians disagree on what happened next. Most versions of the story have the five men pausing in the alley to don false beards and mustaches as disguises, since the Daltons were known in Coffeyville. However, some doubts have been raised about this. For one thing, Bob Dalton had planned to leave the horses in front of the Condon Bank. The gang never would have been in the alley if Bob's original plan had worked out. And if their aim was to keep people from noticing them, it seems unlikely they would have stood in front of the bank where any-one could see them and put on false beards. The disguise story seems doubtful for another reason that will be dealt with shortly.

Whether they were wearing beards or not, the five men walked out of the alley carrying Winchesters and split up. Grat Dalton, Bill Powers, and Dick Broadwell went to the closer Con-don Bank, while Bob and Emmett Dalton headed across Union Street to the First National Bank. They went inside to start the robberies.

Unknown to the outlaws, they had been seen and recognized, and already the word was streaking around town that the Daltons were robbing the banks. This wasn't totally unexpected; for the past couple of weeks rumors had been floating around that the gang would try to hold up some bank in the area. Men who weren't already armed hurried into hardware stores and empori-ums to grab rifles, shotguns, and handfuls of ammunition. Then these armed citizens started closing in on the banks.

Inside the First National, things were going fairly smoothly for Bob and Emmett. They had taken four bank employees pris-oner and forced one of the men to stuff $21,000 in a sack. Across the way in the Condon, however, Grat and his companions had run into trouble. A fast-thinking bank cashier insisted that the vault was on a time lock and could not be opened until 9:30. When Grat, never the smartest of the brothers, asked him what time it was, the man told him it was 9:20. Grat decided they could afford to wait another ten minutes.

In reality, though, the time was 9:40 and the vault could have been opened. And the Daltons didn't have ten minutes to waste. In fact, time had run out for them.

Shots rang out as the citizens of Coffeyville opened fire on the First National just as Bob and Emmett herded their hostages out the front door. The bullets flying around their heads made Bob and Emmett duck back inside the building. Freed, the four hostages ran for cover down the sidewalk, darting into Isham's Hardware Store next door in search of weapons.

Bob and Emmett dashed through the bank and out the back door into an alley. There they ran into Lucius Baldwin, a clerk who worked in Isham's. Baldwin had a rifle in his hands, having run out into the alley in hopes of taking a shot at the robbers. Instead, Bob cut him down, killing him with a single shot. Bob and Emmett turned and ran north along the alley, intending to circle around the block of buildings and take a roundabout route to get back to their horses.

Across the plaza, gunfire was peppering the front of the Condon Bank by now. Inside, Powers and Broadwell fought back against the citizens while Grat finished grabbing whatever cash was easily available behind the bank counter. He never did force anyone to open the vault. Broadwell was wounded in the shoulder. Things began to look desperate for the three outlaws.

Bob and Emmett reached the end of the block and started west along Eighth Street. When they got to the corner they could look south along the sidewalk in front of the First National Bank. A man with a rifle was standing in front of Rammel Brothers Mercantile. Bob paused and shot him dead on the spot. The man's name was George Cubine, and he was the second victim of the

Dalton Gang on this bloody day in Coffeyville. A moment later a third was added as one of Cubine's friends, Charles Brown, stepped out into the open to check on the fallen man. Bob Dalton killed him, too, with a single shot. Bob might not have been the brilliant tactician he thought he was, but he was a fine marksman.

Before Bob and Emmett could move on, another man with a rifle appeared on the porch in front of Isham's. This was Tom Ayres, the First National's cashier. Bob fired at him, too, but this time instead of inflicting a fatal wound, the bullet just creased Ayres on the head, knocking him unconscious. With that little bit of opposition taken care of, Bob and Emmett dashed along the back of the Condon Bank.

Inside the bank, Grat, Powers, and Broadwell were ready to make a break for it, knowing that they couldn't stay where they were. But as they ran out into the street and turned toward the alley where their horses were tied, bullets clawed at them from all sides. Witnesses to the battle told of how dust leaped from the clothing of the outlaws as slugs smacked into them. The three men managed to keep going, stumbling through the hail of lead.

As Grat, Powers, and Broadwell moved along the alley, Town Marshal Charles Connerly stepped out in front of them. Incredibly, though, Connerly was facing the wrong direction, evidently thinking that the outlaws had already passed his position. Grat shot him in the back, killing him. The three desperadoes kept moving toward their horses. Bob and Emmett were approaching the spot, too, coming along a narrow space between buildings that led into the alley from the north.

Powers reached his horse, but was cut down by gunfire as he tried to swing up into the saddle. Broadwell was hit yet again, but managed to get on his horse and gallop off. He was riddled with bullets, though, and barely reached the edge of Coffeyville before he toppled out of the saddle and died.

Back in what came to be known as Death Alley, Bob and Emmett reached Grat's side. Emmett was still carrying the sack containing over twenty thousand dollars. A liveryman who owned a stable there along the alley, John Kloehr, fired from behind a fence and hit Bob. Kloehr next drew a bead on Grat and triggered again. The round ripped through Grat's throat, killing him at last.

Emmett was the only one of the brothers to reach the horses. He had a couple of minor wounds, but was moving pretty well. He got into the saddle and might have been able to race away, but instead he turned his horse and rode back to Bob's side, where he reached down to try to help his brother. A final point of dispute in the story of the Daltons is whether or not Bob was already dead when Emmett made this courageous gesture. But even if Bob still lived at that moment, Emmett never had a chance to save him. One of the citizens, a barber named Carey Seaman, dashed up at that moment and emptied both barrels of a shotgun into Emmett, knocking him off his horse. Emmett sprawled bloody and unconscious in the street.

Less than fifteen minutes had passed since the five members of the Dalton Gang rode into Coffeyville. The death toll stood at eight: four citizens and four outlaws. Emmett Dalton was not expected to live, but he was taken to a nearby hotel room and tended to by several local physicians.

Bill Powers's body was discovered at the edge of town and carried back to the alley, where it was laid alongside the other owlhoot corpses. The four dead men were propped up and photographed lying side by side. This happened only a few minutes after the shooting stopped, and in the famous photograph not a sign of any false beard or mustache is visible, another indication that the story of the gang's disguises, while colorful, might not be true after all.

Against the odds, Emmett Dalton survived not only his wounds but also the inevitable talk of lynching. When he recovered sufficiently, he went to trial and was found guilty of armed robbery. He was sentenced to twenty-five years in prison, and served fourteen of them before being pardoned by President

Theodore Roosevelt. After being released from prison, he moved to California and became not only a successful builder but also the author of two books about his outlaw days. He also served as a consultant on a silent motion picture about the ill-fated Coffeyville raid, and appeared as an actor in several silent films. He lived until July 13, 1937, a truly reformed man who spoke often on the message that crime does not pay.

On that October morning in Coffeyville, it certainly didn't pay for the Dalton Gang . . . except in lead.

BAT MASTERSON AND THE
BATTLE OF THE PLAZA

wo men walked along the tracks of the Atchison, Topeka & Santa Fe Railroad in Dodge City, Kansas, just before noon on Saturday, April 16, 1881. In the distance, a locomotive's whistle shrilled, and the two men looked at each other in grim understanding. The eastbound train was due at noon, and from the sound of that whistle, it was on time.

The two men reached under their coats and checked to see that the six-guns they carried moved freely in their holsters. In a matter of moments, if all went according to plan, those guns would be drawn and would commence doing their deadly work.

On board one of the Santa Fe's passenger cars, a stocky, handsome man sporting a dark mustache and wearing a derby hat pulled a turnip watch from his pocket and checked the time. The train was on schedule, but the man was still worried. He had been in Tombstone, Arizona, dealing faro in Wyatt Earp's Oriental Saloon, when the telegram summoning him to Dodge City had reached him. It had taken quite a while for him to make his way back here. He hoped he wouldn't be too late. His brother's life was on the line.

The passenger's name was William Barclay "Bat" Masterson, and he was on his way to a date with destiny.

BAT Masterson was born in Canada, on November 27, 1853, and was christened Bartholomew. The nickname "Bat" came from that, and it stuck with him even after he later changed his name. The family, including several brothers, moved from farm to farm across the Midwest and finally settled in Kansas. As a young man, Bat became a buffalo hunter and took part in the battle at Adobe Walls, in the Texas Panhandle, in which a few dozen buffalo hunters successfully defended a handful of sod shacks against a force of over five hundred Comanche, Kiowa, Arapaho, and Cheyenne warriors led by Chief Quanah Parker.

Bat's growing reputation as a tough, competent frontiersman led to a stint as a civilian scout for the Army, aiding in General Nelson Miles's campaign against the Indians in the Panhandle. In January of 1876, he was in Mobeetie, Texas, a new settlement on Sweetwater Creek. It was here that he began to acquire a name as a fast, deadly shootist. He was dancing in the Lady Gay Saloon with a woman named Mollie Brennan when an angry Corporal Melvin King barged into the place. King was posted at nearby Fort Elliott, and he considered Mollie his girl. Seeing her with Bat, he pulled a gun and opened fire on them. Mollie was hit and killed by one of King's bullets, which passed through her body and then tore through Bat's leg. But Bat was able to stay on his feet and kill King with a coolly placed shot.

For a while, Bat had to use a cane as his leg healed from the bullet wound, and some have speculated that was how he got his nickname, but the fact is that he was called Bat long before that shoot-out.

The following year, he drifted up to Dodge City, Kansas, where his brother Ed was the county sheriff. Bat went to work for Ed as a deputy, and this was his introduction to law enforcement. When Ed was hired as the marshal of Dodge, Bat decided to run for sheriff himself, and he won.

A shooting scrape between Ed and two Texas cowboys resulted in Ed's death, strengthening Bat's resolve to maintain law and order. Bat kept Ford County cleaned up while he was the top lawman there. But when the next election came, he was voted out of office, which bitterly disappointed him. He had always been a keen gambler, and even owned an interest in one of Dodge City's saloons, the Lady Gay (the same name, but a far different place than the West Texas saloon where Bat had killed Corporal King).

Following Ed Masterson's death, a man named Charley Bassett had been appointed marshal of Dodge City. Bassett later left the job to go to Arizona, and at that time, the marshal's badge was turned over to yet another Masterson brother, Jim. When Bat left, also for Arizona, he gave his interest in the Lady Gay to Jim, who had recently been dismissed as city marshal. So Bat was gone and Jim had nothing to do except run the Lady Gay along with his partner, A. J. Peacock.

Right from the start, Jim and Peacock didn't get along. The main bone of contention between them was Al Updegraff, Peacock's brother-in-law. Peacock hired Updegraff to tend bar in the Lady Gay, and it wasn't long before Jim Masterson suspected that Updegraff was skimming money from the till. Not only that, but Updegraff was an unusually heavy drinker, even for a town where so much whiskey flowed that the place was sometimes called "a bibulous Babylon." Jim thought that Updegraff was not only stealing profits, but he was drinking them up as well. He asked Peacock to fire his brother-in-law.

Peacock refused, leading to hard feelings between him and Jim Masterson. Updegraff, knowing that he had been accused of wrongdoing, hated Jim, too. As the bad blood between the parties grew worse, it also spread, with many denizens of Front Street taking one side or the other in the argument. Knowing that the situation was building up to the point where violence was inevitable, one of Jim's friends decided that it might be a good idea to call for help. He sent a telegram to Bat in Arizona, telling him that he ought to hurry back to Dodge City because his brother's life was in danger.

That was all it took to get Bat to leave the Oriental Saloon and head for Dodge as fast as he could get there. But as the train approached the station, Bat didn't know if his brother was still alive or not. He didn't know if he would soon be fighting to help Jim—or to avenge him.

A. J. Peacock and Al Updegraff had friends, too. One of them had gotten wind of the telegram sent to Bat Masterson, and also had heard that Bat was supposed to be on the noon train on April 16. Neither man wanted to face Bat in a fair fight. Despite the fact that Bat had killed only one man in his career as a gunman, he was still feared and respected as an enemy. They would be waiting for him with pistols drawn when the train rolled in. It would be easy to claim self-defense after they gunned him down. After all, Bat Masterson was a famous shootist.

But Bat's instincts were about to serve him well. As the train approached the depot and began to slow down, Bat stood up from his seat and moved to the platform between cars. He grasped the iron grab-bar on the side of the train and swung to the ground. The train was going slowly enough now so that he was able to keep his feet without any trouble. He started walking toward the station as the cars clattered past him.

The train rolled on by, and as the caboose cleared Bat, he looked across the tracks and saw two men walking toward the station as well. Instantly, he recognized them as A. J. Peacock and Al

William Barclay "Bat" Masterson, one of the few Old West figures who lived up to his reputation as a lawman and a gunfighter, though it's likely he killed only one man in a shoot-out in his career. He lived well into the twentieth century, becoming a newspaperman in New York City.

(Courtesy of Old West Photos)

Updegraff, the men whose threats to his brother had brought Bat back to Dodge City. He called out to them, telling them to stop, that he wanted to talk to them.

Peacock and Updegraff hesitated only a second, then turned and ran for the nearby jail, a sturdy, blockish building constructed of heavy timbers. As they sprinted for cover, one of the men yanked out his gun and threw a shot back toward Bat.

Sensing that he had foiled the ambush Peacock and Updegraff had planned for him, Bat was reacting to the danger already. His gun was out as he heard the wind-rip of a bullet passing close beside his head. He snapped a shot after Peacock and Updegraff, hurrying them on their way to the jail. Then he looked around, hunting for some cover himself.

The Santa Fe rails split Front Street just about in half as they ran east and west through Dodge. On the north side of the street, about fifty yards from the tracks, were the more respectable businesses of Dodge City, including several saloons. To the south, also about fifty yards away from the tracks, were the gambling halls and the brothels. The area along the tracks in between, approximately a hundred yards wide, was known as the Plaza and was open, sandy ground. The only building in the Plaza was the train station, and it was too far for Bat to reach safely, because by now Peacock and Updegraff were behind the corner of the jail blazing away at him, each man emptying his six-gun in turn and then reloading while the other took up the fusillade.

With bullets whipping around his head, Bat did the only thing he could. He hit the dirt, flinging himself down behind the railroad embankment. It was high enough to give him decent protection from the flying lead, but he couldn't stand up to move around without risking being hit. All he could do was poke up his derby-hatted head, trigger a few quick shots at the jail where Peacock and Updegraff were hiding, and duck back down again.

As he lay there engaged in this desperate fracas that would become known as the Battle of the Plaza, Bat had to be wondering about his brother Jim. Had Peacock and Updegraff already killed him? Was that why they had started the ball as soon as they saw Bat Masterson? Bat didn't know, and under the circumstances, he couldn't spend too much time worrying about it. He continued returning the fire of Peacock and Updegraff.

The three of them weren't the only ones involved in this fight. A lot of bullets were flying through the air, back and forth across the railroad tracks. The shots carried easily to the buildings on either side of the street. Not only did the shooting cause a great commotion, but suddenly, bullets began thudding into the buildings where the citizens of Dodge City had been going about their business in peace only seconds earlier. Pedestrians on the boardwalks had to dive for cover. Customers in the saloons and stores along both sides of Front Street beat a hasty retreat toward the rear doors of the establishments as windows shattered under the assault. Inside the Long Branch Saloon, the owner opened the heavy door of his safe and crouched behind it, knowing the thick metal would stop a slug.

As the brisk firing continued, curiosity won out over caution, and some of the men in the saloons on the north side crawled up to the broken windows and risked a quick look. Someone spotted the figure lying behind the railroad embankment and shouted, "Bat! It's Bat Masterson!"

Meanwhile, along the south side of the street, men in those buildings had looked out, too, and seen Peacock and Updegraff shooting toward the railroad tracks. It didn't take a genius to figure out what was going on. The feud between the two men and the Mastersons had erupted into gunplay. The bystanders from the south side might not know exactly who Peacock and Updegraff had pinned down out there in the Plaza, but they wanted to get in on the action anyway. They opened up with pistols and rifles, directing their shots toward the man behind the embankment—and toward the north side of the street as well.

Bat had to hunker even lower as a veritable storm of lead ripped through the air a short distance above his head. Seconds later, the din grew worse as the men in the buildings along the north side of the street joined the fray. It's a good bet that most of the combatants on both sides didn't really know what they were shooting at, but that lack of knowledge didn't stop them. For long minutes, gun thunder rumbled and roared in Dodge City, and a thick haze of burned powder smoke floated over the Plaza.

Bat Masterson thumbed more shells into his Colt and lifted himself enough to fire over the top of the railroad embankment. His slugs chewed into the beams that formed the jail and sent splinters flying through the air. Suddenly, a figure stumbled out from the cover of the jail, pressing one hand to his chest while the pistol in his other hand slipped from his fingers. The man pitched face-first to the ground after a couple of steps, but not before Bat recognized him as Al Updegraff, Peacock's brother-in-law and the man whose hollow leg and light fingers had started this whole mess. A second later, the hammer of Bat's gun clicked on an empty chamber. The revolver was empty again, and now Bat was out of cartridges. The shooting on both sides began to die away as the men who had been firing wildly a moment earlier took in the stark picture of Updegraff lying there in the dusty Plaza. For all they knew, he was dead, and it was a sobering sight.

A sturdy figure emerged from one of the buildings on the north side and trotted toward Bat, shotgun in hand. Bat turned to watch him coming, and recognized Ab Webster, the mayor of Dodge City. Webster came up to Bat, red-faced from the effort of running, and pointed the twin barrels of the shotgun in the general direction of the former sheriff of Ford County. "You're under arrest, Bat," Webster said breathlessly. "Give me your gun."

Bat climbed to his feet and hesitated before complying with the mayor's order. The gun was empty anyway. Bat asked what had happened to Jim, whether or not his brother was still alive. Webster assured Bat that Jim was not only alive, but also hale and hearty. A much-relieved Bat allowed himself to be arrested and taken to the office of the new city marshal, Fred Singer. By this time, Jim Masterson had heard about the small-scale war that had broken out upon his brother's return to Dodge City, and he was waiting to greet Bat warmly.

Meanwhile, Al Updegraff was receiving medical attention. The bullet that had passed through his chest had punctured one of his lungs. The doctor's face was grave as he tried to stem the flow of blood and deal with the wound. Anyone looking at the medico would know that the man didn't hold out much hope for Updegraff's survival.

But that afternoon, as Bat Masterson was brought to an extremely speedy trial, Updegraff was still hanging on tenaciously to life. Bat was charged with illegally discharging a firearm in the city limits. No one really knew whose shot had struck Updegraff, so it was impossible to charge Bat with attempted murder or anything like that. Solemnly, Bat pleaded guilty and was fined eight dollars and court costs. After paying the fine, he suggested to Jim that it might be a good time for both of them to leave Dodge City.

Jim agreed and went to find A. J. Peacock. A gunfight was one thing, but business was another. Jim suggested that Peacock buy out his share in the Lady Gay, and Peacock agreed. Jim must have made him a good price. Now that he was out of the saloon business, there was nothing to hold him in Dodge City.

That very afternoon, Bat and Jim caught a westbound train and left Dodge City behind them. They left behind as well a fast-growing legend about the Battle of the Plaza, a legend in which Peacock and Updegraff were said to have murdered Jim Masterson, prompting Bat to return to Dodge and kill both of them. The numbers grew until the story had Bat killing not only Peacock and Updegraff, but a horde of their gunfighting henchmen as well.

Despite the later exaggerations, what happened that day in the Plaza really was a battle, albeit a small one. And it was a battle with no fatalities, because in spite of the odds, Al Updegraff survived and slowly recovered from his wound. He always insisted that he was a victim in all this, that he hadn't stolen any money from the Lady Gay nor drunk up its supply of whiskey. None of Updegraff's protestations really mattered. There's no arguing with a legend.

Bat Masterson knew that as well as or better than any man who ever walked the streets of the Old West.

THE YOUNGER BROTHERS-
PINKERTONS SHOOT-OUT

I n the mid-1870s, no band of outlaws was more sought after by lawmen and detectives than the gang that included two brothers from Missouri, Frank and Jesse James, and their cousins the four Younger brothers, as well as assorted other relatives and hangers-on. These men had been forged into warriors in the crucible of the Civil War, taking part in the bloody guerrilla clashes that wracked the Border States of Kansas and Missouri. After the war, the harsh iron fist of a Reconstruction government in cahoots with the ruthless power of banks and railroads drove them over the line into lawlessness.

That's the way the romantic legends of those times tell the story, and there is some truth to them. The years following the Civil War were a bad time for those who had supported the Confederacy. The victorious Union, though it wrapped itself in the cloak of self-righteousness, could hardly be considered a good winner. But the response to the excesses of Reconstruction by men such as the Jameses and the Youngers was equally violent and bloody. The Border States continued to be a battleground after the war was over, only now the battles were between the outlaws and the men who set out to bring them to justice.

Beginning in 1866, the James-Younger Gang robbed banks and held up trains across several states. These crimes were well planned and carried out with ruthless efficiency. Though they styled themselves as guerrillas fighting against the banks and railroads, and had friends and admirers far and wide among the common people, they were hardly benevolent Robin Hoods. They never hesitated to gun down anyone who got in their way, including innocent bystanders, and while they may have used some of their loot to help out poor families, most of it went into the pockets of their trademark long dusters to be gambled and drunk away.

With each looted bank and derailed train, the efforts to capture the Jameses and the Youngers intensified. The banks and railroads could afford to hire the best manhunters available, and in this era, that meant the Pinkertons.

The Pinkerton Detective Agency, headquartered in Chicago, was founded by former police detective Allen Pinkerton, who had created the United States Secret Service during the Civil War at the request of President Abraham Lincoln. Famous for their sign, which featured a large eye, and their motto, "The Eye That Never Sleeps," the Pinkertons spread out all across the country to track down criminals, assist local law-enforcement agencies, and serve as strikebreakers. Though a private business, they served as a quasi-official national police force. Backed by the fortunes of their main employers, the banks and the railroad lines, they went where they wanted and did whatever was necessary to accomplish their aims.

Early in 1874, the James-Younger Gang held up the Iron Mountain Express as it rolled into the station at Gads Hill, Missouri. Earlier, they had rounded up all the inhabitants of the tiny village and marched them into the depot, taking them prisoner along with the agent in charge of the place. The loot that the gang took off the train wasn't all that great, only around three thousand dollars, but the brazen nature of the robbery, plus the fact that Jesse James told the prisoners to be sure to give him and his men credit for the job, made the news spread quickly around the country.

This infuriated the Pinkertons. They had a reputation to uphold, and it made them look bad to have the Jameses and the Youngers running rings around them like this. Following the robbery at Gads Hill, even more Pinkerton operatives flooded into the Border States to search for the outlaws, willing to take any chances to catch up with their quarry.

Two of these Pinkerton detectives were Louis J. Lull and James Wright. In March of 1874, they rode into St. Clair County, Missouri, a rugged, sparsely populated area in the Ozark Mountains. The landscape was heavily wooded and cut by dark valleys through which numerous small streams flowed into the Osage River. The county seat and the only real settlement was the small town of Osceola. The two detectives were accompanied by E. B. Daniels, a former deputy sheriff who knew the area about as well as any outsider could.

Lull and Wright had received a tip that some of the Younger brothers were hiding out in St. Clair County. To conceal their identity, they took on false names—Lull called himself W. J. Allen and Wright pretended to be a man named John Boyle—and attempted to pass themselves off as traveling livestock buyers. This was just the same sort of ruse that some of the outlaws pursued by the Pinkertons had used in the past. As they rode through the mountains, they stopped at every small farm and asked seemingly innocent questions that were designed to find out if anyone had seen the Youngers in the area. These men had to be aware that many of the people they talked to were friends, if not relatives, of the outlaws, and it had to be quite nerve-wracking to know that if their disguise were to be penetrated, they would be in mortal danger from these hill folk. Though many of the activities of the Pinkerton Agency have been called into question over the years, the bravery of most of the individual operatives is beyond question.

The three manhunters spent the night of March 16, 1874, at Monegaw Springs, west of Osceola. While they were there, one of the locals saw them and recognized Daniels as a former lawman. The word spread like wildfire through the mountain grapevine. Given Daniels's former profession, it seemed likely that the men with him were hunting outlaws, not looking to buy livestock as they claimed. Unknown to the three men as they rode out of their camp the next morning, they were in greater danger than ever before.

That afternoon, James Wright stopped to visit a friend, and told Lull and Daniels that he would catch up to them later. Lull and Daniels proceeded on down a trail called the Chalk Level Road, and came to a small farm belonging to a man named Theodorick Snuffer. Hearing horses, Snuffer emerged from his farmhouse, which had an unfinished attic.

Lull and Daniels had no way of knowing that just a few minutes earlier inside the Snuffer house, Jim and John Younger had been sitting and eating lunch with the farmer, who was a distant relative and a friend of theirs. When the men rode up outside, the two Youngers had climbed into the attic to check out the strangers and see what they wanted.

Lull and Daniels continued their pose as stock buyers. They asked their usual questions, but got little response from the laconic Snuffer. One of the detectives mentioned that they were on their way to a farm owned by the Widow Simms. This was a lie, and a risky one, because when Lull and Daniels left the Snuffer place, they rode off in the wrong direction to be going to the Simms place. This as much as anything seems to have convinced Jim and John Younger that the visitors were detectives. As soon as Lull and Daniels were out of sight, the Youngers climbed down from the attic and hustled out to the barn to saddle their horses and ride after the detectives.

Meanwhile, James Wright had met his companions on the road and rejoined them. All three men were riding along when they heard the sound of rapid hoofbeats behind them. Reining in, they turned in their saddles and saw two men on horseback galloping after them. One man carried a shotgun while the other was armed with a brace of long-barreled pistols. Though the detectives could not be sure of it at the time, John Younger was the man with the scattergun and his brother Jim carried the pistols.

Wright's nerve broke as he saw the men racing toward him. With a yell, he yanked his horse around and tore out across the fields. Jim Younger brought his mount to a skidding halt and drew his pistols, snapping a shot after Wright. The bullet hit Wright's hat and sent it sailing off his head. It was quite a shot, just not quite good enough to bring Wright down. He was almost out of range of the pistols and shotgun already, so the Younger Brothers let him go.

Lull and Daniels stayed where they were, evidently thinking that it would be futile to flee. They were covered by John Younger's shotgun as the two outlaws came closer. By now, the two detectives probably suspected who their captors were. They stuck to their story, though, claiming to be itinerant cattle buyers when the Youngers demanded to know who they were. The Youngers also disarmed them, forcing them at gunpoint to drop their pistols in the dirt of the road.

Those pistols interested John Younger. When he asked why the two men were traveling around so well armed, Daniels responded that any traveler would be wise to carry weapons in that part of the country.

The Youngers didn't know just how well armed one of their prisoners was. Lull had a third pistol concealed behind his neck, under his shirt. Jim Younger got down to collect the dropped guns, while John Younger crowded closer on horseback, menacing the two detectives with the shotgun. Fearing that they were about to be blasted with buckshot at close range, Lull made a

The Younger brothers—Bob, Jim, and Cole from left to right—along with their sister, Henrietta, in an 1889 photo, long after the James-Younger Gang's disastrous raid on Northfield, Minnesota.

(Courtesy of Denver Public Library, Western History Collection)

desperate play. His hands were raised already; he reached behind his neck and grasped the pistol hidden there. The move took the Youngers by surprise. Lull didn't try to disarm them. He fired instead, sending a bullet ripping through John Younger's neck.

The impact of the slug made John Younger reel back in the saddle. But as he did so, his finger clenched on the triggers of the shotgun he held. The Greener roared, flame geysering from both barrels. The double charge of lead smashed into Lull, but failed to knock him off his horse. However, the animal was spooked by the noise and smoke and bolted, running past a tree where a low-hanging branch hit Lull and dislodged him from his saddle.

On the ground, Jim Younger brought up his pistols and shot Daniels, killing the former deputy sheriff. As Daniels fell, a few yards away the wounded John Younger rode over to Lull, who was trying to struggle to his feet, and pulled out a pistol to shoot him again. Then John turned his horse and rode back to Jim, slipping out of the saddle to fall at his brother's feet.

John Younger's neck wound proved fatal. He died there, his blood gushing out into the road where he fell. A furious, grieving Jim Younger lifted his brother's body and draped it over the saddle of his horse. He rode away, leaving Lull and Daniels where they had fallen, and when he came to a small apple orchard on Snuffer's land, he buried his brother there.

Despite his wounds, Lull was not dead. He lay there senseless for quite some time, until a farmer in a wagon came along and found him. Not knowing the circumstances or the identity of Lull and the other man, the farmer loaded Lull in the wagon and took him to the village of Roscoe, where he was taken care of by some of the locals. He regained consciousness and asked for the law to be summoned. Before Justice of the Peace James St. Clair, a member of the family for which the county was named, Lull told his story, swearing to an affidavit that gave the details of the shoot-out. For a couple of weeks, Lull clung to life, but finally the wounds proved too much for him to overcome. He died there in Roscoe.

Jim Younger told Theodorick Snuffer what had happened, and it turned out that there was another witness to the gunfight, a local man named G. W. MacDonald. All three versions of the story were in substantial agreement.

This incident, plus another in which a captured Pinkerton operative was tortured and killed by the gang, made the agency more determined than ever to bring the Jameses and the Youngers to justice. In their zeal to do so, they blew up the cabin where Frank and Jesse's mother lived. Some say the explosion was an accident, some say it was deliberate. Either way, it was deadly. Frank and Jesse's young half brother Archie Samuels was killed, and their mother's right arm was blown off at the elbow. And as it turned out, Frank and Jesse James were nowhere near the cabin when the Pinkertons tossed a flare—or a bomb— through the window.

This shocking violence turned most of the Pinkertons' supporters against them, and the Pinkertons withdrew from the case. The James-Younger Gang didn't have a free hand after that, however. They were still pursued by hundreds, if not thousands, of local lawmen as they kept on robbing banks and trains.

Jim Younger and his brothers Cole and Bob continued riding with the James Gang until the disastrous raid on the bank at Northfield, Minnesota, on September 7, 1876. All three of the Youngers were badly wounded and captured during the epic gunfight that resulted from this botched bank robbery. All survived and were sent to prison. Bob never breathed free air again, dying of tuberculosis behind the cold gray walls of the Minnesota State Penitentiary at Stillwater in 1889. Cole and Jim served twenty-five years each of their life sentences before being paroled. Unable to cope with life on the outside, Jim committed suicide soon after being released from prison. Cole got religion and wrote extensively about his career as an outlaw before finally dying in 1916.

The body of John Younger, first of the outlaw brothers to die, was moved from the apple orchard on Snuffer's farm to the Younger family plot in the cemetery at Lee's Summit, Missouri, a short distance from the home where the four brothers grew up.

5

THE SAM BASS GANG'S
LUCK RUNS OUT

It was warm on the afternoon of Friday, July 19, 1878, as four men rode into the outskirts of Round Rock, Texas, fifteen miles north of the state capital at Austin. Their eyes never stopped moving as they scanned the landscape around them. They were young, in their twenties, but hardly children. In fact, their eyes were older than their years. They were the eyes of men who had been both the hunters—and the hunted.

The man in the lead was better dressed than his companions, sporting a dark brown suit and a flat-crowned hat of the same shade. Like the others, he wore a mustache. His mouth was wide and had a look about it as if he were quick to smile, though he wasn't smiling today. He was concentrating too much for that. He rode a fine horse; he had always been a good judge of horseflesh. On more than one occasion, riding a good horse had saved his life, so he made sure to always be well mounted.

The other three men wore range clothes and could have been taken for cowboys. As the riders passed a feed store, one of the men reined his horse to a halt. He told the others that he would pick up some grain for their horses and also keep an eye out for trouble. They nodded in agreement, because trouble was one thing these men had known in abundance and expected at all times. Being careful meant staying alive.

Leaving the first man at the feed store, the other three rode on. If all went as planned, there would be no trouble today. They were just going to take a look around, and didn't intend to rob the bank until the next morning.

But rob it they would, because Sam Bass and his gang had come to Round Rock to claim some more of the glory that had made Sam the Robin Hood of Texas.

———————◆———————

SAM Bass wasn't a Texan. He was from Indiana, having been born on a farm near the town of Mitchell on July 21, 1851. The childhood he spent there was not an overly tragic one, but it was not without its hardships. Sam's mother passed away when he was only ten years old, and Sam's father died three years later. Sam and the other Bass children, two boys and four girls, were taken in by their uncle, David L. Sheeks. There is no evidence that Sheeks mistreated the children, but life on the farm was full of grinding chores and dull disappointment for Sam anyway. Reasonably intelligent despite his lack of schooling, he possessed a fertile imagination and a dislike for work—a dangerous combination.

At the age of eighteen, he left his uncle's farm to make his own way in the world. His wanderlust took him first to Mississippi, where he worked for a while in a mill. The money he made there enabled Sam to travel west, to Texas. He wound up in Denton, a community about halfway between Fort Worth and the Red River, the border between Texas and Indian Territory. Needing a job whether he really wanted one or not, Sam went to work for the sheriff of Denton County, W. F. "Dad" Egan. The sheriff hired Sam not as a deputy or jailer, but to do odd jobs and drive a wagon. Egan also owned a freighting company, and Sam proved to be a dependable teamster.

He loved horses, though, especially racehorses. Not far outside of town was a dirt track where horses were trained, and Sam started spending more time there. The idea that he wanted to own a racehorse grew in his mind. One of the local farmers had a chestnut-sorrel mare that he wanted to sell. Sam thought that with the proper training, which he, of course, would provide, the mare would be a champion. Lacking the money to buy the mare on his own, he went into partnership with Armstrong B. Egan, the sheriff's younger brother, and bought the mare, which he named Jenny.

Dad Egan didn't like the idea of his brother owning a racehorse and being involved in a sport known for its shady characters. So he loaned Sam the money to buy out Armstrong's share in the mare. Sam quit his other jobs to concentrate on training Jenny. He hired an experienced jockey, a black man named Charley Tucker, and it wasn't long before Jenny was winning races—and Sam was winning the bets he made on those races.

During a trip to San Antonio for a race held there, Sam met Joel Collins, who was working temporarily as a bartender though his main occupation was that of cowboy. In fact, Collins had been part of four cattle drives up the trail from Texas to the railheads in Kansas. The two young men struck up a friendship, and Collins devised a scheme whereby they could make more money off Sam's mare. Collins pretended to be Jenny's owner, while Sam posed as a racetrack tout and conned other owners into racing their horses against the speedier mare. They were able to keep this up for a year before the denizens of the Texas racetracks caught on to them. Rather than risk trouble, Sam sold Jenny and prepared to accept the dreaded idea of going back to honest labor.

Joel Collins wasn't out of ideas, however. He and Sam and another acquaintance named Jack Davis bought a herd of cattle—

on credit—and headed north to Kansas with it. They sold the cattle in Ogallala for eight thousand dollars, but rather than going back to Texas to repay the men who had financed the drive, the three young men kept going north. There was gold in the Black Hills of Dakota. Deadwood was where they would make their fortune, Collins promised.

But after spending the winter of 1876–77 in Deadwood, Sam and Collins were nearly broke. Davis had drifted on elsewhere. Sam and Collins tried to establish a freight line between Deadwood and Cheyenne, but wound up losing even more money. Times were desperate for them now, so Sam made the only suggestion he could think of.

They would go into the robbing business.

AT first nobody knew who was holding up the stages around Deadwood. Four times, Sam Bass, Joel Collins, and their newly recruited gang pulled holdups, but the loot they came away with was pathetic. One of the robberies netted only a basket of peaches. But at least nothing went wrong, and the robberies were carried out with no violence. On the fifth try, it was different. Gunplay broke out when guards inside the stagecoach opened fire on Sam and his companions. The driver, John Slaughter, who was a popular and well-known figure in the Black Hills, was killed in the exchange of bullets. Now the miners, who hadn't really cared that much about the holdups, were angry and began talking about posses and vigilance committees. Deadwood had gotten unhealthy in a hurry for Sam and his friends. They headed south, toward Nebraska, and Sam had a new idea about what they would do when they got there.

Like the famous Reno Brothers, whom Sam had heard of when he was a kid growing up in Indiana, they would rob trains instead of stagecoaches. The money had to be better.

It was, at least at first. On September 18, 1877, Sam Bass and

Joel Collins, along with their stage-robbing cohorts from Dakota, Bill Heffridge, Tom Nixon, and Jim Berry, as well as Jack Davis, who had rejoined the gang, held up a Union Pacific train as it stopped to take on water at Big Springs, Nebraska. For once, Sam's gang was successful. They rode away with sixty thousand dollars in twenty-dollar gold pieces. It was the most lucrative train robbery in history until that time.

The group of outlaws split up, thinking it would be more difficult that way for the law to track them down. Sam and Jack Davis headed south in an old buggy, pretending to be farmers. Their share of the loot was cached under the floorboards of the vehicle. They ran into a cavalry patrol searching for the men who had held up the train, but the soldiers were looking for six men on horseback, not two men in a disreputable buggy. The ruse worked. After pleasantly passing the time of day with the soldiers, Sam and Davis continued on south, across the Red River and back into Texas.

Joel Collins and Bill Heffridge, also traveling together, might have gotten away if not for two strokes of bad luck. An acquaintance of Collins's had been on the train that was held up and had recognized him, passing along his name to the authorities. And while stopped in a trading post at Buffalo Station, Collins dropped an envelope with his name written on it. He picked it up and likely thought nothing of the incident, but a man in the store had seen the name and recalled that Joel Collins was wanted for his part in the Union Pacific holdup. A sheriff's posse happened to be camped nearby. Tipped off that two of the train robbers had been at the station, the posse went after Collins and Heffridge and caught up to them only a few minutes later. Protesting their innocence at first, the two outlaws started to return peacefully to the station with the lawmen. Then, obviously knowing they were going to be found out, Collins grabbed for his gun, and Heffridge followed suit. The resulting gun battle was short but fierce, and ended with Collins and Heffridge lying dead on the ground.

Later, Jim Berry, another member of the gang, was killed by a lawman in Missouri. Tom Nixon, with his share of the loot and most of Berry's as well, disappeared and was never caught.

Down in Texas, Sam Bass was back in Denton and living high on the hog, spreading the story that he had hit it rich in the gold fields of Dakota Territory. He had plenty of money, but he had tasted success as an outlaw and wanted more. To accomplish that, he would need a new gang. He knew plenty of men from the time he had spent around the racetracks and in the gambling dens before going north to the Black Hills. His first recruit was an old acquaintance named Frank Jackson. Henry Underwood soon joined the gang, as did Seaborn Barnes and Tom Spotswood. Early on, the group pulled several stagecoach holdups around Fort Worth, but the pattern that had been established in the Black Hills around Deadwood repeated itself: Sam couldn't seem to pick the right coaches to rob, and though the gang got more from the holdups than peaches, the loot still wasn't much compared to the sixty grand Sam and his friends had taken from the U.P. train up in Nebraska. It was clear to Sam that the time had come to go back to robbing trains.

Up in the Black Hills, Sam had gotten a bit of a reputation for himself. During his stagecoach robberies, he'd boldly stated that he would not leave any man destitute. So after robbing the passengers on a stage, he would return a dollar to each of them. The story got around, establishing for the first time Sam Bass's status as a sort of frontier Robin Hood. Sam continued that tradition in Texas, and when the newspapers began to print stories about him, he enjoyed the newfound fame. Here he was, a simple, uneducated farm boy from Indiana, and the reporters wrote about him like he was some sort of bandit king. He became as famous in Texas as Jesse James was elsewhere (though Jesse had Texas

The famous outlaw Sam Bass, seated between his trusted second-in-command, Seaborn Barnes (on Bass's left) and the man who betrayed the gang leading to the bloody shoot-out in Round Rock, Jim Murphy (on Bass's right).

(Courtesy of Texas State Library and Archives Commission)

connections, too, and was always good for a newspaper story or three).

In January and February of 1878, Sam and his men robbed trains from the Texas Pacific line and the Houston & Texas Central Railroad. The loot wasn't bad, but still nothing like what Sam had gotten from that one robbery in Nebraska. But the press loved him, the law-enforcement community was up in arms, and Sam was happy.

He knew Denton County like the back of his hand and had several hideouts there. One was at Pilot Knob, a large, wooded hill south of Denton that gave a good view of the surrounding countryside. No posse could sneak up on the Bass gang while they were camped on Pilot Knob. The gang's other main hideout was in neighboring Cooke and Wise Counties, a deep, thickly wooded ravine known as Cove Hollow that stretched for six miles. Near the ravine was a ranch owned by two brothers, Bob and Jim Murphy. Jim Murphy was one of Sam's friends from the old days in Denton, and Sam knew he could count on Jim to warn him if a posse was in the area.

Lawmen didn't like the way Sam and his gang eluded pursuit with such seeming ease, and they didn't like the newspaper stories about him, either. Neither did the executives of the railroad and stagecoach companies that had fallen prey to the Bass gang. Under pressure from these businesses, the governor of Texas, R. B. Hubbard, assigned Major John B. Jones, head of the Frontier Battalion of the Texas Rangers, to track down Sam Bass. Major Jones formed a special company to carry out this task, and put Dallas lawman Junius "June" Peak in charge of it. This special force, composed of both Rangers and local lawmen, was written up in newspapers across the state.

The law had gone to war on Sam Bass.

———————————

IF a war was what the star-packers wanted, Sam was only too happy to give it to them. Confident in his ability to get away from any posse, he pulled off two more train robberies and led the Rangers and the locals on a merry chase through the woods and gullies of several counties in North Texas. More than once, the posses came close enough to throw lead at the outlaws, and on one occasion a bullet ripped Sam's cartridge belt from around his waist. In the same encounter, another slug smashed the stock of his rifle. But despite that, the gang got away again. Sam had quite a few men riding with him now, young cowboys drawn by the twin lures of adventure and wealth. They were willing to risk the danger to be part of the gang led by the famous Sam Bass.

During their quest to capture Sam and the rest of the bandits, the special force under June Peak brought in everyone they could think of who had any connection with Sam. One of the men arrested in this sweep was Jim Murphy. Murphy was suspected of being a rustler and likely faced a stretch in the pen. Unwilling to be sentenced to prison if he could avoid it, Murphy hatched a plan that he shared with the authorities. He knew Sam Bass, was trusted by Sam Bass. Sam would welcome him into the gang. Then Murphy could tip off the law the next time the gang was about to pull a robbery. The Rangers could be waiting in ambush, and the Bass War would be over.

The law went along with the scheme. Jim Murphy was released, though the official story was that he had skipped out on his bail. With that reputation as a wanted fugitive, Murphy had no trouble persuading Sam to take him into the gang the next time Sam and his comrades stopped by the ranch near Cove Hollow. Murphy rode off with Sam and the others, waiting for his chance to betray them.

During the gang's last holdup of a Texas & Pacific train at Mesquite, near Dallas, shots had been exchanged. Seaborn Barnes was wounded, and one young outlaw was killed. The robbing business wasn't as much of a lark as it had once been. Sam began to think maybe it would be a good idea to get out of North

Texas for a while. That idea was reinforced one day when he and his friends chanced upon a gallows by the side of the road. It had been erected for an execution but was unused, the prisoner having committed suicide in his jail cell. Sam didn't know that, but he knew the gallows was a bad omen for a man in his profession.

Not only that, but other than the one big haul in Nebraska, none of Sam's holdups had netted the gang much money. He had tried robbing stagecoaches and then trains. Perhaps the time had come to move on to something bigger: a bank. In the summer of 1878, Sam decided to combine both ideas. He headed south toward Central Texas, aiming to find a good bank to rob. His gang had dwindled to three by now: Seaborn Barnes, Frank Jackson, and the treacherous Jim Murphy.

Barnes was suspicious of Murphy, having heard from contacts in the owlhoot underground that Murphy might be working for the law. The simplest thing to do would be to kill him and get it over with. Jackson and Murphy were friends, though, and Sam himself was fond of Murphy. Letting Murphy live might have been against Sam's better judgment, but that was what he did. He was willing to give Murphy the chance to prove himself. That would come when the gang held up the bank in Round Rock, north of Austin.

The four men reached the area on Monday, July 15, 1878. Already, while they were passing through the town of Belton, Murphy had managed to mail a letter to the authorities without any of the others knowing, passing along the information that the gang was heading for Round Rock. "For God's sake, get there!" Murphy concluded his letter.

Sam was in no hurry. The men made camp outside of Round Rock and hung around the town all week, looking it over and figuring out exactly how they would go about robbing the bank and getting away. Meanwhile, alerted by Murphy's letter, the Texas Rangers and other lawmen converged on the place. Three Rangers, Dick Ware, Chris Conner, and George Herold, drifted into town dressed as cowboys, their star-in-a-circle badges concealed. Major Jones rode up from Austin, along with Travis County Deputy Sheriff Morris Moore. Ranger Captain Lee Hall and a company of men were nearby, ready to pursue the gang if needed. And a local deputy sheriff, A. W. "High" Grimes, was also part of the group on the lookout for the infamous Sam Bass.

Late on Friday afternoon, July 19, Sam decided it was time for one last look around Round Rock before he and the others hit the bank the next morning. They mounted up and rode into town . . . and into history.

JIM Murphy swung down from his saddle in front of the feed store and stepped up onto the porch. His worried eyes followed the other three riders down the street. He glanced around nervously, knowing that there could be lawmen hiding almost anywhere. If this was the day that shots would ring out, Murphy wanted to be as far away from the flying lead as possible. He ambled into the store, casting glances over his shoulder.

Down the street, Sam Bass, Seaborn Barnes, and Frank Jackson turned their horses into an alley off Georgetown Avenue. They dismounted and tied the animals in the alley, then walked along the street to Kopperal's General Store. Texas Ranger Dick Ware, still not wearing his badge, crossed Georgetown Avenue at the same time, bound for a barbershop and a shave. The outlaws and the Ranger must have passed each other, but Ware didn't recognize Sam and the other men.

Ware wasn't the only lawman on the spot, however. Deputy Morris Moore saw the three strangers as well, and noticed that one of them had a gun under his coat. Carrying a gun was a violation of a town ordinance. Moore walked down the street, ran into Deputy A. W. Grimes, and commented on what he had just seen. Grimes started toward Kopperal's Store, intending to investigate.

Inside the store, Sam, Barnes, and Jackson were standing at

the counter, buying some tobacco, when a stern voice from behind them asked, "Do you have a pistol?" The voice belonged to Deputy Grimes, and Sam must have known at that moment that the law had caught up to him at last. He said, "Yes, I do," and there was a smile on his face as he turned around, reaching for the butt of the revolver under his coat.

Barnes and Jackson followed suit, spinning around and drawing their guns just as Sam did. All three men opened fire. Their bullets smashed into Grimes, knocking him backward. The lawman's gun was still in its holster, untouched. He was dead when his body crashed to the floor.

Deputy Moore, who had been waiting just outside, burst through the door and opened fire. His first shot struck Sam Bass's gun hand. Then one of the other men shot Moore through the body, driving him off his feet. Sam, Barnes, and Jackson charged out of the store and headed for the alley where they had left their horses.

Hearing the sudden flurry of gunshots, Dick Ware bolted out of the barber's chair and rushed into the street, white lather still on his face. He spotted the three outlaws and opened up on them, slowing them down as his slugs whipped around their heads. They returned the fire, their bullets chewing splinters from a hitch rack that offered Ware scanty cover.

Major Jones was in a nearby telegraph office. He stepped out to join the fray, firing only a single shot at the bandits before their fierce return fire forced him to retreat. Meanwhile, Ware emptied his six-shooter at the fleeing outlaws, and a local citizen, a one-armed man named Stubbs, came out of Kopperal's carrying the revolver belonging to the dead Deputy Grimes. Stubbs fired the gun after the outlaws as well.

As this storm of lead raged around him, Sam Bass stumbled, hit in the back by one of the bullets, probably fired by Dick Ware. Sam and his companions reached the alley and lunged for their horses. Before they could get there, Seaborn Barnes pitched to the ground, shot through the head. Jackson grabbed the reins, jerked them loose, and held the horses while his wounded leader climbed painfully into the saddle. At the same time, Jackson kept up the fire at the Rangers, trying to hold them off until Sam was mounted. Rangers Chris Conner and George Herold came rushing onto the scene then, and added their fire to the fusillade in the alley and on Georgetown Avenue. Once Sam was mounted, Jackson sprang into his own saddle, and the two men galloped their horses out of Round Rock. Along the way, they passed the feed store where Jim Murphy waited. Murphy watched them go, not knowing exactly what had happened or what his fate would be.

The Rangers pursued Sam and Jackson, but cautiously, not knowing at the time whether Sam had more men waiting outside of town. Night fell not long after that, and the search was called off until Saturday morning.

Unknown to the lawmen, Sam had stopped fleeing almost as soon as he and Jackson reached the woods just outside Round Rock. He was in too much pain to go on. Jackson didn't want to leave him, but Sam implored him to do so, giving Jackson all his money, guns, and ammunition and also swapping horses with the younger man. Reluctantly, Jackson rode off, leaving Sam behind.

The search resumed the next morning, as posses spread out through the countryside. One of the searchers, Deputy Sheriff Milt Tucker, spotted a man sitting under a tree and rode over to him. The man lifted a hand in greeting and said, "Don't shoot. I am unarmed and helpless. I am the man you are looking for. I am Sam Bass."

At last, the law had caught up to the Robin Hood of Texas.

———•◆•———

SAM was brought into Round Rock in the back of a wagon and carried into an empty shack. The Rangers gave him medical

$10.000⁇ _____ Reward

Omaha Train Robbers

Description

William Heffridge als Bill Heffery 5 feet 8 or 9
inches high 145 or 150 28 to 30 years old light Brown
hair light Beard and mustach front tooth gone
Tattoo on hand and dancing girl Tattooed on
arm

Sam Bass 5 feet 7 or 8 inches high 140 or 150
pounds 23 to 25 years old described as quite
young and boyish looking dark complexion
hair black and cut short mustach cut short
Beard black thin and not very stiff has very white
teeth shows his front teeth when laughing is slow
talker and dont talk much drinks very little
does not use Tobacco is called a Texas man

Jack Davis 5 feet 11 inches high some think 6 feet 190
pounds 30 years old large heavy Broad Shouldered
man brown eyes dark hair and beard mustach
not very heavy slow in his walk and has habit
of walking with his hands behind his back
Talks and drinks a great deal Rode a dunn
colored horse with a glass eye

A $10,000 reward notice from Omaha, Nebraska, offering that bounty on Sam
Bass, William Heffridge, Jack Davis, James Berry, and Tom Nixon. Note that
Davis rides "a dunn colored horse with a glass eye."

James Berry 5 feet 9 inches high 180 pounds 30 or 35 years old Sandy or Red hair with a little gray in it Sandy Beard and mustach chin Beard quite long Red or Florid complexion Blue eyes full round face which gets very red when he has been drinking Talks a great deal

Tom Nixon 5 feet 8 inches high 140 to 150 pounds 25 years old Light Hair and Beard not very long or heavy Blue eyes was riding a horse with a H and a heart Brand

E. M. Mosman
Supt U.P.R.R.
Omaha Neb.

$500.00/100.

Chas H. Foulk.
                    Description
41 years old 6 feet high 180 pounds Brown hair light colrd goatee about 3 or 4 inches long which covers chin pretty well. long face thin cheeks high chest bones Blue eyes scar on right side of upper lip large shot lodged in back part of one of his hands think it in the left upper front teeth far apart and have conspicuous gold plugs in them large feet and very long always wears shoes generally fancy ones when walking he takes long steps has a rolling gait gambler by Profession faro dealing favorite
                    Saml J. Anderson Carlisle P.A.

attention, but also questioned him about the other members of his gang. Sam refused to name anyone or cooperate in any way. "If a man knows anything, he ought to die with it in him," he told Major Jones. Mortally wounded, he lingered until Sunday, July 21, 1878. Failing fast, he was told by the doctor attending him that the end would not be long in coming. "Let me go," Sam Bass said, and a few minutes later, he gasped and started up from the bed, exclaiming, "The world is bobbing around me!"

Those were the last words he spoke. He sagged back, dead.

It was his twenty-seventh birthday.

Sam Bass was buried in the Round Rock Cemetery, along with Seaborn Barnes. There was some discussion about taking Sam's body to Austin and displaying it to the state legislature, but that idea was discarded due to the summer heat and the lack of ice in which to pack the corpse. After the small funeral, attended by only a handful of observers, a man who may or may not have been Frank Jackson rode up to the grave and spent a moment alone there before riding on. Plenty of stories circulated in later years about where Jackson went and how he ended up, but no one knows the truth.

Deputy Morris Moore recovered from his wound, and like the rest of the surviving lawmen, became famous for taking part in the gun battle that ended Sam Bass's life.

Jim Murphy spent the rest of his days in fear that someone would try to kill him to avenge his betrayal of the much-loved outlaw. A year after the already legendary shoot-out in Round Rock, Murphy accidentally drank some medicine that had been prescribed for an eye problem he had. The stuff was poisonous, and he died in horrible pain less than a day later. Or maybe, considering his guilty conscience and the fear in which he lived, it wasn't an accident at all. . . .

Sam Bass's grave was unmarked for several years, until his sister made the trip to Texas from Indiana and paid to have a tombstone put up. The epitaph chiseled on the stone read: "A brave man reposes in death here. Why was he not true?"

That monument is long gone, chipped away into nothingness by souvenir hunters.

PART THREE

POSSES

I'm a wild wolf from Bitter Creek,
and it's my night to howl!

—*George "Bitter Creek" Newcomb*

DIABLO CANYON
TRACKDOWN

Gushing smoke from its stack, the Atlantic & Pacific Railroad's Number 2 eastbound slowed to a stop at Diablo Canyon Station, Arizona Territory, on March 20, 1889. The station was about halfway between Flagstaff and Winslow, just south of the rugged Northern Arizona landscape that makes up the Navajo Indian Reservation. There wasn't much to Diablo Canyon Station. Trains stopped there to take on more wood and water, but that was about all.

Today, though, there was more waiting for the train. Four young cowboys who worked for the Aztec Land and Cattle Company—the famous "Hashknife" outfit—rode up while the train was stopped. Their names were John Halford, Dan Harvick, J.J. Smith, and Bill Stiren. The four punchers swung down from their horses, pulled guns, and swarmed aboard the train, holding the conductor, engineer, and fireman at gunpoint while they forced the express messenger to open the express car. These cowboys-turned-train-robbers made quick work of looting the safe. Their loot consisted of about seven thousand dollars in cash and a considerable amount of jewelry, including a set of diamond earrings. With exuberant whoops at the success of their daring robbery, they threw themselves on their horses and galloped off to the north, across the Navajo reservation toward Utah.

Unfortunately for these young desperadoes, they had committed their crime in Yavapai County, setting in motion one of the longest manhunts in terms of distance in the history of the Old West. They hadn't reckoned on the fact that they would be pursued by Yavapai County Sheriff Buckey O'Neill. . . .

WILLIAM Owen "Buckey" O'Neill was born in Ireland on February 2, 1860. When he was still young, his family emigrated to America and wound up in St. Louis, Missouri. Well educated for the time and skilled as a printer and typesetter, when he moved to Phoenix, Arizona Territory, in 1879, O'Neill became editor of the *Arizona Gazette* despite his youth. A couple of years later he started his own newspaper, *Hoof and Horn*, which emphasized the ranching industry in the territory.

At the same time, despite being a respectable citizen, O'Neill became an enthusiastic gambler and picked up the nickname "Buckey" because of his habit of "bucking the tiger" at faro. From all accounts, he was one of those rare individuals who is at home in any level of society, every bit as comfortable with gamblers, gunmen, and prostitutes as he was with politicians and business leaders. He was soft-spoken, modest, cultured, and possessed the knack of making just about everyone like him. But he also had a strong sense of fair play and never hesitated to stick up for the underdog.

At this time, the Atlantic & Pacific was extending its rail line through Arizona. A gang of graders, who prepared the right-of-way for the tracks to be laid down later, took over a waterhole, running off a band of peaceful Navajos who watered their sheep there. Buckey O'Neill found out about this and rode out to confront the railroad workers and ask them to restore the waterhole to the Navajos. The foreman of the grading crew laughed in Buckey's face and invited him to make them leave. Buckey rode off, leaving the railroad men to think that he had been buffaloed. But a little while later, he was back, this time at the head of the Navajos, whom he had armed and offered to lead into battle. Not wanting a full-scale Indian war on their hands, the railroad workers skedaddled, leaving the waterhole to its rightful owners.

This was, perhaps, the incident that turned Buckey O'Neill against the railroads, which at the time were the most powerful political force in the territory. Buckey had political ambitions of his own, and in 1886 was elected the probate judge of Yavapai County, east of Flagstaff. A couple of years later he ran for county sheriff on the platform that he would enforce the tax laws and make the railroad pay its full share. The railroad owned every other section along its right-of-way, having been ceded the land by the territory, so the money in question added up to a considerable amount. Accustomed to having the local law in their back pocket, the railroad barons hadn't been paying their share for quite some time, and they didn't want to return to that practice. So they opposed Buckey's campaign and did everything they could, short of outright violence, to see that he wasn't elected. Nothing worked, as the citizens of Yavapai County voted Buckey into the sheriff's office.

Given their enmity toward the sheriff, it's no surprise that when the eastbound was held up and robbed at Diablo Canyon Station, officials of the Atlantic & Pacific did not ask the sheriff to go after the outlaws. The loss from the express car was not huge, and the officials believed, rightfully so, that if O'Neill pursued and captured the robbers, his standing in the county would increase even more. They feared that he had his sights set on some higher office in the territory, and they were probably right about that, too.

But more than anything else, once Buckey heard about the

robbery, his pride and his devotion to duty would not allow him to ignore it. He set off for Diablo Canyon Station to pick up the outlaws' trail, taking with him a posse consisting of deputies Jim Black and Ed St. Clair, as well as railroad detectives Fred Fornoff and Carl Holton. Some historians say that noted scout, tracker, Indian fighter, and hired killer Tom Horn also accompanied O'Neill on this pursuit, but others dispute that. Horn did work for O'Neill for a short time as a deputy sheriff, so he could have been part of the posse, but if so, no concrete proof of his participation exists.

Whoever served as tracker for the posse, quite possibly Buckey O'Neill himself, was able to pick up the trail of the outlaws. The lawmen rode north, trailing the outlaws through the reservation toward Utah. For two weeks the chase continued, made longer by the fact that the train robbers doubled back several times in an attempt to throw off any pursuit. By the time both groups reached the vicinity of Kanab, Utah, a Mormon settlement, the outlaws had to be aware that a posse was on their trail. They stopped and set up an ambush.

The shots that suddenly rang out forced O'Neill and the other posse members to hunt for cover, but none of them were hit. For several brief but furious minutes, they threw lead back at the outlaws, who finally fled again, still heading north.

If anything, this fracas must have made Buckey O'Neill more determined than ever to catch up to his quarry. The posse rode on, deeper into Utah, sticking to the outlaws like a burr. By now, the mounts of both parties were worn out. The chase couldn't continue much longer.

O'Neill was riding a sturdy buckskin horse named Sandy, and it lived up to its name, having more sand than the other horses. The sheriff was able to pull ahead of the other members of the posse. Accounts differ as to what actually happened when Buckey rode into Wah Weep Canyon. Some say that he came upon the outlaws sitting around a campfire, evidently thinking that they had lost their pursuers at last, while other versions of the story claim that the robbers were waiting for O'Neill and that he rode into another ambush. Whichever is true, there's no doubt that gunshots blasted that day, echoing back from the walls of the canyon as Buckey O'Neill swapped lead with the outlaws he was chasing.

O'Neill's horse went down, falling on the sheriff's leg and pinning him to the ground. Things didn't look too good for O'Neill, but at that moment the rest of the posse caught up. Carl Holton, one of the detectives working for the railroad, leaped to the ground and pulled O'Neill free. The rest of the posse continued peppering the outlaws with gunfire, and once he was on his feet again, O'Neill rejoined the fight. Outnumbered, with exhausted horses, the young cowboys-turned-outlaws finally did the only thing they could: They surrendered, throwing down their guns and lifting their hands as they emerged from the rocks where they had taken cover. When the posse searched their saddlebags, they found nearly all the money taken in the Diablo Canyon holdup, as well as much of the stolen jewelry. The diamond earrings were gone, though, and were never recovered.

Buckey O'Neill had caught the men he was after at last, but now he was faced with the problem of what to do with them. He was hundreds of miles away from Yavapai County, far out of his jurisdiction. (Most county sheriffs in the Old West would not pursue fugitives beyond the boundaries of their own county, let alone into another state as O'Neill had done.) Worried that if he and the posse tried to take their prisoners all the way back to Yavapai County on horseback the outlaws might have a chance to escape, Buckey decided to push on north instead of going south. Riding to Salt Lake City would be closer than heading home.

The posse reached Salt Lake City without incident, and once they got there, O'Neill went straight to the train station. He bought tickets for all of them on the next Denver & Rio Grande eastbound that would take them to Denver. This was a round-about way of getting back to Arizona, but O'Neill considered it safer. When the party reached Denver, O'Neill purchased more train tickets, this time on a Santa Fe westbound headed for Prescott. O'Neill paid for all these tickets himself, but it's not known whether he had that much cash on him or if he persuaded the railroad agents to let him and his companions charge their fares. By the time the posse and the prisoners got back to Prescott, though, Buckey O'Neill had spent eight thousand dollars in out-of-pocket expenses.

Unfortunately, Buckey got back with only three prisoners, not four. While the train was stopped at Raton, New Mexico, at the tail end of the Sangre de Cristo Mountains, J. J. Smith had gotten loose somehow and escaped. Still, Sheriff O'Neill brought back three of the four outlaws following a chase that had lasted for weeks and taken the posse through four different states. It was a feat of law enforcement practically unheard of, and it garnered considerable attention to O'Neill. It probably didn't hurt matters, either, when Smith was recaptured in Vernon, Texas, a short time later and sent back to Arizona Territory to stand trial with his three partners in crime. All four of the men were convicted of armed robbery and sent to prison.

But it turned out to be an expensive trip for the sheriff. Buckey had been careful to get receipts for all his expenses, but when he took those receipts to the county board of supervisors and asked to be reimbursed for them, the board refused to pay up. The supervisors claimed that as a county employee, O'Neill should have asked their permission before leaving the county on official business. Since he hadn't done that, the cost of the pursuit was his responsibility, the board declared. While they were per-haps technically correct in their ruling, the real reason the super-visors refused to reimburse the sheriff was because they were all

cronies of the railroad barons, who hated Buckey for his opposition to them. O'Neill sued the county in an attempt to recoup his
loss, pursued the case through the courts with the same zeal with
which he had pursued the outlaws, but ultimately lost on appeal.
His legal quest brought him considerable sympathy from the
public, but no money.

Buckey O'Neill tried to use the favorable publicity from the
whole affair as a springboard to higher office, just as the railroad
barons had feared he would, but it didn't work out. Twice,
O'Neill ran for Congress, but each time he was defeated. He continued serving as sheriff for a time. The lost money obviously
didn't make him change the way he carried out his duties,
because several more times he pursued fugitives out of the
county and caught them, though none of the chases were as long
and spectacular as the one that started at Diablo Canyon Station.
When he finally gave up the badge, he moved to Tombstone and
edited a newspaper there for a while, then returned to Prescott
and ran for the office of mayor in 1897. This time he won.

When the Spanish-American War broke out in 1898, Buckey
O'Neill was one of the first volunteers from Arizona. He became
a captain in the Arizona troop of Teddy Roosevelt's famous
Rough Riders, and served with distinction in Cuba. As his men
lay in a trench near the city of Santiago, Buckey entertained them
by reciting Walt Whitman's poem "Captain, My Captain." Carried away by what he was doing, Buckey lifted himself a bit too
far from the trench, ignoring a warning voiced by one of his men.
A second later a shot rang out as a Spanish sniper fired, and the
bullet struck O'Neill in the head, killing him instantly.

O'Neill was buried at first there on the island, but later his
body was moved to Arlington National Cemetery. In Prescott,
Arizona, a statue was sculpted by Solon Borglum, brother of the
sculptor famous for Mount Rushmore, and placed in front of the
county courthouse to honor the Arizona Rough Riders. Though

this statue of a horseman was intended to represent all the Rough Riders, Buckey O'Neill's reputation was so great and he was so respected in Arizona that over the years it has come to be known as the Buckey O'Neill monument. A fitting tribute for one of Arizona's greatest lawmen and a sheriff who, once he started after an outlaw, never gave up the chase.

CALIFORNIA'S MOST
WANTED OUTLAW

In the history of the Old West, Bakersfield, California, just doesn't have the same ring to it as Tombstone, Dodge City, Deadwood, or Cheyenne. The name "Bakersfield" doesn't conjure up images of fierce gunfights between lawmen and desperadoes. And yet, in April of 1903, sleepy little Bakersfield was indeed the scene of one of the West's last great shoot-outs.

The story begins in Farmersville, another small California town, some twenty years earlier. A young man who lived there named Jim McKinney became incensed when his younger brother was paddled by the local schoolteacher. McKinney had drifted in and out of the San Joaquin Valley, and already had an unsavory reputation. It was even rumored that he might have gunned down a man in Leadville, Colorado. But in Farmersville, McKinney's first documented brush with the law took place as he confronted the teacher. Losing his temper, McKinney drew his gun and pistol-whipped the teacher, knocking him out. As the unconscious man lay at his feet, McKinney holstered his revolver and pulled a bowie knife. He leaned over and with a swift slash cut off a chunk of the schoolteacher's ear. The angry words exchanged between the two men had drawn the attention of the townspeople, and a deputy sheriff rushed up just as McKinney was straightening up from the grisly mutilation. McKinney whirled in response to the lawman's challenge and slashed the deputy's arm with the bowie. Despite his injury, the deputy managed to take McKinney into custody.

In one of those strange outcomes that litter the judicial history of the West, McKinney was found not guilty of assaulting the teacher and the lawman. He wasn't welcome in Farmersville anymore, though, so he moved on.

Over the next two decades, McKinney drifted around the West, always on the shady side of the law. He was said to be wanted for several killings down in Arizona, and it's known that for a time he was an outlaw in Wyoming and may have ridden with the Wild Bunch. But he always came back to California. In Visalia, the San Joaquin Valley town that was also the home of famous train robbers Chris Evans and John Sontag (see "Gunfight at Stone Corral" elsewhere in this volume), McKinney aroused the ire of the locals when he lost his temper in one of the local saloons and shot a woman in the rump because he didn't like the way she danced with him. McKinney was drunk at the time—he was a hard drinker and many of his violent actions occurred when he was "likkered up"—and after he sobered up, he paid to have the young woman's wound treated by a doctor. According to some versions of the story, the two even became lovers . . . presumably after the injury healed.

McKinney's next notorious incident took place in Bakersfield in 1899. It also involved a woman, but this time she wasn't the object of McKinney's ire. She helped provoke a fight instead by complaining to McKinney, who was her lover, about her treatment at the hands of one Long Tom Sears, a gambler who considered himself one of McKinney's friends. Sears was about to learn how fleeting McKinney's friendship could be. The gunman braced Sears in an alley behind one of Bakersfield's general stores and began trying to goad him into a fight. Knowing McKinney's reputation, Sears wanted no part of that. He drew his gun, but only to throw it on the ground in front of him and beg for mercy, making excuses for his behavior toward McKinney's mistress. (Exactly what Sears did to offend the woman is unknown ... but McKinney's history makes it plain that it didn't take much to set him off.)

McKinney was in no mood to listen to Sears's pleas. Faced with McKinney's gun, fear and frustration made Sears exclaim that if they couldn't be friends, McKinney might as well go ahead and shoot him.

McKinney obliged.

The shot that killed Long Tom Sears was heard by Deputy Sheriff John Crawford, who was otherwise occupied in an outhouse close by. Crawford hustled out of the privy and ran into the alley as he was still pulling up his pants. McKinney turned and triggered a couple of shots at him. Both slugs nicked Crawford's mostly bare backside and sent him fleeing. (Why McKinney kept shooting at that particular part of his victims' anatomy can only be speculated upon, doubtless with few meaningful conclusions.)

McKinney was tried for the killing of Long Tom Sears, but was acquitted. The incident just added to his reputation. By the turn of the century, Jim McKinney was well known in the San Joaquin Valley and elsewhere in California as a dangerous man with a hair-trigger temper, though his reputation had not spread much beyond the boundaries of the state. In July of 1902, he was in the town of Porterville, and one night when he was drinking heavily, as usual, in Zalaud's Saloon, the urge to cut loose and raise a little hell was too strong for him to resist. He drew his gun, let out a whoop, and started blasting away at the slowly revolving blades of the ceiling fan overhead. No doubt many of the customers in Zalaud's that night knew McKinney's unsavory reputation and hurriedly hunted for some cover. With the ceiling fan shot to pieces, McKinney turned his attention to the lamps in the place and the whiskey bottles arrayed on the back-bar. Glass flew in the air as shot after shot smashed the bottles and knocked out the lights.

The town marshal, drawn by the commotion, rushed into the saloon carrying a club. He swung the bludgeon at McKinney and hit the outlaw over the head. The blow wasn't hard enough to put McKinney out of action, though, and the next instant the gun in McKinney's hand exploded again. The bullet hit the marshal in the face, entering just beside his mouth and bursting out the other side, no doubt a bloody and painful wound but not life-threatening.

As the lawman collapsed, probably with crimson bubbling from his bullet-torn face, McKinney stalked out of the saloon. There's no record of anyone trying to stop him.

McKinney wasn't finished raising a ruckus, though. Perhaps fearing that other lawmen would come after him, or that some of the townspeople would appoint themselves vigilantes and try to bring him to justice, he armed himself with a shotgun and came back down the street toward the saloon. As he approached, a man came out of the shadows toward him. Thinking that he was being attacked, McKinney swung the scattergun up and cut loose with both barrels.

The other man was thrown backward, practically torn in half by the double load of buckshot. McKinney reloaded and went over to his victim, discovering that he hadn't gunned down an enemy at all, but rather one of his few friends, a man whose name has been reported variously as Will Linn or Billy Lynn.

This wild night in Porterville still wasn't over. Instead of charging back into the saloon with the shotgun, McKinney headed out of town instead, but on the way, he shot and wounded two more men as he rode out. One of them was a local pressman who had printed up some flyers urging the people of Porterville to run McKinney out of town because he was "an undesirable citizen." McKinney's behavior on this night was certainly proof of that. The wounded printer got his wish, though. Jim McKinney didn't come back to Porterville.

Instead, the outlaw and gunman returned to the Bakersfield area. Knowing that he was no longer welcome in town because of the murder of Long Tom Sears, McKinney kept a low profile and hid out with a friend, Al Hulse, who rented a room in an establishment known variously as a "joss house" and "hop joint," where some of the Chinese who lived in Bakersfield went to gamble and smoke opium.

When word got around town that the infamous gunman Jim McKinney had returned, the local lawmen decided to find and arrest him, since he was still wanted for the killing in Porterville. They received a tip that McKinney was hiding out in the joss house on L Street, and on the morning of April 19, 1903, a posse of nine officers closed in on the place. City Marshal Jeff Packard and Deputy Sheriff Bill Tibbet went in to search the building, while the other badge-toters spread out around it in case McKinney tried to escape.

Several tense minutes went by before gunfire suddenly erupted inside the house. Packard and Tibbet had broken into Hulse's room, but as they kicked the door open, McKinney and Hulse met them with rifle fire. Packard was hit and thrown back as he tried to rush through the doorway. Tibbet made it into the room, but as he entered, Hulse shot him from the side. The two outlaws vaulted the fallen forms of the lawmen and headed for the back of the house, intending to get out that way.

Deputy Sheriff Bert Tibbet, brother of Bill Tibbet, was behind the building, and rushed toward the rear door in response to the shooting. As he and another deputy approached the door, McKinney appeared, rifle in hand. McKinney got off a shot or two before Bert Tibbet fired his shotgun, hitting McKinney in the head and neck. McKinney staggered back, already mortally wounded, and the other deputy finished him off with a shot through a window.

The lawmen poured into the house, arresting Al Hulse and dragging him off to jail. Both Jeff Packard and Bill Tibbet were still alive, though badly wounded. They were carried down the street to the Southern Hotel and given medical attention, but Tibbet died a short while later. Packard lingered for more than twelve hours before succumbing to his wounds.

Jim McKinney was dead, his habit of getting into violent altercations having caught up to him at last. But before dying, he had been responsible for the killing of two more men, just another reason why, in the very early days of the twentieth century, he was the most wanted outlaw in the whole state of California.

3

GUNFIGHT AT STONE CORRAL

Late in the day on June 11, 1893, a beautiful summer Sunday, two men walked down a hill in California's Sequoia Forest, an area known locally as the Big Trees that recently had become a national park, only the second one in the country. This was a rugged landscape where dozens of hiding places could be taken advantage of by men who did not want to be found, such as the two who approached an old, abandoned cabin that had been built by a long-gone settler named Billy Bacon. Once there had been a barn near the cabin, but it had been torn down. What was left of a haystack stood nearby. The place was known as Stone Corral because at one time a stone fence had closed off the end of one of the nearby canyons, so that horses could be penned up there. Not far away was the road that led to the prosperous community of Visalia, in the San Joaquin Valley west of the Big Trees.

The two men were both bearded and heavily armed. Both limped from recent injuries. Though one was in his forties and the other in his thirties, they looked older, the result of months spent in these heavily wooded hills. They had an air of wariness about them, like wild animals tentatively drawing near to civilization. As they came up to the old haystack, the older man sighed and sat down, steadying himself by bracing the butt of the rifle he carried against the ground as he lowered himself. Exhaustion and the strain of hiding out in the hills had etched deep lines in the man's face. His companion stood nearby, shifting restlessly, evidently anxious to move on to the abandoned cabin.

Suddenly, with no warning, a rifle shot blasted through the stillness of the gathering dusk. The older man lurched forward with a cry of pain and surprise as a heavy slug plowed a furrow across his back. As he twisted to try to bring his rifle to bear on the cabin, a shotgun roared. The wounded man tumbled backward, struck in the head by several buckshot pellets. One of them smashed his right eye, blinding it. But he was still conscious and alert, and as he stretched out on the ground, blood pouring from his wounds, he began to return the fire that came from the cabin, which, despite appearing deserted, obviously was not. The second man also lay on the ground, having thrown himself behind the haystack when the shooting started. He joined in the fight, lifting up just enough to be able to throw some rifle shots at the tumbledown shack.

What had been a peaceful mountain meadow a few minutes earlier was now a battlefield. As the shadows of evening gathered, muzzle flashes split the gloom and sharp reports echoed back from the towering trees. From now on, whatever happened, no one who was there that day would ever forget the gunfight at Stone Corral.

Chris Evans was born in Canada, the son of a large farming family, and like many young men left home at the age of sixteen to seek his fortune. He started by crossing the border into the United States and joining the Army. The fact that he was not an

American citizen does not seem to have been much of a barrier to his enlistment. The Civil War was being fought, and armies on both sides needed all the recruits they could get.

Evans did not take part in the War Between the States. Instead, his troop was sent west to the Great Plains, to guard against Indian attacks, and stayed there after the war was over. Evans became well known in the Dakota Territory as a scout. Having killed a Sioux warrior who snuck into the cavalry camp one night, Evans decided to impress a lady friend back in Canada, so he scalped the Indian and mailed the hunk of hide and hair to her. The horrid smell emanating from the package caused it to be opened before it ever reached its destination, and when it was traced back to Chris Evans, it took away any chance of promotion for him. The Army wasn't for him anyway. He took French leave, walking away one day with a friend and never returning. He left behind the outfit where he had spent several years: the U.S. Seventh Cavalry, under the command of Colonel George Armstrong Custer.

After he deserted from the Army, Chris Evans's wandering path led him to California. He found work in the San Joaquin Valley with a family named Byrd, on a place that was known as Rattlesnake Ranch. The Byrd family had a pretty young daughter named Molly, and inevitably she and Evans wound up getting married. Despite his earlier footloose ways, Evans seemed ready to settle down here in California's verdant, fertile San Joaquin. He worked as a teamster and ferryboat captain, and with money saved from those jobs he bought a tract of land that was heavily forested with large redwood trees, naming the place Redwood Ranch. Over the years, several children came along, including a daughter, Eva, on whom Evans doted all his life.

About this time, two connected events happened that would have a large impact on Chris Evans's life. The first was the expansion of the Southern Pacific Railroad into the San Joaquin Valley. Despite all the advantages of the railroad, not everyone hailed its coming. Many homesteaders and settlers were forced to move, and their resentment led to open hostility and violence between the settlers and the railroad. This friction created a tension that filled the valley, and although Evans did not have any trouble directly with the railroad, he supported the settlers and thought that the Southern Pacific was running roughshod over the common people.

The second event was the meeting, in 1887, between Evans and a younger man named John Sontag. Sontag had been working for the Southern Pacific as a brakeman, until one day in the yards an engineer mistakenly slammed two cars together while Sontag was between them trying to uncouple them. One of the cars carried a load of iron bars, and the sudden lurch caused one of the bars to rip through Sontag's body, almost destroying one of his lungs. The injury easily could have proven fatal, but somehow Sontag survived, though his recuperation was long and painful and he was left with a sizable depression in his back where the bar had struck him. The ordeal was made even more painful by the fact that the Southern Pacific refused to take any responsibility for the accident. Sontag was left nearly penniless, with no job and in such bad physical shape that his chances of finding another one were slim indeed. When Chris Evans was introduced to the young man, Evans immediately took pity on him and felt a genuine liking for him. He invited Sontag to live with the family on the Redwood Ranch. At the time, Evans was working for the Bank of California as the manager of one of their grain warehouses, and had to be away from the ranch quite a bit. He needed someone he could trust to look after things there, including his family, and John Sontag seemed to fit the bill.

Sontag got along well with the Evans family, especially Eva. At first any romance between them was mild, though, barely more than platonic. Sontag didn't want to take advantage of Chris Evans's kindness toward him. Some things will not be denied, however, and as several years passed, Sontag and Eva grew closer.

She was still in her middle teens, but an understanding developed among the family: When Eva reached the age of seventeen, which was deemed old enough to marry, she and John Sontag would be wed. The fresh air, decent food, and gradually harder work had strengthened Sontag, repairing much of the damage done to him by the horrible injury in the rail yards.

It was a peaceful time for the Evans family and their boarder, who was by now more like a member of the family himself. They took frequent camping trips into the nearby Sequoia Forest. Chris Evans was an avid reader, especially of the classics, and could often be found stretched out under a tree with a leather-bound volume in his hand, enjoying life.

The only blot on this otherwise tranquil existence was the fact that someone had started holding up Southern Pacific trains as they passed through the San Joaquin Valley. Two someones, to be precise. One tall, one short. One who moved like a somewhat older man than his companion. The two bandits were always masked, and their daring robberies fueled much speculation about their true identities. Some people had the idea that the train robbers were two of the famous Dalton brothers, who were indeed in California at the time, visiting their brother Bill—and carrying out a few crimes while they were at it.

Meanwhile, with money they had gotten from some unknown source, Chris Evans and John Sontag bought a livery stable in Visalia and became partners in its operation. The stable was successful to start with, and Evans and Sontag made it more so. Then, in January of 1891, the bad luck that seemed to follow the two men, especially Sontag, struck again. The stable caught fire and burned to the ground, leaving its owners destitute. Evans owned a not-so-successful mine up in the mountains. He went to work it, hoping to eke a living out of the ore he took from it, when he wasn't busy nursing Sontag through an attack of pneumonia that was more dangerous than usual, seeing as how Sontag had only one good lung.

Somehow both men, and the rest of Evans's family, made it until the summer of 1892. The mine was keeping them alive. And there was the occasional train holdup, too, because all along it had been Evans and Sontag stopping those Southern Pacific trains. Some of Evans's relatives by marriage had lost land to the railroad, and Sontag had his own grudge against the Southern Pacific, of course. Why shouldn't the railroad help support some of the men it had damaged through its callous, high-handed ways, they reasoned.

Unfortunately, John Sontag's brother George lived in the area and knew what was going on. Indeed, he may have even taken part in some of the robberies. He tended to drink too much, and when he drank too much he also talked too much. His boasts got back to the authorities and made them suspicious of Chris Evans and John Sontag. Will Smith, a railroad detective who worked for the Southern Pacific, and George Witty, a local deputy sheriff, went to the Evans house in Visalia to question the two men.

Finding Eva Evans apparently alone in the house, Smith and Witty began to question her. She denied knowing where Sontag was. (He was hiding only a few feet away behind a screen between two rooms, in fact.) Chris Evans entered from the rear of the house, a revolver in his pocket. Furious at what he saw as Eva's refusal to cooperate, Smith began shouting at her, and this seems to have momentarily unhinged Deputy Witty, who yanked out his own pistol and loosed a shot for no reason. As the bullet whipped past the head of the startled girl and went on out an open door behind her, Chris Evans pulled his gun. At the same instant, John Sontag burst into the room from his hiding place, carrying a shotgun in each hand. The two lawmen, suddenly confronted with two armed, furious opponents, turned around and made tracks, taking off for the tall and uncut as fast as their legs would carry them. That didn't stop Sontag from unloading a charge of birdshot into the rump of Detective Smith. Evans opened fire on Deputy Witty, ventilating him through the shoulder. Even wounded, the two lawmen managed to keep running.

They had come to the Evans house in a wagon. Evans and Sontag piled into the wagon and escaped in it, Sontag whipping up the team. They made a clean getaway, and could have headed for the forest and the mountains, an area they knew so well that it was unlikely any posse could have found them without a great deal of difficulty and danger. The evidence connecting them to the train robberies was slight; they might have bluffed their way through the trouble if Deputy Witty hadn't opened fire and started a gunfight. Now, though, the whole San Joaquin Valley was in an uproar as word spread of the shooting. No one doubted anymore that Evans and Sontag were responsible for the series of holdups . . . as, of course, they really were. The hue and cry got even louder when the two of them tried to sneak back to the Evans house that very night, only to encounter a group of deputies who were keeping an eye on the place. More shots were exchanged, and this time, one of the lawmen was killed.

Now, Chris Evans and John Sontag really were fugitives, and they had no choice but to head for the mountains.

------◆◆◆------

THE many camping trips into the Sequoia Forest paid off for Evans and Sontag. They knew this rugged terrain better than any of the lawmen who were hunting them.

And there were plenty of those lawmen. During the fall of 1892 and the spring of 1893, as Evans and Sontag led them a merry chase, a veritable army of badge-toters descended on the area. It was the biggest manhunt California had ever seen, one of the biggest in the entire country. Not only hordes of sworn deputies and marshals, but also railroad detectives and men who were just out for the bounty on the heads of the two fugitives, joined the great hunt. Somehow, though, Evans and Sontag continued to elude the wolfpack baying at their heels. In fact, it was later discovered that they had returned to Visalia, where the Evans family lived, and spent two weeks at Christmas with them before slipping back to the hills!

The manhunt assumed epic proportions and was in the news from coast to coast. A melodramatic play was written about the two outlaws, and actors portraying Evans and Sontag hit the boards in some of the country's leading theaters. U.S. Marshal Vernon C. Wilson was sent to California to take charge of the effort to capture the fugitives. He took with him two Apache Indians who had worked for the Army as scouts. They would help Wilson track down Evans and Sontag.

While dodging posses, Evans continued to check on his mine, evidently hoping that someday the fuss would die down and he could return to working the shaft. A cabin belonging to a friend of Evans's named Jim Young stood in the vicinity, and Evans and Sontag visited there from time to time. One morning, while Evans and Sontag were there with a friend named Sam Williams, a visitor showed up, an Englishman named Edward Mainwaring, who was one of Young's neighbors. Young had left the cabin and gone to town to replenish his supplies.

Williams had stepped out the back of the cabin when Evans, standing at a window, spotted a group of men approaching. He recognized the newcomers as members of a posse looking for him and Sontag. In fact, both Marshal Wilson and Will Smith, the railroad detective, were with the posse, along with several local deputy sheriffs and the Apache trackers. Gunplay was inevitable, as Evans and Sontag could not leave the cabin without being seen.

Not wanting Mainwaring to be caught in the crossfire, Evans quickly ordered him to take a couple of buckets and walk out to a nearby spring. The posse, seeing the buckets, wouldn't think anything of Mainwaring's actions. The apparent normality of the scene might even lull the lawmen into thinking that Evans and Sontag weren't there. Mainwaring agreed. He left the cabin with a bucket dangling from each hand and strolled toward the spring, taking care to conceal the nervousness he must have felt.

About then, Sam Williams stepped back into the cabin from the rear, and Evans ordered him to get out, too. Williams was reluctant to do so; he knew that hell was about to pop and wanted to watch it. Evans forced him to go, however, leaving the two outlaws alone in the cabin as the posse approached. Breakfast was on the stove, and the lawmen must have been able to smell the food cooking.

Evans crouched at the window with a shotgun, letting the posse get closer. Sontag stood by the door, rifle in hand. Finally, when he judged the moment was right, Evans smashed the glass in the window with the shotgun and let go with both barrels. The double charge of buckshot slammed into the belly of Marshal Wilson and almost cut him in half. At the same instant Sontag kicked the door open and drilled one of the other lawmen, a former friend of Evans's named Andy McGinnis.

Instead of returning fire at the cabin, most of the posse members fled. The Apache trackers and another deputy sought cover behind some rocks and logs. They threw a few blind shots at the cabin, but the bullets came nowhere near their intended target.

Sontag's shot had only wounded Deputy McGinnis. Recognizing his old acquaintance, Evans went out of the cabin to check on him. He felt no sympathy for McGinnis, who, as Evans saw it, had turned on him. Sontag followed, covering his partner. The one deputy who hadn't run off when the shooting started loosed a shot at Sontag, hitting him in the arm. Meanwhile, the wounded McGinnis was begging Evans not to kill him. Seeing that Sontag had been wounded, Evans opened fire again on the deputy who was hiding behind a pile of logs. A bullet clipped Evans as well, grazing his skull and almost knocking him out. As he struggled to stay conscious, Evans caught a glimpse of McGinnis trying to bring his gun to bear. Evans fired first, blasting his former friend into oblivion.

Now both fugitives were wounded. Helping each other, they hurried into the woods behind Young's cabin. The Apaches and the lone remaining deputy didn't go after them. Those three posse members probably felt they were lucky to have escaped with their lives.

Evans and Sontag had many friends among the settlers in the area, and were able to get help from them. They hid out and recuperated from their injuries, and the manhunt continued throughout the winter.

The Apache trackers, having clashed with Evans and Sontag, decided that the better part of valor would be returning to the San Carlos Reservation in Arizona. But there were still plenty of other men searching for the notorious fugitives. Evans and Sontag were doing some searching of their own. They regarded Will Smith, the detective who worked for the Southern Pacific, as the source of most of their troubles. Having been tipped off by a friend that Smith was going to be traveling on a particular stagecoach, they stopped the stage, intending to settle the score with Smith. They found that the detective was not on board, having changed his mind at the last minute about taking the stage. They held up the passengers anyway, adding stagecoach robbery to their list of crimes.

Finally, in June of 1893, a posse led by another U.S. marshal, George Gard, came to Stone Corral and made the old Bacon cabin their headquarters as they searched the surrounding area. They kept a low profile any time they were at the cabin, so it would continue to appear deserted. As Evans and Sontag approached the cabin on the evening of June 11, it looked like no one was there. Evans suggested firing a few shots into the cabin, just to make sure it was unoccupied, but Sontag talked him out of it, saying it was not necessary. Besides, Sontag said, young people in the area sometimes used the old cabin as a lovers' rendezvous, and he didn't want to be responsible for any innocents coming to harm. Evans agreed, and the two outlaws walked down the hill toward the cabin. Tiring before they got there, Evans sat down beside an old haystack, intending to rest for a moment before pushing on.

Inside the cabin, the lawmen had seen Evans and Sontag approaching and recognized them. Marshal Gard ordered his men to hold their fire and let the outlaws get closer, but one of the posse, a deputy named Fred Jackson, got overeager and fired too soon, wounding Evans and opening the ball. Like it or not, the fight was on.

The old haystack concealed Evans and Sontag from the view of the posse, but didn't do anything to stop the bullets the lawmen poured into it. Still, the fugitives put up a hot fight. Jackson, whose premature shot had started things, tried to leave the cabin and circle around the haystack. Evans shot his leg out from under him, shattering the deputy's knee with a well-placed bullet. Another member of the posse, a half-breed Indian scout, did manage to get around behind them, and he sent a bullet through Sontag's one good lung, knocking him out of the fight.

Darkness fell, but the shooting continued, most of it coming from the cabin. Evans was still able to make the posse men duck with an occasional return shot. Sontag was alive, but injured too badly to take part in the fight. Toward morning, after Evans was wounded in the right arm and could no longer use his rifle, Sontag regained consciousness and asked his friend and partner to put him out of his misery with a revolver. Evans refused, unable to bring himself to do such a thing even though Sontag requested it. Sontag then urged his friend and partner to save himself if he could. Reluctantly, Evans crawled off in the darkness, leaving Sontag behind the haystack.

When dawn came and no shots had been heard from the fugitives for quite some time, the lawmen rushed the haystack, guns ready. They found Evans gone and Sontag unconscious.

Incredibly, as badly wounded as he was, Chris Evans had managed to crawl and walk for six miles up nearby Wilcox Canyon. He reached the cabin of some settlers named Perkins and begged the family to help him. They bandaged his wounds as best they could while Evans passed out from shock and loss of blood. Fearing what might happen if they didn't notify the law about their unwanted visitor, the homesteaders sent a rider galloping for help. Word got around quickly that the notorious Chris Evans was at the farm, and several groups of lawmen converged on the Perkins place. For a moment, it seemed that there might be more violence, this time among the authorities themselves as they argued over who would have the honor of arresting the infamous outlaw. When the squabbling was over, Evans was loaded in a wagon and taken to Visalia, where he was placed in jail. A doctor was sent for to care for his injuries. In the next cell lay John Sontag, who, still clinging to life, had been brought to the jail in Visalia, too.

Sontag would not live to stand trial. He died in jail several weeks later, on July 3, 1893.

Evans's right arm had to be amputated because of the wound he had suffered there, and the buckshot lodged in his head caused him great pain the rest of his life. Put on trial for his crimes, he was convicted and sentenced to life in prison. Chris Evans was not finished causing trouble for the law, however. While in the jail at Fresno, before being transferred to the state penitentiary, he managed to escape in December 1893, and remained at large for several months before he was recaptured. The law caught up to him when, unable to bring himself to stay away from his wife and children, he tried to visit them on the sly. Chris Evans, robber of trains and killer of lawmen, was always a devoted family man as well, contradictory as that may seem.

John Sontag lying in a pile of hay after being shot by the posse assembled behind him, on June 11, 1893.

(Courtesy of National Archives and Records Administration)

In 1911, wracked by poor health as a result of age and the injuries he had received, Chris Evans was pardoned by the governor of California and released from prison. He went to live with his wife Molly and several of their children in Oregon. In the intervening years, his daughter Eva had achieved some fame as an actress, even playing herself in the melodrama based on the exploits of Evans and Sontag. Evans's remaining years, though few, were at least peaceful. He died in 1917, hardly resembling the daring outlaw who years earlier had been one of the objects of the biggest manhunt in the history of California.

4

THE DOOLIN BUNCH VS.
THE U.S. MARSHALS

The six men who rode into the Oklahoma Territory hamlet of Ingalls on the morning of September 1, 1893, were hardly strangers to the townspeople. The group of horsebackers was led by tall, handsome Bill Doolin, once a cowhand on the nearby HX Bar Ranch owned by Oscar Halsell, but lately an outlaw. Doolin had ridden with the famous Dalton gang, but he missed their disastrous raid on Coffeyville, Kansas, when his horse pulled up lame on the way there. Following the destruction of the Daltons at Coffeyville, Doolin returned to Oklahoma and began organizing his own gang from the survivors of the Dalton bunch and some newcomers who had ridden into the area.

George "Bitter Creek" Newcomb was Bill Doolin's right bower. He had ridden with the Daltons as well, and had picked up his nickname during that period of his life. Exuberant by nature, when the gang was celebrating a successful robbery, Newcomb liked to sing, "I'm a wild wolf from Bitter Creek, and it's my night to howl!" Big, reasonably handsome, good with a gun or his fists, Bitter Creek really fit the accepted image of a dashing young desperado.

Bill Dalton had not ridden with his outlaw brothers, preferring instead to strike out on his own. He went to California, and even began a career there in politics, only to be drawn back to Oklahoma by the deaths of his brothers (except for Emmett, who was seriously wounded and captured at Coffeyville). While there, an embittered Bill gave up on his own dreams of respectability and drifted into a life of crime, joining up with Bill Doolin and Bitter Creek Newcomb to form the nucleus of Doolin's new gang.

The others with Doolin, Dalton, and Newcomb on that fateful morning were Jack Blake, better known as Tulsa Jack; Dan Clifton, called Dynamite Dick because he had a habit of hollowing out his bullets and placing a small quantity of dynamite inside them; and Roy Daugherty, a young outlaw who hero-worshipped Bill Doolin and used the alias Arkansas Tom Jones. There were others who came and went from the gang, but these six were the core. Some called them the Oklahombres, after the territory; others referred to them as Doolin's Wild Bunch. To most they were simply the Doolin gang.

The gang's primary hideout was a cave on the Cimarron River, some twenty miles south. The outlaws were known and liked in Ingalls, where for the last several months they had been coming to stock up on supplies, drink in the saloons, and visit old friends. Ingalls was a small community with approximately two dozen businesses and homes scattered around a spacious town square. The only two-story building was Mary Pierce's hotel. Arkansas Tom headed there as the group rode into town. He was sick and wanted to lie down in one of the rooms on the hotel's second floor. The other five outlaws made their destination Ransom and Murray's Saloon, where they intended to spend a pleasant day drinking and playing cards.

Unknown to Bill Doolin and his companions, another group was headed toward Ingalls on this warm late summer morning.

Responding to the reign of banditry that the Doolin gang had unleashed on the territory in recent months, President Grover Cleveland had appointed Evett Nix U.S. Marshal for the Oklahoma Territory. Nix recruited other well-known lawmen to help him bring the gang to justice. Foremost among them were Bill Tilghman, Heck Thomas, Chris Madsen, and Bud Ledbetter. Others in the inner circle of marshals charged with tracking down the outlaws were John Hixon, Jim Masterson (Bat's brother), Frank Canton, Charlie Colcord, Lafe Shadley, Tom Houston, and Dick Speed. Acting on a tip that Doolin and his compadres often could be found visiting Ingalls, Nix sent two wagons full of deputy marshals to the small community. John Hixon was in charge of the operation, and he had almost a dozen men with him, including Masterson, Canton, Colcord, Shadley, Houston, and Speed. There were plenty of other covered wagons moving around the countryside, and the lawmen hoped that they would be taken for itinerant farmers, rather than U.S. marshals. The wagons arrived in the vicinity of Ingalls on August 31, 1893. The next morning, the star-packers started into town, hoping to catch some or all of the Doolin gang there.

By mid-morning on September 1, Arkansas Tom was ensconced in a second-floor room in the Pierce Hotel. The rest of the boys were drinking in the saloon. The wagons carrying the marshals skirted the town to the east and then circled back to approach from the north. When they reached the outskirts of the settlement, they came to a stop in front of Light's Blacksmith Shop. The heavily armed marshals hopped out of the vehicles and began spreading out along the street and across the town square, picking positions from which they could open fire on the gang if necessary.

Suddenly, down the street toward the saloon, a young man started to run across the dusty thoroughfare. Who he was and what he was really doing are uncertain; chances are he had nothing to do with the Doolin gang. But Marshal Dick Speed spotted him, jumped to the conclusion that he was going to warn the outlaws that a posse was in town, and snapped his rifle to his shoulder to fire at the young man. The bullet sent the young man spinning off his feet. It also opened what came to be known as the Battle of Ingalls.

Hearing the shot, Bitter Creek Newcomb stepped out the door of the saloon to see what was going on. Immediately, he spotted the gun-toting lawmen spreading out through the town, and started to lift the Winchester he carried. One of the marshals fired first, the bullet striking the breech of Bitter Creek's rifle and ricocheting downward into his thigh. The leg wound knocked him off his feet.

Now hell really began to pop. Having seen Newcomb come out of the saloon, the marshals assumed that the rest of the gang was inside and opened up on the place. With lead flying around him, Bitter Creek struggled to his feet and made it to his horse, which was tied at a hitch rail nearby. He jerked the reins loose, grabbed the saddlehorn, and managed to pull himself onto the animal's back. With his leg bleeding from the hole that the ricocheting slug had gouged in it, he galloped off toward the southwest, putting Ingalls behind him.

Escaping would prove to be more difficult for the rest of the outlaws. Bullets crashed through the thin walls of the saloon and shattered the glass in the windows. Doolin, Dalton, Tulsa Jack, and Dynamite Dick hugged the floor. George Ransom, one of the proprietors of the place, was hit in the leg as he crouched behind the bar. The outlaws crawled to the front of the saloon, rose up enough to use the barrels of their six-guns to rake the rest of the glass out of the windows, and began returning the fire. Most of the time they were shooting blind, though, because they couldn't risk looking out to aim. They were at a definite disadvantage here.

As the firing died down for a moment, another citizen of Ingalls, Jerry Simonds, tried to dash across the street, probably in

search of a safer place to go to ground. It was a fatal miscalcula-
tion. More shots roared from both sides, and Simonds tumbled
off his feet, mortally wounded. Whether it was outlaw or lawman
lead that found him didn't matter. He was just as badly wounded
either way. He was able to crawl into a nearby grocery store
before he died.

The marshals continued their assault on the saloon. They had
the members of the gang pinned down in there, and they had
enough ammunition to keep up the attack all day. It looked like
everything was on the side of the law today.

But they had reckoned without Arkansas Tom, up on the second floor of the hotel. That was the highest point in town, and
from there Tom could see everything that was going on spread
out before him. He might have been sick, but that didn't seem to
affect his shooting eye. Hearing the sounds of battle outside, he
took his Winchester and moved to the windows of the room. He
began sniping at the marshals, who had no idea one of the gang
was in the hotel. At first, probably none of them knew where the
bullets were coming from that suddenly whipped past them. Jim
Masterson was leaning against a tree near the blacksmith shop
when slugs started thudding into the trunk and knocking bark
flying. Masterson did some flying himself then, leaping away
from the tree and diving into a ditch where Marshal John Hixon
had taken shelter. Both lawmen poked the muzzles of their rifles
out of the ditch and, spotting Arkansas Tom, opened fire on the
window of the hotel. Tom had to retreat, but there was another
window in the room, so he just moved over there, out of the line
of fire from Masterson and Hixon, and resumed taking potshots at
the other marshals.

Meanwhile, Bill Doolin had realized that he and his companions couldn't maintain their precarious position in the saloon.
They had to reach the stable where they had left their horses.
Though they knew they were taking their lives in their hands,
they dashed out a side door of the saloon and made a run for the

stable, zigzagging back and forth, dropping behind cover to throw some more lead at the marshals, then leaping up to run a few more yards before doing it all over again. It was a desperate race. A bullet ripped a gash across the back of Doolin's neck, striking him with enough impact to send him tumbling off his feet. But he rolled over and came up again, still running. Somehow, through the storm of lead that surrounded them, Doolin and the others reached the stable and threw themselves inside.

Arkansas Tom was still firing hot and heavy from the hotel. Marshal Tom Houston tried to reach a better spot across the street, but a bullet from Arkansas Tom's Winchester caught him in the belly, doubling him over. Several of the marshals risked their own necks to dash out and grab Houston where he lay sprawled in the dusty street. They pulled him to cover, but it was too late. He was already dying.

Hixon, who was in charge of the posse, had made a mistake by not heading straight for the stable with the wagons. If the lawmen had secured the stable first, so that the gang could not reach their horses, Bill Doolin and his companions would have been well and truly trapped in Ingalls. Instead, the outlaws now had their mounts, and they had a stronger place to fort up and do some damage of their own. The marshals concentrated their fire on the sturdy barn, but the outlaws' return fire was so fierce that the lawmen were forced to pull back a little.

The town pump and public watering trough were located near the stable. Marshal Dick Speed thought that if he could reach it, the trough would give him good cover and an angle from which he would be able to fire into the stable. He made a dash for it, but Bill Doolin, bleeding from his neck wound, stepped into the doorway of the stable just then. Flame bloomed from the muzzle of the Colt in Doolin's hand. His first shot missed, but the second one struck Speed and killed him. The luckless lawman fell face-forward in the street.

Doolin pulled back into the barn, where the other three men

were mounted up and ready to make a run for it. Swinging up into the saddle, Doolin joined them. Thinking it would be better to give the lawmen more targets, Doolin and Dynamite Dick went out the rear door of the stable while Dalton and Tulsa Jack thundered out the front.

Marshal Lafe Shadley was crouched close to the front of the livery barn, ready for the escape attempt. As Dalton and Tulsa Jack emerged, Shadley opened fire. One of his bullets hit Dalton's horse in the jaw, shattering it and causing the animal to fall. Dalton was thrown out of the saddle and rolled clear, shaken up but otherwise unhurt. His gun was still in his hand. He snapped a shot at Shadley, and the marshal went down. It's just as likely, however, that he was picked off by Arkansas Tom rather than hit by Dalton. Maybe both of them hit him. Whichever outlaw was responsible, Lafe Shadley was fatally wounded, the third lawman to fall on what should have been a peaceful morning in Ingalls.

Dalton escaped on foot to a ravine near the settlement, where he was picked up by one of the other outlaws. They galloped off, leaving the stunned community behind them. Bill Doolin and Bitter Creek Newcomb had been wounded, neither seriously. Those were the only injuries sustained by the outlaws.

The posse hadn't been so lucky, and neither had the citizens of Ingalls. Dick Speed was dead, Tom Houston and Lafe Shadley so badly wounded that they would not recover. Two innocent bystanders were dead. The raid for which the lawmen had had such high hopes was a disaster. But for the time being, there was still one outlaw in Ingalls—Arkansas Tom Jones. With Doolin and the others gone, the surviving marshals were able to turn all their firepower on the second floor of the hotel where Tom was holed up. He no longer dared to show his face at the windows, and couldn't do anything except hunker on the floor and hope none of the slugs smashing into the building found him.

The wounded lawmen were tended to by one of the local doctors. After a while, Mary Pierce, the owner of the hotel, begged the other marshals to stop shooting the place to pieces. She was told that unless Arkansas Tom surrendered, the lawmen intended to set the building on fire and burn it down around him. The marshals were filled with rage at what had happened to their fellow badge-toters. Mary called up to Tom to surrender, but he refused. Finally, though, seeing that he had no choice, he agreed to put down his guns and turn himself over to the law. He insisted that the local minister be present, however, so that the furious marshals wouldn't dare to hang him or shoot him out of hand, as they surely wanted to after what he had done. They settled for clapping a pair of handcuffs on him and throwing him into the back of one of the wagons.

The great Ingalls shoot-out between the Doolin gang and the posse of U.S. marshals was over—and it wasn't even noon yet.

—◆—

Roy Daugherty, alias Arkansas Tom Jones, was convicted of manslaughter and sentenced to fifty years in prison. He was paroled after seventeen years behind bars, and tried to live a law-abiding life once he was on the outside. That lasted for a while, but then he robbed a bank in Missouri and was killed in Joplin as he swapped shots with some lawmen trying to arrest him.

The Doolin gang continued to pull robberies across Oklahoma Territory, but their numbers began to decrease. Bitter Creek Newcomb and Charlie Pierce were caught in a posse's trap and gunned down as they rode up to a barn on the farm of a man they considered a friend. One by one, Dynamite Dick, Tulsa Jack, Red Buck, and the others fell as the marshals tracked them down. Bill Doolin and Bill Dalton both dropped out of sight for a while, lying low in hopes that the crusade to catch them would die down. It never did, though. Dalton was located living near Ardmore. As a posse closed in on the house where he was hiding, he tried to climb out a window and escape. A single shot from one of the deputies killed him instantly.

Bill Doolin was still on the loose, living under assumed names in Kansas and Arkansas with his wife Edith, whom he had married in secret several months before the Ingalls fight. Of the forces of marshals after him, Bill Tilghman was the most relentless manhunter. In January of 1896, more than two years after the Ingalls shoot-out, Tilghman traced Doolin to Eureka Springs, Arkansas, where he had gone to find relief for his arthritis in the town's famous mineral baths. Tilghman confronted him, and after a few tense moments when it appeared that Doolin might try to shoot his way out of this predicament, the outlaw surrendered instead. Under heavy guard, Tilghman took Doolin back to Guthrie, Oklahoma, which at that time was still the territorial capital.

Tilghman's efforts went for naught. Doolin escaped from the jail in Guthrie before he could be brought to trial, releasing all the other prisoners in the lockup at the same time to distract the authorities and help cover his escape. Only one member of his gang was still alive, the bandit called Little Dick West. It was rumored that Doolin and West had joined forces again and were pulling bank robberies here and there in the territory.

Marshal Heck Thomas received a tip that Doolin was going to be visiting his wife and child at their home near Lawson. Thomas led a posse there. It was night, and Doolin, who had indeed been visiting his family, was about to leave. As the outlaw walked out onto the road in front of the house carrying a rifle, Heck Thomas stepped out of concealment and leveled a shotgun at him. Thomas called on Doolin to surrender, but Doolin tried to make one more fabulous escape. He flung the rifle to his shoulder and snapped a shot at Thomas—and missed.

A split second later, the shotgun in the lawman's hands roared, and Bill Doolin was smashed to the ground by the withering charge of buckshot that tore into him. He died on the spot, finally laid low by the law.

The fight at Ingalls became one of the most famous battles

between outlaws and lawmen in the history of the West. Many of the details have been exaggerated and romanticized, including an almost certainly fabricated love story between Bitter Creek Newcomb and a local girl named Rose Dunn, the stepdaughter of one of the town's doctors. In a wildly inaccurate but very popular epic poem written years after the battle, she was characterized as a tragically romantic figure known as the Rose of the Cimarron, who carried Bitter Creek's rifle to him and bound up his wound as she stayed by his side during the battle. Historians agree that nothing of the sort ever happened.

Which is not to say that historians agree on everything about the battle. Many angles of it are still in dispute, such as the location of the various participants, the number of shots fired, and which of the outlaws actually killed the three marshals who met their deaths at Ingalls. Also, some versions of the story portray the settlement as a wild outlaw town, when in reality it seems to have been little more than a sleepy little farming and ranching community most of the time. Many members of Bill Doolin's gang had worked as cowboys in the area and knew most of the townspeople as friends. Instead of coming to Ingalls to raise a ruckus and howl at the moon, they usually rode in on much more mundane errands, such as getting their hair cut at Sherm Sanders's barbershop. But that didn't stop the legends from growing. The facts seldom do.

In this case, though, the real-life battle at Ingalls was plenty violent and colorful enough to start with.

PART FOUR

HOLDUPS

I'll be in hell before you start breakfast, boys!

—Black Jack Ketchum

BUNGLED BANK ROBBERY

The town of Meeker, Colorado, is located in the northwestern part of the state, about seventy-five miles from the rugged area known as Brown's Park. In the 1890s, Brown's Park was notorious as the hideout of the Wild Bunch, the famous outlaw gang led by Butch Cassidy. By all accounts, Butch was a charming, voluble fellow, and after the gang pulled off a successful robbery of the bank in Montpelier, Idaho, in the summer of 1896, it was natural that Butch would boast about the holdup to the members of the gang who hadn't taken part in the job.

A colorful desperado like Butch Cassidy drew a lot of admirers to him. Several of these novice members of the Wild Bunch, after sitting around the campfire and listening to Butch's brags about the Montpelier robbery, decided that they ought to try to pull off something like that themselves. After all, they must have reasoned, when it came to bank robbery they had learned from the master himself. There was no reason they couldn't knock off a bank of their own.

So, probably after talking about it among themselves for quite a while, three of the less experienced members of the Wild Bunch rode off toward Meeker. They were George Law, Jim Shirley, and a youngster known as "the Kid," whose real name may or may not have been Pierce.

Their plan was to pull off this job just like Butch Cassidy would have. They got their hands on some extra horses and stashed them several miles outside of town so that they could change to fresh mounts for their getaway. They rode into Meeker on the morning of Tuesday, October 13, 1896, and familiarized themselves with the layout of the town and the bank that was their intended target by hanging around the local livery stable. If anyone in Meeker was suspicious of the three strangers, no record of it has come down through history. More than likely, Western hospitality dictated that they would be welcome to sit around and shoot the breeze with the townies.

The three outlaws had their eyes on the Bank of Meeker, which was owned by the J. W. Hugus Company, a business enterprise that operated numerous banks and mercantiles in Colorado and Wyoming at the time. The bank was housed in the Hugus Building on Meeker's Main Street. A Hugus general store also occupied the same building. That afternoon, still acting unsuspiciously, George Law and the Kid wandered, apparently aimlessly, into the bank/store while Jim Shirley came in through the back door. They split up even more, George Law heading toward the left, where the bank counter was located, while the Kid went to the right and Jim Shirley advanced into the center of the room. At the counter Joe Rooney, who clerked at the Meeker Hotel, was making a deposit.

George Law calmly stood in line behind Rooney, as if he were waiting to conduct some normal business, but when Rooney finished making his deposit and turned to leave, Law went into action. He drew his gun as he stepped up to the counter. Thrusting the weapon through the teller's window, he ordered the man to put up his hands. To punctuate the order, Law fired a shot past the teller's head.

The teller, David Smith, who was the bank's assistant cashier, didn't follow the order quickly enough to suit Law, so, amazingly, the robber fired again, this time sending a slug whistling past Smith's other ear. If the idea was to rob the bank without arousing the attention of the rest of the town, the outlaws were in the process of failing miserably. Two gunshots going off in the bank were bound to cause a commotion.

Some say that the shots were accidental, that Law was so nervous he fired them without meaning to. It's impossible to know the exact truth, but no one can argue with the fact that the shots galvanized the town of Meeker.

Inside the bank, Jim Shirley and the Kid threw down on C. W. Moulton, the manager, and the other employees, holding them at gunpoint, while Law kept an eye on Smith and Rooney, who still stood nearby with his hands up, and tried to open the door of the bank office. The door was locked and wouldn't budge.

Shirley ordered Moulton to unlock the door. The bank manager cooperated, producing a key and opening the office door. Law crowded into the room and pulled out the cash drawer in Moulton's desk. Yanking a crumpled sugar sack from his pocket, Law dumped the cash from the drawer into the sack. While he was busy doing that, Shirley made sure all the prisoners were disarmed, and also broke the actions of all the rifles in the mercantile that adjoined the bank.

All this was taking too much time. The earlier shots had already alerted the townspeople that something was wrong at the bank. Tom Shervin, who worked at the Meeker Hotel with Joe Rooney, ran down the boardwalk and peeked in the bank window to see what was going on. Spotting the hostages with their hands up, Shervin leaped to the obvious conclusion that the place was being robbed. He signaled as much to a man passing in the street, C. J. Duffey, who dashed away to spread the word. By the time

Shirley, Law, and the Kid finished their work inside the bank, a group of armed men led by Town Marshal Ben Nichols had surrounded the entrance to the building, using whatever cover they could find as they leveled rifles and shotguns at the door.

Jim Shirley was the oldest and most experienced of the bandits, and he knew trouble likely was waiting for them outside. Their best chance to escape would be to take hostages with them to serve as human shields. Shirley grabbed Joe Rooney, jammed a gun in his back, and forced him out the door onto the sidewalk. Seeing one of their fellow Meekerites in the lead, the townsmen held their fire as the outlaws and their prisoners pushed out of the bank. It was a tense moment, and it became even more so as Jim Shirley spotted a man with a rifle crouched at the corner of a nearby grain warehouse. Shirley snapped a shot at the man, hitting him in the chest and wounding him, but not fatally.

Given the circumstances, that shot could have been the match that touched off an explosion of gunfire. If that had happened, there would have been a massacre there on Meeker's Main Street. Some or all of the hostages probably would have been killed. Somehow, the townsmen managed to rein in their taut nerves and hold their fire. The group of hostages began shuffling down the street, herded along by Shirley, Law, and the Kid.

Their destination was a wagon belonging to the Hugus Company that was parked alongside the boardwalk. The outlaws' horses were tied to the wheels of the wagon. When they got there, Law and Shirley started jerking the reins loose while the Kid covered the prisoners with his rifle.

Suddenly, one of the hostages—impossible to say which one, at this late date—couldn't stand it any longer. The man lowered his arms and broke away from the group, dashing for safety. That unexpected development caused the Kid's nerve to crack. The young outlaw opened fire, spraying lead at the hostages as fast as he could work the lever of his rifle.

Naturally enough, when the shooting started the rest of the hostages stampeded, too, trying to get out of the way of the flying lead. One man was hit in the arm, another in the leg, and a third had a finger grazed by a wild bullet. But despite their injuries, the hostages kept moving, and suddenly the three outlaws found themselves without their human shields.

Guns roared all around them as the citizens of Meeker opened up with all barrels blazing.

The Kid was thrown backward, his body ripped through by five bullets. One of them found his heart and killed him instantly. Jim Shirley stumbled against the wagon, shot through the lungs. He managed to lift his gun and jerk the trigger as he fell. He continued firing even as he sprawled on the ground, blood puddling on the dirt underneath him, until the revolver was empty.

George Law was the only one still on his feet. Instead of trying to get on one of the spooked horses, he lit out on foot. He had to have known that the odds were against him getting away, but he did his best. He hadn't gone far, though, before he stumbled, shot through the body. A second later, a slug smashed his left leg out from under him and he tumbled to the ground. Slowly, the armed townsmen began to emerge from their concealment and cautiously approach the fallen desperadoes.

Jim Shirley and the Kid were dead. George Law was alive but in bad shape, obviously mortally wounded. The county attorney and the editor of the local newspaper tried to get a dying statement out of him, but all Law managed to do was to give them phony names for himself, Shirley, and the Kid. It was only later that their real identities were discovered. Law lived for less than an hour after the shoot-out that ended the botched bank robbery.

Oddly enough, when the bank employees returned to the bank, they found the sack of money sitting there. In the excitement of herding the hostages out of the bank, the outlaws had left the money behind. Even if they had gotten away, they would have done so empty-handed. They had bungled this bank robbery up one way and down the other. When it came to following in the lawless footsteps of Butch Cassidy and the rest of the Wild Bunch, this hapless trio never had a chance.

THE CAPTURE OF "BLACK JACK" KETCHUM

Stars glittered brightly in the sky above the town of Folsom, New Mexico Territory, on the night of August 16, 1899. The hour was just past ten o'clock, and the eastbound train was late. It rolled into the depot of the Colorado & Southern Railroad to take on coal and water at 10:20 P.M. While it was stopped, a stealthy figure slipped up on the blind side of the train, away from the depot. The man swung aboard and concealed himself in the shadows of the platform between the baggage car and the coal car. A short time later, the train lurched and rumbled into motion, leaving Folsom behind but taking with it an unknown—and unwanted—passenger.

A few miles out of town, the train approached a distinctive landmark, a pair of mesas known variously as Twin Mountain or Twin Butte. As the train rolled along the mostly flat landscape south of the buttes, the man who had boarded at Folsom climbed onto the coal car and began crawling over the mound of black rocks. As he neared the front of the car, he drew the revolver he wore holstered on his hip and poised himself to leap down into the cab of the locomotive.

His gang had broken up and he was alone, but he was about to attempt something that few if any other desperadoes of the Old West had accomplished. He was going to hold up a train single-handed. He was already well known, but what happened tonight would assure that no one would ever forget the name Black Jack Ketchum.

———◆·❖·◆———

BLACK Jack wasn't really Black Jack. The name belonged to someone else, and it wasn't really that man's, either. Black Jack Ketchum was born Thomas Ketchum in San Saba, Texas, in 1863. He was the youngest of three brothers, the oldest of whom became a successful and well-liked horse trader in the area. Tom and the middle brother, Sam, were cowboys, uneducated and rather unstable, given to fits of rowdiness and troublemaking. They drifted into a life of crime, but didn't commit any serious offenses until 1895, when they and several friends shot to death a local rancher, John N. "Jap" Powers. Powers's wife paid to have her husband killed, but while she was sent to prison for her part in the crime, Tom and Sam Ketchum lit out for the tall and uncut, in this case New Mexico Territory.

About this time, the area along and on both sides of the border between New Mexico and Arizona began to be plagued by the lawless activities of an owlhoot gang known as the Black Jacks. The gang took its name from its leader, William "Black Jack" Christian. How Christian came by that nickname is unknown, but for a while, his success as an outlaw was unquestioned. He and his men held up trains and stagecoaches, robbed banks, post offices, and stores. They shot it out with posses and citizens. No one seemed able to catch them, and the task was made even more difficult by the ranchers in the area, who helped Christian and his men escape from the law on several occasions. Some of the ranchers no doubt liked and sympathized with the bandit and aided him for that reason, while others simply feared him and wanted to stay on his good side. Faced with this problem, New Mexico authorities appealed to the Justice Department in Washington for help. A group of Federal marshals arrived in the area and teamed up with local lawmen, private detectives hired by the railroads and banks, and even a troop of Mexican soldiers, sent by the Mexican government because Christian also raided across the border in Sonora and Chihuahua.

Oddly enough considering what happened later, Christian and his men might not have been guilty of all the outrages attributed to them. It's possible that some of those crimes were committed by two brothers who had drifted into the territory because Texas had gotten too hot for them—Tom and Sam Ketchum.

Fate took another twist when Tom and Sam ambled farther west and started riding with the Black Jack Gang. Shortly after that, the combined efforts of the lawmen finally paid off. A posse caught up with the bandits near Clifton, Arizona. It isn't known if Tom and Sam were on hand for this fight, but it's certain that William "Black Jack" Christian was, because he went down with more than enough star-packer lead in him to assure that he would never get up.

Some of the outlaws escaped, but now they were leaderless. Tom Ketchum stepped into that breach, assuming command of the gang and decreeing that from here on out, he would be known as Black Jack Ketchum. And known far and wide, too, because he planned on being an even more notorious desperado than his namesake.

The gang actually grew in numbers under Tom Ketchum's leadership. For a while, there was even an unofficial partnership with Butch Cassidy's Wild Bunch, though Butch himself thought Tom was crazy and never trusted him. A few members of the Wild Bunch continued to ride with the Black Jack Gang from time to time, however.

After killing a postmaster who pursued them from the scene of a post office robbery, the gang concentrated on trains, holding up several of them in New Mexico, Arizona, and even back over the line in the Ketchum brothers' home state of Texas. None of the robberies proved to be very lucrative. On one occasion, the gang used so much dynamite to blow open a stubborn express safe that they blew up most of the money inside it, too.

That may have been an omen. The gang's luck began to turn. A shoot-out with a posse in southeastern Arizona resulted in the deaths of several of the outlaws. Tom, Sam, and the remaining members of the group retreated across the border into Mexico. They stayed there for the most part until July of 1899, when they returned to New Mexico to hold up a Colorado & Southern train near Folsom. They got away with a good haul and, thinking themselves safe from pursuit, made camp for the night in a draw along Turkey Creek.

Unknown to Tom and the others, a posse led by U.S. Marshal Creighton Foraker was hot on their trail. The lawmen swooped down on the gang's camp, leading to a ferocious battle. The outlaws scattered, but several of them were seriously wounded. Wild Bunch member Elza Lay, who had been in on the train robbery, was hit a couple of times and was soon captured at a nearby ranch. Sam Ketchum, Tom's brother and long-time partner in crime, was also shot up during the battle and captured soon after. He was sent to prison, but had not been there long when he died from blood poisoning, a result of the wounds he had suffered during the fight with the posse.

Tom Ketchum was alone now. Embittered, outraged by what he considered a cruel fate, and none too stable to start with, he quickly conceived a plan to strike back at the forces of law and order. It would be bold, it would be daring, it would show everyone that he was still Black Jack Ketchum, by God, and still a force to be reckoned with.

His idea was simple: He would hold up a train . . . by himself.

TOM "Black Jack" Ketchum bounded down from the coal car, into the locomotive. Brandishing a rifle, he called out to the engineer to stop the train. Faced with a wild-eyed desperado waving a gun around, neither the engineer nor the fireman thought it would be a good idea to argue. The engineer hit the brakes.

Ketchum's plan called for the express and mail cars to be uncoupled from the passenger and freight cars behind them. Then he would force the engineer to run that part of the train on down the tracks to a spot well away from the rest of the cars. That way he would have to deal only with the engineer and fireman and could loot the express and mail cars at his leisure.

Ketchum forced the engineer and fireman out of the cab and prodded them along the tracks at gunpoint to the rear of the mail car. Right away, it became apparent that something was wrong. The train had come to a stop on a curve in the tracks, and with the mail car sitting at a slightly different angle than the car directly behind it, the coupling could not be undone because of the way its parts were binding together.

While Ketchum was trying to figure out what to do next, the door of the mail car opened and a clerk stuck his head out, trying to see why the train had come to an unexpected halt. Reacting instinctively, Ketchum fired, his bullet ripping away the unfortunate mail clerk's jaw.

Unlike the clerk, the train's conductor, Frank Harrington, knew all too well what was happening. Three times before, his trains had been stopped and held up by robbers. Now, unknown to Ketchum, Harrington was making his way along the train with a shotgun clutched in his hands. The shooting of the mail clerk proved to be the distraction Harrington needed. He stepped into the open only a few yards from Ketchum and leveled the scatter-gun.

The outlaw's speedy reactions enabled him to get off the first shot, but his slug only grazed Harrington's neck. The conductor pulled the triggers of the shotgun an instant later, and the double charge of buckshot ripped into Ketchum's right arm, destroying his elbow. The impact also knocked Ketchum backward down the embankment along the roadbed.

Only slightly wounded, Harrington hustled the engineer and fireman back aboard and ordered the engineer to get the train moving as fast as he could. It pulled out as Ketchum, dazed by the pain of his wound and only half-conscious, crawled into the brush along the tracks.

That was where he spent the night, drifting in and out of awareness. His horse was nearby, but he lacked the strength to mount up and get out of there. He knew that the train crew would spread the alarm, and by morning posses would be out searching for him. But there was nothing he could do about it. His grand scheme had failed.

Early the next morning, still in great pain, Ketchum heard a freight train coming along the tracks. He found his hat and put it on the end of the rifle he had dropped earlier when he was shot. He waved the hat in the air to signal the men on the train, which ground to a halt. As the crew jumped down and ran out into the brush, Ketchum summoned up a final display of defiance, menacing them with the rifle as they approached him. The wary trainmen backed off and threatened to leave him there, and finally Ketchum relented. He called out, "I am all done. Take me in."

He was loaded on the train and taken into Folsom to the doctor's office. Marshal Creighton Foraker was summoned, and arrived to place Ketchum under arrest. The outlaw's wounded arm was bound up, and he was taken to San Rafael Hospital in Trinidad, Colorado. The doctors there knew immediately it would be impossible to save Ketchum's right arm. It was amputated without delay.

New Mexico state law made it a capital offense to hold up a train, though no one had ever been executed for that crime alone. When Ketchum stood trial in Clayton, New Mexico, the prosecuting attorney pressed for a death sentence, and when Ketchum was convicted, that was what he received. More bitter than ever, the now-one-armed Ketchum awaited his execution in the Clayton jail, where he wrote letters to various officials protesting what he considered the unfairness of his fate and the cruel nature of his sentence. He was interviewed as well by numerous reporters, and repeated his harangue to them. None of it did any good. Early on the morning of Friday, April 26, 1901, he was led to the gallows wearing a new black suit.

Fate had one more unusual twist in store for Black Jack Ketchum.

The lawmen in charge of the execution were inexperienced at such things. They miscalculated the length of rope they needed, and to make matters worse, after testing the gallows the night before with a two-hundred-pound sack of sand, they left the sack hanging overnight so that the rope was stretched out even more. An unrepentant Ketchum told his executioners as they fastened the rope around his neck, "I'll be in hell before you start breakfast, boys!" Then he stood there as a black hood was lowered over his head and pinned to his vest.

This was no fancy gallows with a lever to spring the trapdoor. A rope had to be cut in order to drop the prisoner through the opening. It took the hangman two swings to cut the rope and spring the trap. One can only speculate what must have gone through Ketchum's mind when he heard the first blow strike but the trapdoor failed to open. At any rate, the second stroke of the ax did the trick, and Ketchum plummeted through the trap.

But the extra length of the rope meant that he fell farther than usual, almost so far that his feet touched the ground, in fact. When he finally reached the end, the tautening rope jerked him

The hangman fits the noose around the neck of Black Jack Ketchum on April 26, 1901. Unfortunately, he didn't do a very good job of it, and a few minutes later, Ketchum lost his head.

(Courtesy of National Archives and Records Administration)

so hard that instead of cleanly breaking his neck, as intended, it tore his head completely off his shoulders. The hood attached to his vest kept the head from falling and rolling away, but it was still a grotesque sight to the onlookers, of whom there were many because this was quite an occasion in Clayton, New Mexico. All the businesses closed down except for the saloons, and some of the people who witnessed the execution of Black Jack Ketchum undoubtedly were grateful for that exception.

After what they had seen, they probably needed a good stiff drink.

THE BANK-ROBBIN'EST
OUTLAW IN AMERICA

In some places, the Old West hung on for longer than most folks might have thought possible. Well past the turn of the nineteenth century into the twentieth, in a day when automobiles had become a common sight and paved roads were beginning to extend across what had been open prairie only a few years earlier, vestiges of the frontier remained. It wasn't that unusual to see men riding on horseback. So no one on the streets of Stroud, Oklahoma, paid much attention when seven men rode in on the morning of March 27, 1915. They drew rein and dismounted in front of the local stockyard. Six of the men walked on down the street, while the seventh stayed there to hold the horses.

Stroud was a small town about halfway between Oklahoma City and Tulsa, but it boasted of having two banks, the First National and the Stroud State Bank, both of them on Main Street some two blocks apart. Those two banks were the reason the seven strangers were here on this cold morning when the temperature was still below freezing despite the fact that spring had started less than a week earlier. They had come to do what no other outlaw gang had ever accomplished, not Frank and Jesse, not the Youngers, not the Daltons. They were going to hold up two banks at the same time.

And they were led by Henry Starr, the bank-robbin'est outlaw in America.

———————

HENRY Starr's career in banditry began many years earlier. He was born of Cherokee-Scotch-Irish descent on December 2, 1873, near Fort Gibson, Indian Territory. He was related to the infamous Belle Starr only by marriage; her husband was Henry Starr's uncle. He was educated at the Cherokee school in Tahlequah and was a good student, quick-witted and intelligent. But when he was a young man working as a cowboy, trouble began to dog him. He was arrested by Cherokee Nation police for selling whiskey when he claimed he was just holding a suitcase belonging to someone else; the suitcase had two bottles of Who-hit-John in it. Another time he was accused of horse thievery when, according to Henry, he had just borrowed the animal with the full knowledge of its owner.

He was jailed because of these scrapes with the law, but on both occasions he was released a short time later. Maybe he really was innocent; he always claimed to be, even later on when he freely admitted to other crimes. But one way or the other, the pattern had been set for Henry Starr's life. He began pulling holdups of railroad stations and small country stores, in company with several other young men he had met in the Verdigris Valley, which seemed to be a breeding ground for outlaws. He had jumped bail on the horse-stealing charge, which led to a warrant being sworn out for his arrest. Floyd Wilson, one of the deputy marshals who worked for the famous hanging judge Isaac Parker, set out with an express-company detective, H. E. Dickey, to track down the fledgling desperado.

Wilson and Dickey rode to the XU, a ranch owned by Arthur Dodge. Henry Starr had worked there as a cowboy in the past, and the two lawmen thought he might be hiding there. Dodge told them that he had not seen Henry for weeks, and they had no reason to disbelieve him.

Dodge's honesty was confirmed the next day. Wilson and Dickey were still at the XU, conducting a search of the area. They had stopped at the ranch house for a midday meal when Dodge rode in and told them that he had just seen Henry. Wilson jumped on Dodge's horse and galloped off in the direction the rancher indicated. Dickey had to stay behind to saddle a horse for himself.

Dodge was right: Henry Starr was riding across XU range. Wilson caught up to him along a winding stream known as Wolf Creek. The deputy was a brave man, but also a foolhardy one. Instead of waiting for help, he confronted the fugitive alone.

Armed with a rifle, Henry swung down from the saddle as Wilson galloped up to him, halting no more than thirty feet away. Wilson called out for Henry to surrender and said that he had a warrant for him. Henry had no intention of surrendering, but apparently he didn't want to start a gunfight with Wilson, either. He kept his rifle pointed toward the ground.

The impatient deputy whipped up his own rifle and fired. He may have been trying to frighten Henry into giving up, or he may have been aiming at the outlaw. Whatever the case, Wilson's shot missed, though it passed very close to Henry Starr's head. Henry acted then, lifting his rifle and firing as fast as he could lever fresh cartridges into the chamber.

The bullets knocked Wilson off his feet and made him drop his rifle. He reached for his revolver and managed to draw it from its holster, but Henry Starr shot him twice more before he could fire. Then, in the only act of his life that could be called brutal, Henry walked up to Wilson's fallen form, held the Winchester one-handed next to the deputy's body, and fired one last shot into him, killing him.

Dickey, who had been delayed in joining the pursuit by a balky horse, was close enough to witness the battle but too far away to do anything about it. By the time he reached Wilson, Henry was gone.

Now a killer as well as an outlaw, Henry rode for a time with a small but well-organized gang led by a man named Bill Cook. After splitting from them, he organized his own gang and orchestrated the holdup of the People's Bank in Bentonville, Arkansas. The qualities that made Henry Starr such a successful bank robber were becoming apparent. He studied each bank before he attempted to rob it, and his heists were meticulously planned. Not only that, but he was also very cool under fire and though possessed of a temper, was always able to keep it under control.

Despite his crimes, it seemed at times there was an honest man inside Henry Starr, struggling to get out. For quite a while he had been romancing a young woman named May Morrison. Henry decided that he and May would leave Indian Territory and head west to establish an honest life for themselves in California. It was a good plan, but it didn't work out. In company with Kid Wilson, one of the young men who had been part of Henry's gang, they made it as far as Colorado Springs, Colorado, but they were recognized there and arrested. Henry and the Kid were returned to Fort Smith, Arkansas, to stand trial in front of the Hanging Judge.

Kid Wilson was found guilty of robbery and sentenced to prison. Henry, on the other hand, faced murder charges because of the shooting of Deputy Floyd Wilson (no relation to the Kid), and the prosecutors wanted him to hang. Judge Parker agreed. Come February 20, 1894, Henry Starr was to be hanged by the neck until dead.

His lawyers appealed the case all the way to the United States

Supreme Court, and months dragged by as the execution was postponed again and again. While waiting to see what was going to happen, Henry gained a new sort of notoriety. During a riot in the squalid prison in Fort Smith known as "Hell on the Border," Henry disarmed another inmate called Cherokee Bill, who had gotten his hands on a gun and killed a guard. Now the law was a little more sympathetic to Henry—but that didn't stop him from being convicted again when he finally was granted a new trial. And for the second time he was sentenced to hang.

Once again the Supreme Court intervened, setting aside the murder conviction and accepting a plea of manslaughter from Henry. After all, Deputy Wilson *had* shot at him first. Henry was sentenced to fifteen years in the federal penitentiary at Columbus, Ohio.

He didn't serve the whole time. A model prisoner, he had his sentence commuted by President Theodore Roosevelt and was released in 1903. He went back to Tulsa, started selling real estate, and married a young Cherokee schoolteacher named Ollie Griffin, with whom he had a son they named Theodore Roosevelt Starr, after the president who had freed Henry from prison.

Every time Henry tried to go straight, however, something seemed to interfere. In this case, it was Oklahoma becoming a state. Henry was still wanted for robbing the bank in Bentonville, Arkansas, but there was no way to extradite him as long as Indian Territory remained a territory. As soon as it became a state, things were different. Fearing that he would be sent back to Arkansas to answer to that old charge, Henry left home and hid out in the Osage Hills.

The lure of the outlaw trail was too much for Henry to resist. Riding with his old partner Kid Wilson, who had been paroled by this time, he robbed a bank in Kansas and was suspected of robbing several others, though it's doubtful he was to blame for all the holdups. One robbery he did pull during this time was that of the bank in Amity, Colorado, and it would come back to haunt him. Though a large manhunt had been mounted in Kansas and Oklahoma, Henry eluded his pursuers, robbed the bank in Amity, and drifted on to Arizona, where he received the news that Ollie had divorced him. More bad news was to follow soon, as he was tracked down and arrested.

The Arizona authorities sent him to Colorado to be tried for the bank robbery at Amity. Henry was convicted and sent to the state prison at Canon City. His sentence: no less than seven and no more than twenty-five years at hard labor.

If there was one thing Henry Starr knew how to do other than rob banks, it was how to get along in prison. Once again he seemed to reform, and won over the warden, the chaplain, and everyone else at Canon City. After five years, he was paroled, and walked out of the prison on September 24, 1913, a relatively free man. He still had to report to a parole officer once a month, and was not supposed to leave the state of Colorado.

But there were still banks waiting to be robbed back in Oklahoma. Less than a year after being released from prison, Henry broke his parole and headed home, and on September 8, 1914, sometimes alone and sometimes with the help of an unknown confederate, he embarked on a series of holdups that had the whole Southwest buzzing. From September 1914 to January 1915, Henry Starr robbed fourteen banks and waltzed off with over $26,000 in loot. It was a crime spree unlike any the country had ever seen.

These were brazen, daring, daylight robberies, and Henry was recognized more than once. Rewards—dead or alive—were posted on his head, and the hue and cry was in full swing.

Henry had come up with a plan even more daring, though, and to carry it out, he would need help. There was no shortage of young, lawless firebrands in the Verdigris Valley and the Osage Hills, Henry's old stomping grounds. He gathered up a gang of six men and headed for Stroud, Oklahoma, which had not one but two banks.

A distinguished Henry Starr in 1919, looking more like a successful businessman than the most prolific bank robber in the history of the Old West. Two years later, an ill-advised return to his old profession would result in his death.

(Courtesy of Denver Public Library, Western History Collection)

Two banks . . . and robbing them both at the same time was to be the culmination of Henry Starr's long career as a desperado.

ONE man stayed with the horses, while the other six split up. Henry and two companions went into the Stroud State Bank, while the other three entered the First National Bank at the same time. Henry had a rifle with a sawed-off barrel shoved down one leg of his trousers, with his coat concealing the weapon's stock. He pulled out the rifle as the other two bandits drew six-guns and menaced the bank's employees and customers. In a matter of moments, Henry had scooped $1,600 out of the bank's cash drawers. The bank's employees refused to open the safe, where the rest of the money was kept. One man claimed not to know the combination, while the other explained that the safe had a time lock and could not be opened by anyone until several more hours had passed.

Furious, Henry threatened the men with his rifle, but he was no cold-blooded killer. Best just to take what he could and get out, he realized. He ripped a diamond stickpin off the tie of the bank vice president, and then marched three hostages out of the bank and into the street.

By now the word had spread around Stroud that a pair of bank robberies were in progress. The second group of robbers had netted over $4,200 at the First National, and appeared in the street with their own hostages about the same time as Henry and his companions emerged. The hostages were all herded together and the outlaws headed for their horses.

Guns began to bang as several of the town's citizens fired from concealment in an attempt to stop the outlaws. The hostages, more afraid of their fellow townies than they were of the bandits, dived for cover, leaving Henry and his men out in the open. They returned the fire even though they couldn't see the men who were shooting at them, blazing away up and down the street as they hurried toward the stockyards and their horses.

Across Main Street, a seventeen-year-old boy named Paul Curry crouched in an alley beside a butcher shop, half-hidden behind some barrels. Curry had seen Henry and the others entering the bank and recognized them as outlaws. He ran into the butcher shop and picked up a Winchester 30-30 that the butcher used to kill hogs. Carrying the rifle, Curry left the shop by the back door and took up his position in the alley, waiting for a chance at the robbers.

When he got it, he squeezed off a shot at the retreating outlaws that caught Henry Starr in the left leg just below the hip. The bullet broke the thighbone and knocked Henry off his feet. As he lay on the ground, unable to get up, Henry looked around for the source of the shot that had downed him. Across the street, Paul Curry jacked another round into the chamber of the Winchester and called out, "Throw away that gun, or I'll kill you!"

Henry was no fool. He tossed the revolver aside.

The rest of the gang was still getting away. Caught up in the excitement, Paul Curry ran out of the alley and fired after them, seriously wounding one of them. They all managed to get on their horses and gallop out of Stroud, even the wounded man, but he soon passed out and toppled off his mount. The others abandoned him to the posse that was already after the gang. They brought the wounded outlaw, whose name was Lewis Estes, back to town.

Henry Starr admitted freely who he was. His wounded leg was tended to by the local doctor, and he was placed in the jail. There was some talk of lynching, but nothing ever came of it. Bill Tilghman, the famous marshal, came to Stroud as soon as he heard about the double bank robbery and the capture of Henry Starr. Tilghman was there less as a lawman, though, and more as a motion picture producer. He was already involved in the movie industry, which was trying to get a foothold in Oklahoma, and instead of deputies brought a camera crew with him to film the scene of the robberies.

Hearing about that must have planted a seed in Henry Starr's brain.

Some of the other members of the gang were tracked down and arrested later, while the rest were never caught. In a deal struck with the prosecution, Lewis Estes testified against Henry and the other robbers who were apprehended, and received the relatively light sentence of five years. Henry didn't bother trying to fight the charges. He simply entered a plea of guilty and was sentenced to twenty-five years in the Oklahoma state prison at McAlester.

For the third time, Henry Starr was behind prison bars, and for the third time he was the best prisoner anyone could ever hope to see. His injury left him with a limp, which also engendered sympathy for him. Most helpful of all was the fact that Kate Brainard, Oklahoma's first commissioner of charities and corrections, supported the effort to parole him. Less than four years after entering prison, Henry was back out, apparently rehabilitated yet again.

Now Henry had a plan that didn't involve breaking the law. Prompted perhaps by Bill Tilghman's involvement with motion pictures, Henry borrowed money and became a movie producer himself. He wrote, directed, and starred in the film *A Debtor to the Law*, playing himself in this recreation of the Stroud bank robberies and the resulting shoot-out. Even Paul Curry got to be in the movie, which was a rousing success. Henry went on to make two more pictures, fictional variations on the bank-robbing theme, and they were successful as well. He should have made a lot of money from this venture. He would have . . . except that his partners somehow swindled him out of it.

Reduced to begging loans from friends to live on as he tried unsuccessfully to recoup his losses by legal action against his former partners, Henry Starr was a bitter man by this point. He had tried at various times in his life to be a good man, but something always seemed to go wrong. Early in February 1921, he paid a visit to his seventeen-year-old son Teddy and warned him to stay away from crime at all costs. Later that same month, he drove into Harrison, Arkansas, and with three other men attempted to rob the People's National Bank. In Henry's other robberies, he had always made his getaway on horseback. Now instead of a horse, he had an automobile. Times had changed. But Henry Starr had not. In times of trouble, he just naturally went back to bank robbing.

His luck was played out, though. As Henry and his companions prodded the bank employees into the vault at gunpoint, one of them snatched up a rifle that was hidden there for the very purpose of foiling such a robbery. The man cut loose, firing a single shot that tore through Henry's right side and shattered his spine. As he fell, the other bandits ran out, jumped in the car, and took off at high speed, never to be caught or seen again.

Henry lingered for four days, finally slipping into a coma on

February 22, 1921, and dying a few hours later. He had been an outlaw for almost three decades, and before lapsing into unconsciousness for the final time, he bragged to the doctor who was attending him, "I've robbed more banks than any man in America."

Henry Starr was right about that.

EXPRESS COMPANY
FRAUD

The Canadian River runs from west to east across the Texas Panhandle, and gets its name from the blue northers that roar through the region every winter, dropping the temperature so rapidly that it seems Canada must be just on the other side of the river. In 1887, as the Santa Fe Railroad laid tracks across the Panhandle, the Canadian River gave the name in turn to the town of Canadian. The settlement served as the county seat of newly organized Hemphill County, and quickly became a bustling community as it served the needs of the vast cattle ranches in the area.

When Hemphill County was formed, it needed a sheriff, of course. The winner of the first election for the post was Tom McGee.

Born in 1849 in West-by-God Virginia, McGee came west in 1877 and worked as a cowboy in Colorado. When McGee's employer, Hank Cresswell, the owner of the Bar CC brand, moved his ranch to the Texas Panhandle, McGee went along, helping drive the herd to its new home. Once in the Panhandle,

McGee decided to stay, working at times for several other spreads as well as the Bar CC. Evidently, he was an ambitious young man and wanted a ranch of his own. In 1883, he registered his own brand, the Quarter Circle C. In 1886, he bought the PO Ranch from William Young. Not content to sit back in the ranch house and do the paperwork, Tom McGee ramrodded his own crew. He seems to have been a man with a knack for success. By 1887 he was not only a rancher, but owned and operated a wagon yard and livery stable in the town of Canadian as well. But even that was not enough to keep Tom McGee occupied. He turned his hand to politics, and was elected Hemphill County's first sheriff. His partner in the livery stable, Vastine Stickley, served as his chief deputy.

Since Canadian was a shipping point for the surrounding ranches, it seems likely that most of McGee's official duties consisted of breaking up fights and throwing drunken cowboys in the hoosegow on payday or when herds had been driven in to be shipped. Most of the time, the community was probably a peaceful little place.

All that changed on the evening of November 24, 1894.

THREE men rode up to the Santa Fe depot in Canadian and dismounted, tying their horses at the hitch rail outside the railroad station. It was a Saturday night, so the town was crowded with cowboys who had ridden in from the surrounding ranches to have a good time. Tinny music and raucous laughter came from the saloons. Given the season, it was probably a chilly night in the Panhandle, but that didn't do much to dampen the enthusiasm of the young punchers who had come to town to blow off steam.

The three strangers hadn't stopped at any of the saloons or dance halls on their way into town. They made straight for the depot. Their arrival was well timed. Just minutes before they rode up, the Santa Fe's Panhandle Express had rolled into the station, southbound for Amarillo. The train came to a halt with the express car next to the platform. No passengers were waiting to board. The Panhandle Express had something to drop off tonight, rather than picking up passengers or freight.

For the past couple of weeks, local cattleman George Isaacs had been talking about how he was having $25,000 shipped in by train from his bank in Kansas City. Isaacs seemed to have the habit of talking too much. Nearly everyone in the area knew about the money, and there were even rumors about which train it would arrive on. When the express car door opened and the Wells Fargo messenger carried a package into the depot, anyone watching could have guessed what was in it. Especially when the messenger handed the pouch over to the station manager, who opened the safe to deposit it.

The three men who had just ridden into town certainly knew what was in the package. They drew their guns and moved with grim determination across the platform.

At that moment, fate intervened and Sheriff Tom McGee stepped up onto the platform. One of the sheriff's duties was to meet the trains and keep track of who was coming and going. Enough light came from inside the station for McGee to see the guns in the hands of the three strangers.

It's unknown whether McGee challenged them or simply slapped leather himself. Either way, shots blasted out in a murderous roar. The sheriff never had a chance against the already drawn weapons in the hands of the outlaws. They gunned him down ruthlessly.

The local law was out of the fight, but the outlaws had reckoned without the presence of guards in the employ of Wells Fargo being stationed inside the express car. These armed guards burst out and opened fire, which the three desperadoes returned. In a matter of split seconds, a small-scale war was being waged on the platform of the Santa Fe depot.

The shooting drew the attention of other people in town, of

course, and in this time and place, most men went armed. Gun-toting townspeople and reckless cowboys rushed toward the rail-road station. They couldn't have known exactly what was going on at first, but they must have figured it out in a hurry. They joined in the battle against the three outlaws, who were pinned down on the platform.

With all that shooting going on, it's a wonder that no one except Sheriff McGee was killed. But after several minutes of swapping lead with the express-car guards and the citizens of Canadian, the three would-be robbers fled, making it back to their horses and galloping off into the night. There's no record of whether or not a posse pursued them, but if so, it failed to catch up to them.

Back in Canadian, bystanders carried Tom McGee's bullet-riddled body down the street to the undertaker. Other citizens, shocked by the outbreak of deadly violence, stood around the depot talking things over. It seemed obvious to one and all that the outlaws had been after the pouch that had been carried into the station and placed in the safe. The express messenger con-firmed that the pouch contained five envelopes shipped from Kansas City by George Isaacs. Each envelope contained five thousand dollars, for a total of $25,000, just as the rumors had said. Someone no doubt noted that Isaacs was a lucky man. He had come close to losing a small fortune. If not for the sheriff hap-pening onto the robbery just as it was getting started, the three desperadoes might well have gotten away with the pouch.

It's impossible to know who it was that suggested opening the package to take a look at the money, but the idea was greeted with enthusiasm. After all, it wasn't every day that folks in a small town in the Texas Panhandle got to feast their eyes on $25,000. If Sheriff McGee had been alive, he might have vetoed the sugges-tion, but as it was, the group of townspeople and cowboys trooped into the station and persuaded the manager to open the pouch. Surely the money would be safe enough, surrounded as it was by dozens of well-armed men who had just fought off armed robbers to save it for its rightful owner.

But when the envelopes were taken out of the pouch and opened, gasps of surprise and angry curses filled the depot. Each envelope had only a few real bills in it, carefully placed on top, and the rest of the space was filled with blank pieces of paper cut to the right size to resemble a stack of currency. A quick count revealed the startling fact that there was no more than five hundred dollars inside the pouch, instead of fifty times that much.

It didn't take a genius to figure out what had happened. George Isaacs never shipped $25,000 from Kansas City. He had been in cahoots with the outlaws and had planned for them to carry off the pouch. Then Wells Fargo would have had to replace the supposedly stolen money. It was fraud of the most blatant sort . . . and it had almost worked.

When a posse rode out to his ranch, George Isaacs must have been expecting his visitors to convey the sad news that his money had been stolen. Instead, grim-faced lawmen placed him under arrest on charges of fraud, conspiracy, and murder, since Sheriff McGee had been killed in the robbery that Isaacs had planned. What must have seemed like a sure-fire scheme had blown up right in the cattleman's face.

George Isaacs's trial was moved to Quanah, Texas, on a change of venue, but that didn't help his case. He was convicted and sentenced to life in prison at the state penitentiary in Huntsville. By this time, Isaacs had revealed the identities of the three men who shot up the train station in Canadian: Jim Harbolt (spelled Harbold in some accounts), Dan McKenzie (or possibly Jake McKinzie; again there is some uncertainty), and either George "Red Buck" Waightman or Tulsa Jack Blake, depending on who is telling the story. Those latter two also rode with Bill Doolin's gang at times. Federal marshals went after the men, and captured Harbolt and McKenzie, who were brought back to Canadian, tried, convicted, and sent to prison. If the third man really was either Red Buck or Tulsa Jack, he met a violent end during the next couple of years, as both of those outlaws were killed in gun battles with lawmen elsewhere.

George Isaacs, the man who put the whole thing in motion, escaped from prison and made it across the border into Mexico. What happened to him after that is not known. What is certain is that his scheme to bilk twenty-five grand out of Wells Fargo was a failure. Unfortunately, it cost the life of a good lawman, Hemphill County Sheriff Tom McGee.

PART FIVE

BACK-SHOOTERS

Brown, you've got four sixes to beat.

—Last words of John Wesley Hardin

THE MAN WHO KILLED
THE MAN WHO
KILLED JESSE JAMES

In the summer of 1892, Creede, Colorado, was quite a place. It was a silver-mining boomtown, full of men who were determined to wrest a fortune from the earth, as well as other men—and women—equally determined that whatever wealth the miners took from the ground would wind up in their pockets instead. This latter group included gamblers, con men, prostitutes, and outright thieves and murderers.

And saloon-keepers like Bob Ford.

On June 5, 1892, a fire had broken out in Creede. Fire was perhaps the most feared catastrophe that could befall a frontier town, because in only a short time, an unchecked blaze could destroy an entire community. That was what happened in Creede. Most of the buildings in town burned to the ground.

But the silver was still there, under the ground, in the mines that dotted the mountains around Creede. Despite the destruction, the citizens weren't ready to give up and abandon the town, not while there was still money to be made. So they rolled up their sleeves and started over, Bob Ford included. Within a couple of days, Ford had leased some land, bought a tent, and was back in business, serving up liquor and card games to the miners who flocked into the place.

Bob Ford was a well-known, if not well-liked, figure not only in Creede but all across the frontier. His claim to fame, as he never let anyone forget, was that he had killed Jesse James, the most famous outlaw in the world. A little more than a decade earlier, on April 3, 1882, in St. Joseph, Missouri, Ford shot Jesse James in the back of the head as Jesse stood on a chair dusting a picture in the home he was renting under the false name of Thomas Howard. As a relatively new member of Jesse's gang, Ford betrayed and killed him for the ten-thousand-dollar reward—which he never received. Instead, he and his brother, who was also present at the time of the killing, were arrested, tried, and convicted of murder, only to be pardoned by the governor of Missouri.

Finding that he was not regarded as a hero for his actions, a bitterly disappointed Bob Ford drifted west. He opened a saloon in Las Vegas, New Mexico, in partnership with Dick Liddil, another former member of the James Gang. The business failed, and Ford moved on to Colorado, opening another saloon in Walsenberg. He boasted openly about who he was and what he had done, perhaps thinking that would improve the saloon's business. If so, the tactic backfired. Ford was forced to supplement his income by charging to pose for pictures with people who wanted to be photographed with the infamous slayer of Jesse James. Violent and aggressive when drunk, Ford was involved in several shooting scrapes while he was in Walsenberg. The town must have been happy to see him go when the silver strike in Creede took place and Ford packed up and left for the new boomtown.

Ford's personal popularity wasn't any higher in Creede, but

Robert Ford, "the dirty little coward who shot Mr. Howard, and laid poor Jesse in his grave." The murderer of Jesse James achieved notoriety but never the wealth and acclaim he hoped for. Instead he was almost universally despised until his own violent death.

(Courtesy of Denver Public Library, Western History Collection)

his saloon, the Creede Exchange, was quite a success. He was still a bad drunk, though, and one night, deep in his cups, he stumbled out into the street and started shooting out every light he could find. The townspeople took a dim view of this behavior, and a vigilance committee warned him to be out of town by four o'clock the next afternoon. Bob Ford might not have been the smartest man west of the Mississippi, but he was no fool. He left for Pueblo, Colorado, on the next train.

EDWARD O. Kelly was a Tennessean who had moved to Colorado in 1882. Little is known about his early life, but when he landed in Pueblo, he worked as a streetcar driver and a policeman. The fact that he had a temper is documented by the fact that while working as a policeman, he shot and killed a man he was placing under arrest because the man accidentally stepped on his foot.

Kelly was tried for that killing but acquitted, no surprise considering the rough-and-tumble nature of the times.

Despite living in Pueblo for a decade, Kelly remained a bachelor, living in a rented room. One day he struck up an acquaintance with a man who was newly arrived in town and looking for a place to stay. That man was Bob Ford. Kelly agreed to let Ford share his room. While living in Pueblo, Ford wrote letters to the community leaders in Creede, asking that he be allowed to return and reopen his saloon. He promised that he would be on his best behavior.

Wearing down the opposition in Creede took time, and while he was in Pueblo, Ford continued to share a room with Ed Kelly. One morning, Ford discovered that a diamond ring belonging to him was gone. He accused Kelly of taking it, but Kelly hotly denied the theft. Hard feelings sprang up immediately between the two men, and trouble might have developed then and there if Ford had not received word at last that he could go back to Creede. He departed for the silver boomtown, still smarting over the loss of the ring and leaving an equally angry Ed Kelly behind in Pueblo.

Like scores of others, Kelly was drawn to the Creede area by the silver boom. He didn't strike it rich; in fact, he was accused of claim-jumping. The charge must have been proven groundless, because a short time later Kelly was elected marshal of a nearby community known as Bachelor City.

Still looking to make his fortune, Kelly drifted into the town of Creede and stepped into one of the saloons for a drink, a bustling establishment called the Creede Exchange. Maybe he knew the place was owned by his old enemy Bob Ford or maybe he didn't; also unknown is which of the men saw the other one first. But within minutes of Kelly's arrival, trouble broke out.

Ford strode up to Kelly and demanded that he turn over his

weapons. Kelly was carrying a pistol and a knife and didn't want to give up either one. His refusal prompted Ford to draw his gun, but he didn't fire. Instead he slammed the weapon against the side of Kelly's head in a swift attack, knocking Kelly to the floor. Stunned, Kelly was unable to stop Ford from disarming him. Then Kelly was lifted to his feet by Ford's bartenders and bouncers. While they held him, Ford warned him in a loud voice never to return to the Creede Exchange again. He would be shot on sight if he did so, Ford threatened. Then the humiliated Kelly was given the bum's rush into the street.

Kelly returned to Bachelor City, but hatred for Bob Ford now seethed inside him. A short time later, the fire that nearly destroyed Creede took place. Ford erected his tent saloon to take the place of the building that had been destroyed, and the stage was set for the final showdown between the two men.

On the afternoon of June 8, 1892, a Wednesday, Ed Kelly walked up in front of the tent that housed the Creede Exchange. A horseman rode up beside him, reined to a halt, and handed him a double-barreled shotgun. With his hands wrapped tightly around the weapon, Kelly entered the tent saloon and looked around, spotting Bob Ford on the other side of the place with his back to him. Kelly walked up behind Ford, moving quickly so that no one could call a warning to the saloon-keeper and infamous killer of Jesse James. Kelly called out, "Hello, Bob," and lifted the shotgun.

Ford started to turn around. Before he could do so, Kelly fired both barrels. The heavy twin charges of slugs and buckshot slammed into the side of Ford's neck at close range, tearing his throat out, breaking his spine, and killing him instantly. He went down, flooding the ground around his head with blood as screams and shouts from the Exchange's patrons filled the saloon. Calmly, still holding the now-empty shotgun, Ed Kelly reached down and took Ford's revolver from his back pocket. No more shots were fired, though. Kelly turned toward the saloon's entrance, and got there just as Deputy Sheriff Dick Plunkett rushed up. Kelly handed over the shotgun and the revolver and surrendered to the startled lawman.

A hurried inquest was held right there in the saloon, and the coroner's jury ordered that Kelly be held over for trial on charges of murder. He was locked up in a nearby vacant building, and a deputy named Joe Duvall was posted there to guard the prisoner. Unknown to the authorities, Joe Duvall was a friend of Kelly's, and had, in fact, been the man who rode up and handed him the shotgun.

Instead of letting Kelly escape, though, Duvall fled himself, apparently convinced that his part in the affair would soon come out. Kelly remained in custody, and on July 8, 1892, he was found guilty of murder in the second degree and sentenced to life in the state penitentiary.

For the next nine years, Ed Kelly was a resident of the Colorado state prison at Canon City. He wrote frequent letters to the governor and to the Board of Pardons asking for clemency, and evidently he was a model prisoner, because the warden of the prison supported those requests. Finally, in October of 1902, Kelly's sentence was commuted and he was released. He had several minor scrapes with the law, but nothing that landed him back in jail. Perhaps thinking that a change of scenery would be for the best, he left Colorado in 1903 and headed east to Oklahoma City.

Unfortunately for Kelly, a man named Otto Ewing, who had been in the Creede Exchange on the day of Bob Ford's murder, happened to be in Oklahoma City as well, and informed the police of Kelly's background. The police considered Kelly a potential troublemaker and kept an eye on him. He was picked up several times for suspicious behavior, and this made him even more angry and belligerent. Kelly's temper had always been his downfall, and this was to be no different.

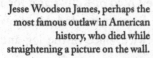

Jesse Woodson James, perhaps the most famous outlaw in American history, who died while straightening a picture on the wall.

(Courtesy of Denver Public Library, Western History Collection)

On the evening of January 13, 1904, Kelly ran into Joe Burnett, a local police officer, on the street. Burnett greeted Kelly pleasantly enough, not knowing that earlier in the evening, Kelly had been arrested and then released in what he considered another instance of the law being out to get him. Something inside Kelly snapped at the greeting from Burnett. He yanked a gun from his pocket and tried to pistol-whip the officer with it. Startled but quick to react, Burnett grabbed the gun and pushed it away from his face. Kelly jerked the trigger, causing the gun to go off so close to Burnett's head that he suffered powder burns on his ear.

It was a deadly wrestling match after that, with Burnett hanging on for dear life to Kelly's gun hand as the berserk man emptied the revolver. Somehow, all the bullets missed Burnett, though several of them came so close that they tore holes in his overcoat. Burnett yelled for help, but none of the passersby would come to his assistance. In fact, one of Kelly's friends saw the fight going on, pulled out a gun, and let off a single shot at

Burnett before thinking better of it and lighting out for safer places. Even with a now-empty gun, Kelly kept fighting, caught up in the grip of his unreasonable anger. He attacked Burnett with fists, feet, and teeth.

Finally, one of the bystanders, an employee of the Frisco Railroad, jumped into the fight and grabbed hold of Kelly's arm for a moment. That was all the respite Joe Burnett needed. He drew his own gun and fired, hitting Kelly twice, once in the leg and once—the fatal shot—in the head.

Bob Ford killed Jesse James hoping it would bring him fame and fortune. But Ed Kelly, who gained a certain amount of notoriety himself as the man who killed the man who killed Jesse James, acted out of irrational anger and an uncontrollable temper. Years later that same temper brought about Kelly's own death. He was buried in Fairlawn Cemetery in Oklahoma City in an unmarked pauper's grave.

MAKE SURE YOUR
MAN IS DEAD!

By the early 1860s, the Overland Stage Company established by Ben Holladay had reached across the country, stretching from St. Louis to California along routes that ran through Texas, New Mexico, Colorado, and Arizona. The line was broken up into divisions, each of which had a superintendent whose job it was to see that all the stage stations were run efficiently and that the coaches were protected from Indians, owlhoots, and anyone else who tried to interfere with them.

The settlement of Julesburg was in the northeastern corner of Colorado, and was home to both a stop on the Overland stage line and a trading post established a decade earlier by Jules Beni (sometimes spelled Reni), who gave the place his name. Beni was still in Julesburg, not only running his trading post but also serving as superintendent of the Overland's Sweetwater Division. The Sweetwater Division stretched for two hundred miles over some of the most rugged, dangerous territory in the West, made even more dangerous by the gangs of outlaws who roamed over it seemingly at will.

The stage stations along the line were plagued by horse thieves and arsonists who set fire to the haystacks that were supposed to provide feed for the stagecoach teams. As Ben Holladay saw it, Jules Beni wasn't doing enough to put a stop to these outrages. In fact, considering that Beni was buying replacement hay from his friends at exorbitant prices and paying generous rewards for the return of stolen horses, a suspicious man might just wonder if Beni had something to do with the lawlessness in the first place.

Ben Holladay was a suspicious man; otherwise he never would have been so successful in his business. He fired Jules Beni and turned to another man to replace him and clean up the Sweetwater Division.

That man was Joseph Albert Slade, to become famous as Jack Slade.

———————◆◆◆———————

JACK Slade was born in Carlyle, Illinois, in 1829, the son of a former Congressman. He served in the Army during the Mexican War before he was even twenty years old. Evidently possessed of the same sort of restless nature that sent so many of his contemporaries roaming over the West, Slade went to work as a freighter along the Oregon Trail, and later became a stagecoach guard. It was while he was working as a guard that he began to acquire a reputation as a frontiersman. He was an excellent shot with a rifle and pistol, and was able to keep a cool head in a fight. Once, when the coach on which he was riding shotgun was attacked by four Indians, Slade calmly killed three of them and took the fourth and final Indian prisoner. Slicing off the ears of the men he had killed, Slade gave them to the surviving Indian with instructions to take them back to the chief of the tribe along with a warning not to bother any more stagecoaches. Slade had plenty of bravado, but he had the fighting ability to back it up.

Naturally, Jules Beni was upset over being fired and replaced by Slade. The evidence suggests that Beni was indeed to blame for the corruption and violence that plagued the Sweetwater Division, and he didn't like being forced out of such a lucrative position. He left the station at Julesburg, but not without threatening Slade first. There is no way of knowing whether Slade took the threats seriously, but given his cocksure attitude, it's doubtful that he was afraid of Beni.

Not long after Slade took over as superintendent of the Sweetwater Division, another haystack was burned. Slade bought a load of hay from a local rancher to replace what had been destroyed. The rancher, who had been part of the scheme with Beni, didn't know that things had changed at Julesburg. He delivered one of the sorriest batches of hay that anyone had ever seen. Slade looked it over, pulled a gun, and had some of the station employees chain the rancher to a log. Pulling out a lucifer, Slade scratched the match into life and tossed it into the pile. The hay might not have been fit for the stage line's horses to eat, but it burned just fine. Within minutes, flames were leaping high in the air. Slade ordered his men to wait a few minutes and then toss the log into the fire—with the crooked rancher still attached to it.

A few minutes later, the rancher, still quaking in horror, was freed from the log and ordered to light a shuck out of this part of the country, which he did without delay. He hadn't been tossed into the inferno, but it was a near thing. Word of his brush with death spread quickly, just as Slade intended, and from then on out, the torching of haystacks came to an end.

Slade moved to put a stop to stage holdups, too, by pursuing the bandits and hanging them whenever and wherever he caught them. Word of that got around, too.

Old Ben Holladay had to be pleased with the job Slade was doing cleaning up the Sweetwater Division. The Overland's passengers appreciated Slade's efforts, too. Slade could be charming whenever he wanted to, such as the day when one of the coaches stopped on its way to California and a young writer shared a meal and a cup of coffee with Slade. The writer found Slade to be a gentleman, describing him as quiet and affable, but at the same time, the division superintendent's reputation as a volatile, dangerous man was well known by now, so the visitor was careful to be on his best behavior. The man's name was Sam Clemens, better known as Mark Twain, and he described the meeting with Slade in his book *Roughing It*.

Jules Beni was still a thorn in Slade's side. The former agent was not involved in any lawless behavior against the stage line at the moment, at least none that Slade knew of, but Beni still had possession of some horses and mules belonging to the company. That stuck in Slade's craw. Finally, taking one man with him, Slade rode out to Beni's ranch near Julesburg to reclaim the livestock.

For one of the few times in his life, Jack Slade was careless on this, the worst possible day to let his guard down. After arguing with Beni about the stock, Slade turned his back on the former agent. Beni hauled out a six-shooter and blasted away. Evidently, Beni was not one to carry his revolver with the hammer resting on an empty chamber, because it was reported that he pumped six slugs into Jack Slade's body in less time than it takes to tell about it.

Somehow, Slade stayed on his feet despite the hammering impact of the bullets. He managed to duck around the corner of Beni's ranch house. Beni went after him, running through the house to snatch up a loaded shotgun on the way. He caught up with Slade and fired both barrels. It isn't known how much of the buckshot hit Slade, if any, but Slade went down, covered with blood. Shot up as he was, he should have been dead already, but he was still breathing. A triumphant Beni told the stage line employee who had accompanied Slade to take him back to the station and bury him.

Legend has it that at this point, Slade came around enough to push himself onto his feet and threaten Beni, vowing that he would live long enough to wear one of Beni's ears on his watch chain. Given Slade's condition, that seems pretty unlikely to have happened. But there is no disputing that Slade's companion got the badly wounded superintendent on his horse and took him back to Julesburg, where a doctor removed some, but not all, of the bullets from his body. The slugs that could not be taken out remained in Slade's body the rest of his life.

Slade refused to die, and when he had regained enough of his strength to travel, he took a stagecoach back to Illinois to complete his recovery. His toughness allowed him to bounce back as strong as ever. When he was healthy enough, Ben Holladay asked him to return to Colorado. The Sweetwater Division was still peaceful, but the Rocky Ridge Division to the west was now having the same sort of trouble that Slade had put a stop to around Julesburg. And for good reason: Jules Beni, now leading a gang of outlaws, had moved his base of operations over to the Rocky Ridge District. Jack Slade wasn't just about to pass up a chance to go after his old nemesis.

Along the way he married a spirited young woman named Virginia, who by all accounts was almost as handy with a six-gun as her husband and didn't mind using one. In fact, when several outlaws captured Slade during the early days of his service as superintendent of the Rocky Ridge Division, he asked only that he be allowed to say good-bye to his wife before he was killed. The outlaws agreed, summoning Virginia to the cabin where Slade was being held prisoner. Unknown to them, she had several revolvers hidden under her skirts, and as soon as she came in the door, gun thunder began to boom. Slade got his hands on one of the guns and pitched in, and soon the gun-handy couple walked out unhurt, leaving the cabin full of dead outlaws behind them.

That yarn may be apocryphal, but it seems to have some basis in truth. Virginia Slade's existence is beyond doubt, as are the reports of her dangerous personality.

Now Slade could turn to dealing with Jules Beni. Beni must have been shocked to learn that not only was Slade still alive, but his old enemy was back in Colorado. Slade recruited a number of tough men to serve as a posse and went after Beni. It was only a matter of time before the outlaw was caught. Slade brought him back to the stage station that served as his headquarters in the Rocky Ridge Division, a place called Virginia Dale, after Slade's wife. Slade had Beni tied securely to a post in front of the station and then left him there, uncertain as to what his fate might be.

All during the long night that followed, Beni must have been tortured by thoughts of what Slade was going to do to him. Surely he must have wished that he had made certain Slade was dead that day on the ranch when he had filled Slade with lead. Any normal man would have died. Why hadn't Slade?

Perhaps it was the thirst for vengeance that kept Jack Slade alive despite his horrible wounds. Certainly it was vengeance that prompted him to leave Beni tied up like that all night, until early the next morning when Slade emerged from the station carrying a gun. He stood in front of the post where Beni was tied, lifted the gun, took careful aim, and fired.

The bullet drilled Beni in the arm, a painful but not fatal wound.

Then Slade turned and walked back into the station, leaving the wounded man there while he went inside and had breakfast. When he was finished with the meal, Slade came outside again.

And shot Beni again, another flesh wound.

Jack Slade must have smiled as he turned and walked away.

This slow, brutal process went on all day. Jules Beni finally expired late in the afternoon, dying from loss of blood, shock, or both. When Beni was dead, Slade pulled a knife and carved off both his ears as souvenirs that Slade would carry for the rest of his life.

Yes, Jules Beni should have made sure that his man was dead.

———•◦•———

THOUGH Jack Slade fought outlaws and brought law and order to two divisions of the Overland stage line, he was something of a menace to the peace in his own right. Prone to violence when he was sober, he was even more so when he had been drinking. When in a drunken rage he smashed up a sutler's store at Fort Halleck, the Army complained to Ben Holladay. It was another case of a man who was brought in to clean up a lawless element wearing out his welcome once that lawless element was gone. Holladay fired Slade.

Slade probably was filled with resentment at this development, but he didn't turn outlaw and go after the Overland Stage Company as he might have. Instead he took his wife and moved to the mining boomtown of Virginia City, Montana Territory. He had no interest in mining. Instead he tried his hand at ranching, and then took over the supervision of a toll road, a job at least similar to the one he had held in Colorado. He was responsible for collecting tolls, maintaining the road, and protecting the safety of travelers. Virginia wound up doing most of the work while Slade spent his time gambling and drinking in Virginia City's saloons. He did more than his share of carousing and fighting, too, galloping his horse up and down the street and into saloons, shooting out windows and street lamps, and generally wreaking havoc whenever he went on a bender. Not only that, but the blame for a series of robberies in the area was laid at Slade's feet, although in actuality he had nothing to do with them.

There was no official law in these mining camps and boomtowns, so the citizens made their own law, forming vigilance com-

mittees to take care of troublemakers. The vigilantes hauled
Slade into a miners' court, where Slade promptly pulled a gun on
the judge and bluffed his way out. In the eyes of most people,
Jack Slade was a badman now, his time as a force for law and
order forgotten even though only a few years had passed since
those days. Not long after that, after another incident in which
Slade assaulted a milkman, another group of vigilantes captured
Slade on March 10, 1864, and decided that the thing to do was
hang him.

One of Slade's friends galloped out to the tollgate to let his
wife know what was happening. Virginia threw a saddle on a
horse and rode toward town as fast as she could, intent on saving
her husband's life yet again. But meanwhile, a noose was put
around Slade's neck, he was lifted onto a packing box, and the
hang rope was attached to the crosspiece of a corral gate. When
the leader of the vigilantes got word that Slade's wife was on her
way, he increased the pace of the execution even more. Odds are,
he had heard the story about how Slade and Virginia had wiped
out a whole gang of outlaws down in Colorado. Probably, the story
had even grown some in the telling, as stories are prone to do.

So, while Virginia was still racing toward town, the box was
kicked out from under Jack Slade's feet and he strangled to death
at the end of a rope. He had some friends among the vigilantes,
and more than one of them brushed away a tear at his passing.

When his wife arrived, all she could do was lambaste the men
who had hanged him and promise that she wouldn't let him be
buried there among them. Having the body placed in a specially
made zinc-lined coffin, she filled it with whiskey as a preservative
and kept it in a Virginia City house until the weather improved
and the snow in the passes melted enough for her to travel. She
hired a wagon and took Slade to Salt Lake City to be buried.
After that, Virginia Slade married one of her late husband's
friends, a union that lasted only a couple of years before ending in

divorce. Following the divorce, Virginia moved to Denver and then vanished into history.

Jack Slade was buried in Salt Lake City, but the exact location of his grave site was unknown for many years until it was discovered that he was buried under the name I. A. Slade, rather than the J. A. Slade that should have been entered in the records and carved on his headstone. Though never the outlaw that he was rumored to be at times, he left behind a reputation, probably deserved, as one of the West's most dangerous gunmen.

And he will always be known as the man who by all rights should have died at the hands of Jules Beni, only to survive and return to exact a terrible revenge on his enemy.

3

PAT GARRETT'S MYSTERIOUS DEATH

The buckboard rolled westward along the road between Las Cruces, New Mexico, and a settlement with the unlikely name of Organ. Two men perched on the wagon seat, while a third man rode alongside on horseback. It was March 1, 1908—winter was dying, spring was on the horizon, but the weather was still chilly here in the Tularosa Valley, south of the vast region of ever-shifting white sand dunes.

Despite the turn of the century eight years earlier, signaling the dawn of a supposedly new age, this was still rugged, sparsely populated country, not that far removed from the frontier days that had seen the wanton blood-spilling of the Lincoln County War some thirty years earlier. Many of the inhabitants of the region still had firsthand memories of that violent conflict. Some had even participated in it, like one of the men who traveled along the Las Cruces–Organ road on this day.

The horsebacker and the passenger on the buckboard were having an animated, almost angry discussion. As the vehicle neared Alameda Arroyo, the driver hauled back on the reins and brought the buckboard to a stop at the side of the road. He hopped down from the seat and stepped off the road to relieve himself. After a moment, the passenger climbed stiffly from the seat and followed suit. He was the oldest of the three men, tall, rawboned, with a thick mustache and piercing eyes. He wore a town suit and hat, but anyone looking at him would know right away that he was a Westerner, not some tenderfoot from back East. He was a famous man in these parts, but his fame was linked forever to someone else, someone whose star had shone even brighter, a young man whose flaming existence had been snuffed out thirty years earlier by this lanky old-timer who now stepped to the edge of the road and unbuttoned his trousers to take a leak.

Even legends had to answer the call of nature. Even legends like Pat Garrett, the man who killed Billy the Kid. . . .

———————

BEFORE he was a Westerner, Pat Garrett was a son of the South. Born in Alabama on June 5, 1850, he was raised in Louisiana after his family moved there a few years later. After the end of the Civil War, times were hard all across the South during the Reconstruction Era. The Garrett family had owned a plantation in Claiborne Parish, but that was surely lost in the war. By 1869, Pat was ready to head for somewhere else, someplace that held more promise for a young, ambitious man.

Like so many others, he chose Texas.

These were the days of the great buffalo hunts, when vast herds of the shaggy creatures darkened the plains of the Texas Panhandle from horizon to horizon. Numbering in the millions, the beasts were an irresistible temptation for the men who hunted them for their valuable hides. Pat Garrett was one of those men. Buffalo hunting was hard, dirty work, but it toughened a man. Garrett took to it and made a success of himself, but

Frontier lawman and rancher Pat Garrett in the 1890s, more than a decade after he gained widespread fame as the killer of Billy the Kid.

(Courtesy of Denver Public Library, Western History Collection)

the seemingly endless herds proved not to be endless after all. As the number of buffalo began to dwindle, Garrett moved on to cowboying, taking a riding job on the LS Ranch, located on the Canadian River near the town of Tascosa, which became known as the Cowboy Capital of the World. Tascosa was also a wide-open town where almost anything went, where cowboys, buffalo hunters, outlaws, gamblers, and all the other wild characters of the Old West came to blow Hell off its hinges.

Whenever Garrett rode into Tascosa, he frequented Ryan's Saloon in Hogtown, the settlement's red-light district. Ryan's was also the watering hole favored by a group of cowboys from across the border in New Mexico. Calling them cowboys is being generous—to be bald-faced about it, they were rustlers, stealing live-stock from the New Mexico cattle baron John Chisum and selling it to ranchers in the Texas Panhandle. They were nothing if not fair in their thievery, though: They also stole cattle from the Panhandle ranchers and sold the animals back to Chisum. It's possible that the same cow might have gone back and forth several times over the course of a few months.

Among those rustlers from New Mexico was a young man with an easy, charming, bucktoothed grin. Born Henry William McCarty in Brooklyn, New York, he had come west with his brother and their widowed mother. Mrs. McCarty remarried in New Mexico, taking as her second husband a blacksmith named Antrim. Though not legally adopted by his new stepfather, Henry McCarty became known as William Antrim. Later, after falling in with the group of young cowboys and rustlers, for some unknown reason he started calling himself William H. Bonney, better known as Billy Bonney.

Even better known as Billy the Kid.

Pat Garrett and Billy Bonney were no more than acquaintances at this stage of their lives, drinking and playing cards together at Ryan's and then going their separate ways. Over the line in New Mexico Territory, the trouble between the McSween-Tunstall faction and the Murphy-Dolan faction that would lead to the Lincoln County War was already brewing, but Garrett had no connection with it. He soon rode into New Mexico, though, as a member of a group of Texas cowboys sent by the Panhandle ranchers to recover several hundred head of rustled stock from John Chisum's Jingle Bob ranch.

This expedition could have been the spark that set off an explosion of violence, but instead, Chisum somehow persuaded the Texas cowboys to throw in with him, thus averting a range war, at least for a while. Pat Garrett, who was to play no direct part in the Lincoln County War, only in its aftermath, remained in

New Mexico, settling down in Fort Sumner to try his hand at ranching. He even took a wife, Apolinaria Guitierrez, to whom he would remain married through a long, eventful life.

With John Chisum backing him and with a reputation as a "law and order" candidate, Garrett was elected sheriff of Lincoln County on November 2, 1880. Since there was no indication until the campaign began that Garrett had any interest in being a lawman, the whole thing may well have been Chisum's idea. A rough, hard-edged character himself, Chisum wanted the uproar in Lincoln County to settle down so that it wouldn't hurt his ranching business. For several months the county had been plagued with lawlessness as the two factions fought it out. Billy the Kid, as an employee and ally of the murdered John Tunstall, had been in the thick of the bloody fracas. With the war mostly played out following an epic gun battle at Alexander McSween's house, Billy and some of his friends were still on the loose. Garrett, as the newly elected sheriff, gathered a posse and went after them.

After a couple of close calls, the posse finally closed in on Billy and his friends as they forted up in an old stone house at Stinking Springs, near Fort Sumner. Charlie Bowdre, one of Billy's companions, was killed in the resulting standoff, and at last Billy surrendered. He spent the next few months in jail, hatching escape plans that didn't work and writing letters to Territorial Governor Lew Wallace in an effort to strike a deal that would free him in exchange for his testimony. None of that worked, and in April 1881, Billy was found guilty of murder at a trial in Mesilla and was sentenced to be hanged. He was returned to Lincoln for the sentence to be carried out.

That never came about, because on April 28, while Garrett was away on business, Billy the Kid broke out of the second floor of the Lincoln County jail, killing Deputies James Bell and Bob Olinger in the process. Once more he was on the run, and once more his old acquaintance from Panhandle days, Pat Garrett, headed up the effort to track him down and bring him to justice.

The end came on the night of July 14, 1881, when Garrett and two deputies rode up to the house of Pete Maxwell, a friend of the Kid's. It was rumored that Billy sometimes visited Maxwell, and Garrett wanted to find out if that was true. The deputies sat themselves down in chairs on the porch of the adobe house, near where a side of beef hung, while Garrett stepped into the bedroom where Maxwell was stretched out on a bunk. While Garrett was talking to Maxwell, another man came around the corner of the house and stepped onto the porch. The newcomer's boots were off, indicating that he wasn't expecting any trouble, and he carried a butcher knife, probably intending to carve himself a hunk of meat from the side of beef. He spoke to the deputies in Spanish, no doubt taking them for a couple of Maxwell's Mexican ranch hands, and then stepped into the doorway of the bedroom.

Inside, Garrett had lowered himself to the edge of the bunk, and was sitting there talking to Maxwell when the shadowy figure appeared in the doorway. The man said, *"Quien es?"* asking in Spanish who Garrett was.

Garrett knew the voice, perhaps even recognized the silhouette of the man who stood there with the starlight behind him. The lawman drew his revolver and fired twice. The first bullet drilled the Kid in the heart. The second missed, probably because Billy was already falling to the floor, dead. The short but notorious career of Billy the Kid was over.

Pat Garrett, however, was still alive, and as the word of Billy's death spread, Garrett found himself a famous man ... though never as famous as the man he had killed there on Pete Maxwell's porch.

The next year saw the publication of a book bearing Garrett's name as the author, *The Authentic Life of Billy the Kid*. The volume was ghostwritten for Garrett by his friend Ash Upson, and despite its claim of being a factual account of Billy's life and death, it was hardly authentic at all. Instead it was a blatant mixture of fact and fiction, designed to appeal to those who saw the Kid as a dashing, romantic figure, and Garrett must have hoped that it would make him a lot of money.

That wasn't the way it worked out. The whole publishing venture was a failure, although in later years, after Garrett's death, the book was reissued and remained in print for many years. Garrett, who had been pondering whether or not to run for re-election as sheriff, decided to try his hand at a higher level of politics instead. He ran for New Mexico Councilman, the equivalent of a state senator, and found himself embroiled in such a messy, vicious campaign that during one confrontation with a supporter of his opponent, Garrett lost his temper, yanked out his revolver, and used it to cold-cock the man.

Garrett lost the election. Not only had he suffered this political defeat, but also at the same time, he was having trouble collecting the reward he felt was due him as the man who brought Billy the Kid to a final justice. Depressed over the election, on shaky ground financially, Garrett returned to the Texas Panhandle to work as a range detective and regulator for the LS Ranch, where he had once been a simple cowboy in the days before he went to New Mexico and became famous. Unhappy with the work, which he had thought would involve catching rustlers, when all his employers really wanted him to do was kill them, Garrett gave up the position and returned to New Mexico.

After being involved for a time with a failed plan to bring irrigation to the Pecos River Valley, Garrett went back to Texas yet again and bought a ranch near the town of Uvalde. He remained there for several years, living peacefully until 1896, when the disappearance and supposed murder of Colonel Albert J. Fountain brought him back to New Mexico and back to prominence.

Colonel Fountain was a lawyer, newspaperman, and political figure always at odds with his political enemy Albert Bacon Fall. In a strange twist of fate, Fountain was also the attorney for the defense when Billy the Kid was tried for murder at Mesilla and found guilty. Pat Garrett was called back to New Mexico by the territorial governor when Fountain and his nine-year-old son vanished after giving evidence to a grand jury concerning A. B. Fall's allegedly illegal activities. Everyone assumed that Fall had had Fountain and his boy murdered, but the governor appointed Garrett a special detective and charged him with getting to the bottom of the case. Garrett was also appointed sheriff of Dona Ana County after the man who had the job was pressured to resign. This gave Garrett more of an official standing to conduct his investigation.

After looking into the matter, Garrett settled on two local ranchers, Oliver Lee and Jim Gilliland, as the most likely suspects, and also thought they had been working for Fall when Fountain was killed. The bodies of Fountain and his son were never found, but no one doubted they were dead. Lee and Gilliland went on the run rather than surrendering to Garrett, who formed a posse and pursued them. After a bloody shoot-out in which the two fugitives gave the posse the slip again, Gilliland and Lee finally turned themselves in. Perhaps Fall had gotten word to them that no jury would convict them. That was exactly how the trial turned out. The two defendants were acquitted, and the disappearances of Fountain and the boy remained a mystery . . . as they do to this day.

Disgusted by this turn of events, Pat Garrett served out the rest of the term as sheriff and then went back to Texas.

The century turned, as centuries do, and in 1901, Garrett applied for the job of U.S. Customs Inspector in El Paso, Texas. President Theodore Roosevelt appointed him to the job, setting off a storm of opposition. After all, said Garrett's critics, with one exception, he had never been any great shakes as a lawman. His one and only claim to fame was that he had shot and killed Billy the Kid. That hardly qualified him for the job of Customs Inspector, claimed those who objected to his appointment.

Teddy Roosevelt stuck to his guns, and Garrett stayed on the job. His term as Customs Inspector was beset with controversy,

and by most accounts, Garrett wasn't very good at the job, preferring to spend his time gambling and visiting with friends in some
of El Paso's many saloons instead of being in his office. When his
term expired in 1905, President Roosevelt decided not to appoint
him to the position again.

Faced once more with failure, Garrett took his family back to
New Mexico and resumed ranching near Las Cruces, in the San
Andres Mountains. He was growing older now, but still got
around all right. This time around, however, ranching did not
work as well for Garrett. After falling in debt and taking out a
mortgage on his land, Garrett was unable to pay the note. A
neighboring cattleman, W. W. Cox, had bought the note, so he
claimed Garrett's livestock in payment and had his cowboys
round up the cattle and drive them off Garrett's range. Garrett
could do nothing to stop this humiliation. He still had his land,
which Cox had decided not to claim, and so in 1907, he leased the
ranch to Wayne Brazel and Print Rhode, two local cowboys. Garrett assumed that Brazel and Rhode planned to run cattle on the
range, but instead the two men moved a herd of goats onto it.
Having a bunch of goats on his land infuriated Garrett, but there
was nothing he could do about it.

A possible way out of this predicament presented itself in the
unlikely person of "Deacon Jim" Miller, the notorious gunman
and killer who sometimes tried his hand at ranching when he
wasn't gunning down his enemies. Miller and one of his relatives,
Carl Adamson, wanted to buy Garrett's ranch—on one condition.
That condition was that Garrett would have to get rid of those
blasted goats. Brazel, who was running things for the partnership
of himself and Print Rhode, balked at the deal.

Garrett, who desperately needed the money that a sale of the
land would bring, asked Brazel and Carl Adamson to go into Las
Cruces with him so that they could hash everything out and
maybe come up with a solution to the problem. Adamson drove

his buckboard, and Garrett rode with him. Brazel rode alongside on horseback. The date was March 1, 1908, and the wagon was about four miles east of Las Cruces, near Alameda Arroyo, when Adamson stopped to urinate and Garrett decided that he might as well, too.

The two men were standing at the side of the road when a shot rang out. Pat Garrett was thrown forward as a bullet crashed into the back of his head. He twisted as he fell, so that he landed on his back. Quite probably he was dead already, so the chances that he felt the second bullet entering his stomach are slim.

The man who had ended the life of Billy the Kid had now met death himself. The question that remained was . . . who killed him?

The story told by Carl Adamson was straightforward. He claimed that when he heard the shots, he turned around and saw Wayne Brazel still sitting on his horse, holding a revolver with gunsmoke curling from the barrel. The two men went on into Las Cruces, and that was the story Adamson told after Brazel turned himself over to the law. Brazel claimed that he had fired in self-defense, knowing Garrett's reputation as a man-killer and knowing that there was a shotgun in the buckboard. They had been arguing, Brazel said, and he had been afraid that Garrett would grab the shotgun and blaze away at him. He had prevented that, he declared, by gunning down Garrett first.

It was a rather weak story, but when Brazel was put on trial in Las Cruces a little over a year later, his lawyer was none other than Albert Bacon Fall, Colonel Fountain's old nemesis. Not only that, but the jury was drawn from the townsmen and cowboys of a county dominated by W. W. Cox, Garrett's enemy. In what must have been no surprise, Brazel was found not guilty of murdering the old former lawman. His claim of self-defense had held up in court.

For years after that, rumors flew around the death of Pat Garrett. Stories placed the gun that had fired the fatal shot in the hands of Deacon Jim Miller, Carl Adamson, Print Rhode, even Cox himself. About the only one who didn't get blamed by somebody for the killing was the shade of Billy Bonney himself, come back from the grave. (There is a whole other controversy about whether Pat Garrett really killed Billy the Kid or whether Billy really lived a long life elsewhere under another name, but that's a story for another time and place.) Garrett's contemporaries were convinced that no matter who pulled the trigger, W. W. Cox paid for the killing and ordered it done. While it's impossible to be one-hundred-percent certain who was responsible for Garrett's murder, the most likely explanation, as usual, is the simplest. Wayne Brazel really did shoot Garrett for the reasons he originally stated: They had been arguing, and whether from fear or anger, Brazel went for his gun and blasted away. After being acquitted, Brazel dropped out of sight, his fate unknown, yet another mystery surrounding the death of Pat Garrett, the man who killed Billy the Kid.

THE END OF THE NOTORIOUS JOHN WESLEY HARDIN

The man standing at the bar in El Paso's Acme Saloon on the night of August 19, 1895, had been handsome once, but time and hard living had taken their toll. He still possessed a sort of dissipated attractiveness. He had thinning dark hair and full black mustaches. His clothes had an air of shabbiness about them. He swayed a little as he shook some dice in his hand. His unsteadiness was testimony to the amount of liquor he had consumed this evening. In that respect, this hot summer night was no different than any other. The man at the bar drank steadily, consistently, day in and day out. He was an attorney, but never practiced much law, and when he did, he wasn't very good at it. But he could drink, Lord, he could drink.

And one more thing: He could kill. There had been a time when he was the best in Texas at killing men, maybe the best in the whole West. Or worst, depending on how you look at it.

His name was John Wesley Hardin.

———◆·◆·◆———

BORN May 26, 1853, in Bonham, Texas, John Wesley Hardin was the son of a Methodist minister. The preacher named his boy after old John Wesley, the founder of the Methodist Church. He probably hoped that young Wes, as he was called, would grow up to be a preacher, too. That wasn't the way it turned out, but of course nobody could know that then. Nobody can see into the future, which is usually a good thing. It probably was in the case of John Wesley Hardin.

But when Wes was twelve years old, folks might have gotten an inkling that he was a little different than the usual kid. A little quicker to fly off the handle, and a lot more dangerous when he did. A scuffle with another boy turned serious when Wes's opponent pulled a knife on him. Wes was carrying a knife, too, and he got it out and used it with surprising speed, stabbing the other boy twice, luckily not fatally. Since the boy had been armed, it was assumed that Wes had acted in self-defense.

That was the first time, but it wouldn't be the last.

Texas was in the grip of Reconstruction, a terrible time that saw the Texans abused and oppressed by carpetbaggers, a state government that was little more than a dictatorship, and the hated Union Army. Wes Hardin's first killing was that of a former slave who bore a grudge against him and came after him with a club. As Wes rode by, the man grabbed the reins of his horse, refused to let go, and poised the club to smash Wes's head. Wes, only fifteen, already was packing iron, a big Colt .44 cap-and-ball revolver. He drew the gun and fired three times, the bullets knocking his attacker away from the horse.

Under the circumstances, Wes knew he would never get a fair trial from a Reconstruction court, even though in his eyes the killing was justified. He went on the run instead of staying to face what passed for justice in Texas at that time. The Hardin family had relatives scattered all over central Texas, so it wasn't difficult for Wes to find places to hide out. The Army was after him, but they couldn't get close to him without some kinfolks warning him so that he could get away.

Wes wasn't one to shy away from trouble, though. The Army was looking for him, so he went looking for the Army, intending to deliver a message. He delivered it in lead, confronting a three-man patrol that was searching for him. Still in his mid-teens, Wes Hardin was a natural-born shootist. He killed all three soldiers in a fierce gunfight.

It came easy to him after that. (Indeed, judging by his previous activities, killing always came easy to John Wesley Hardin.) Though he was a fugitive, Wes loved horse racing, and often turned up at race meets staged throughout Texas. The crowd that followed the ponies was a tough one even then, and it's not surprising that Wes clashed with some of them. Two more corpse-and-cartridge sessions added two more dead men to his tally. Wes always thought he was in the right in these scrapes; the autobiography he wrote late in his life is testimony to that. But right or wrong, by 1870 Wes Hardin had a reputation as the deadliest Coltman in Texas.

That year, 1870, saw the end of Reconstruction government in Texas. The carpetbaggers and scalawags were kicked out of power, but a new state police force was formed that proved to be every bit as big a threat to the common people. The state police were corrupt and brutal, and they came after Wes just like the Army had. His luck turned bad temporarily, and he was arrested in the East Texas town of Longview while he was trying to get to Louisiana, where he would be out of reach of the state police. Two officers tied him on horseback and set out to deliver him to Waco.

Only one of the officers made it to Waco, and without Hardin.

Wes had gotten his hands on a gun, killed the other man, and escaped.

Texas was too hot for him now. He visited some cousins, a family named Clements, and when he heard that three of the Clements boys were about to drive a herd of cattle to Abilene, Kansas, Wes decided to go along. He wouldn't mind seeing some country that was new to him, and besides, the cattle drive would get him out of Texas.

Not surprisingly, trouble followed Hardin to Kansas. As the herd was crossing out of Indian Territory, several Osage rode up and demanded that they be allowed to butcher one of the long-horns as a sort of tribute and toll. Hardin disagreed, and when one of the Indians tried to slaughter a cow anyway, Hardin drew and killed him. Then, supposedly, Hardin threw the corpse over the back of the steer, tied it in place, and left it there as a warning for anybody else who might want to interfere with the herd.

A short time later, Hardin killed several *vaqueros* who were driving a herd up from Mexico. There was bad blood between the Texas drovers and the Mexicans, and as always, the easiest way for Hardin to settle any dispute was with lead.

Arriving in Abilene with the herd, Hardin reacquainted him-self with Ben Thompson and Phil Coe, a couple of gamblers he had known in Texas. He was especially fond of Coe, who nick-named him "Young Seven-up," after a popular card game. Thompson and Coe were partners in the Bull's Head Saloon, and they had been having trouble with the town marshal, the famous James Butler "Wild Bill" Hickok.

Hardin, like practically everyone else in the country, had heard of Wild Bill and knew the sort of reputation Hickok had as a gunman. The idea of going up against Hickok must have intrigued him, but when Ben Thompson suggested just that, Hardin nixed the idea. He didn't mind killing, obviously, but he had to have what he considered a good reason for it. Ridding Ben

Thompson of an annoying lawman wasn't anywhere near a good enough reason.

Hickok and Hardin confronted each other on at least one occasion while Wes was in Abilene. A town ordinance stated that men couldn't carry guns in public. Wes Hardin wore not just one gun, but two. When Hickok asked him to remove the guns, Hardin refused, setting the stage for a classic shoot-out. But instead of letting himself be prodded into gunplay, Hickok suggested that they have a drink together instead. The problem of Wes's guns was put aside for the time being. He continued to wear them, and Hickok continued to ignore them. Evidently the two shootists, with all they had in common, struck up an immediate friendship. Hickok even gave Wes another nickname, "Little Arkansaw."

The story goes that John Wesley Hardin and Wild Bill Hickok had another showdown over Hardin's guns. In this version, Hickok again demanded that Wes surrender his guns. Wes drew the revolvers and extended them toward Hickok, butt-first, but then as Hickok reached for them, Wes stepped back, flipped the guns around—the so-called Border Roll—and pointed them at Hickok. The famous marshal was caught flat-footed for a moment, and would have been easy prey for Hardin had Wes chosen to fire. Instead, Wes holstered the guns. He had made his point and had nothing else to prove.

Down through the years, much argument has gone on about whether or not the Border Roll incident really happened. Hardin tells of it in his autobiography, but nowhere else is it documented. True or not, it's a good story, and it certainly sounds like the sort of thing John Wesley Hardin might have done. He was certainly proud of his ability with his six-shooters.

He was proud of being a Texan, too, as one of the locals in Abilene learned to his regret when he cursed Texas in Hardin's hearing. Hardin's response was to challenge the man to a gunfight, and seconds later he had hung another skin on the wall.

Hardin stayed in Abilene for a while, having been paid by the trail boss to stay there and guard the herd until it could be shipped east. It was during this time that Hardin recorded what was perhaps his only legally sanctioned killing. A *vaquero* named Bideno gunned down one of Wes's friends in a fight and fled toward Indian Territory. Wes got himself appointed as a special deputy and led a posse after the fugitive. They caught up to Bideno in a restaurant in a small town twenty miles north of the border between Kansas and Indian Territory. Hardin even gave the *vaquero* a chance to surrender, and promised that he would not be harmed if he allowed the posse to take him into custody. Bideno grabbed for his revolver instead, and Hardin killed him instantly with a single shot to the head.

It was also while in Abilene that Hardin shot a man for snoring. More than likely, it was an accident—while in the American Hotel, Hardin thumbed off some shots through the wall into the room next door, in an attempt to get that room's inhabitant to roll over and stop sawing logs. But his aim was a little too low, and when the first shot startled the man into sitting up in bed, the second one stopped his snoring permanently. Realizing what he had done, Hardin and his cousin Manning Clements slipped out of the hotel and decided it was time to head back home to Texas.

Despite everything that had gone before, Wes might have been able to put it all behind him and live a peaceful life in Texas if he had kept his temper reined in and his six-gun pouched. He did neither. Shortly after returning, he killed two state policemen who tried to arrest him, then shot down several more members of the posse that came after him. By now, only a little over eighteen years old, he had killed at least twenty-seven men.

With all the gunfighting to occupy him, it doesn't seem that he would have had a chance to romance a girl, but he must have found the time somewhere, because on February 29, 1872, he

A young but already deadly John Wesley Hardin, the most dangerous gunman in the Old West, in a photograph taken in Kansas in the 1870s, while Hardin was working as a cowboy driving cattle up from Texas. This is the period during which he shot a man for snoring and had his famous, perhaps apochryphal confrontation with Wild Bill Hickok.

(Courtesy of Old West Photos)

married fourteen-year-old Jane Bowen. Though he was often gone, helling around the countryside and getting into shooting scrapes, he managed to have a child with Jane, a daughter named Molly.

A dispute over a game of tenpins resulted in the only serious wound Hardin received in any of his gunfights. His opponent, a man named Sublett, came after Hardin with a shotgun. Though Wes put a couple of bullets through him, Sublett was able to hit Wes in the belly with a charge of buckshot. Neither man died from his wounds, but it was Hardin who wound up being charged with attempted murder, one of the few indictments against him that actually does seem unjustified.

Wounded and slow to recover from his injuries, Hardin decided he couldn't run from the law this time. He surrendered and was jailed in Austin for a while, until he recuperated enough to escape. Back on the loose, Hardin continued his powder-smoke parade, slaying lawmen who came after him and getting involved for a while in the bloody, infamous Sutton-Taylor feud. Then Wes headed for the central Texas town of Comanche, where he planned to gather up a trail herd in partnership with his brother Joe. Some horse races were also scheduled to take place in Comanche, and Wes never could resist the lure of a race.

Deputy Sheriff Charles Webb of neighboring Brown County had run into Wes before and didn't like him. There was no particular bad blood between the two men; Webb just didn't like the fact that Hardin was a shootist and a man-killer and had run free for several years. While Hardin was in Wright's Saloon on Comanche's town square, Webb came up behind him but didn't challenge him. Nudged by one of his companions, Hardin turned around and asked Webb if he'd come to arrest him. Webb denied having that intention. Hardin then invited the deputy to have a drink with him and his friends. Webb seemed to accept, but as he came closer, he suddenly started to draw his gun.

One of Hardin's friends shouted a warning. Hardin spun around and reached for his own Colt. Webb cleared leather first and got off a shot that grazed Hardin's side. Hardin returned the fire, hitting Webb in the face. Hardin's companions joined the fray, pumping more slugs into the luckless deputy. Webb crashed to the floor, dead.

Wes might have been lynched then and there, since Comanche was crowded that day because of the races and not everyone was a friend or relative to the Hardin family. But the Comanche County sheriff showed up and backed the mob off. Wes grabbed a horse and galloped off while he had the chance, on the run from yet another killing.

This time he didn't have the state police after him. That group had been disbanded recently, and the Texas Rangers had been re-established as Texas's statewide law-enforcement agency. The Rangers weren't as corrupt as the state police had been, and they were even better manhunters. Wes must have thought twice about crossing them.

Also, a tragedy struck the Hardin family following the shooting of Charles Webb in Comanche. Most of the Hardin relatives in the area were rounded up and jailed so that they couldn't help Wes escape from the law. Once again a lynch mob formed in Comanche, and this time it was successful. Wes's brother Joe and two of his cousins, Tom and Bud Dixon, were taken out of the stone building that was being used as a jail and strung up from the wide-spreading branches of a live oak tree on the town square.

Faced with being pursued by the Rangers and distraught over the hanging of his brother and cousins, Hardin decided to leave Texas behind, for good this time. Taking Jane and Molly with him, he moved to Florida, assumed the name J. H. Swain, and settled down to lead a new life. Jane had another child, a son, and then later, a second daughter. Wes still gambled and caroused, but didn't kill anybody for a while. Maybe, sooner or later, he would have straightened out for good.

But the Texas Rangers were still on his trail, and they were able to track him down to Alabama, where the family had moved after living for a time in Florida. Ranger Lieutenant John Armstrong was sent to bring back Hardin. Armstrong and some local lawmen confronted Hardin and a gambler friend of his, Jimmy Mann, on a train as Hardin was returning home from a gambling trip. In the resulting shoot-out, Mann was killed and Hardin was arrested. He was brought back to Austin in chains, surrounded by heavily armed guards. Charged with murder in the death of Deputy Sheriff Charles Webb, Hardin was found guilty and sentenced to twenty-five years in the state prison at Huntsville.

Hardin no doubt thought he would escape, just as he had on

The document that pardoned and restored citizenship to John Wesley Hardin, following his release from prison on February 14, 1894. He had served fourteen years of a twenty-five-year sentence for the killing of a deputy sheriff in Comanche, Texas.

(Courtesy of Texas State Library and Archives Commission)

numerous occasions in the past. This time, however, the law succeeded in keeping him behind bars despite several escape
attempts. The effort netted Hardin nothing except some brutal
whippings and a long stay in solitary confinement. He even had
to wear a ball and chain attached to his ankle.

During his incarceration, the realization that this time he
wasn't going to get away finally soaked in on Wes Hardin. Jane
and the three children were living on a small farm, a hard life but
a law-abiding one. Hardin, knowing that good behavior might
shorten his sentence, now behaved himself behind bars. He even
tried to educate himself, reading every book he could get his
hands on, including quite a few law books. An idea began to
sprout in his head. When he got out of prison, maybe he could
become a lawyer.

That was what happened. He was paroled in February 1894,
and shortly after that received a pardon from the governor of
Texas so that his rights were restored, including the right to practice law once he had passed the bar examination, which he did
later that year. But now he was a widower, Jane having died at the
age of thirty-six while Wes was still in prison.

A second marriage, to a woman much younger than him,
didn't work out and was extremely short-lived. Hardin moved to
El Paso, about as far west as he could go and still be in Texas.
Even this late in the nineteenth century, El Paso was a frontier
town, full of gamblers, whores, and fast guns. The fastest of
them all was Wes Hardin, but he was more interested now in
writing a book about his life, giving his side of all the bloody stories about him.

Wes always had an eye for the ladies. Although he didn't do
much legal work, one of his clients was a woman named Beulah
M'Rose, whose husband Martin was a wanted man hiding out in
Mexico. M'Rose wanted to come back across the line and surrender, but was afraid he would be killed out of hand by the law. His

wife hired Hardin to work out an arrangement so that M'Rose could cross the Rio Grande and turn himself in without having to fear for his life. But a romance quickly developed between Hardin and his client, and Beulah no longer cared if her husband came back from Mexico or not. When M'Rose tried to slip into El Paso, he was caught and killed by local lawmen, just as he feared would happen. His death left Beulah a widow, and naturally she turned to her attorney, John Wesley Hardin, for consolation.

She also turned to the bottle, and ultimately, that was Wes Hardin's downfall. Beulah was arrested for being drunk in public by a young El Paso policeman, John Selman, Jr. Selman's father, John Sr., was an El Paso constable at the time, but like many another frontier star-packer, he hadn't always been on the right side of the law. In the past he had been a rustler and an outlaw. Selman, Sr., was well known as a gunman, too, though he was never on the same level as Wes Hardin.

Hardin was furious that young Selman had arrested Beulah, and he didn't keep his anger to himself. As he drank in El Paso's saloons, he vented his spleen about what had happened, and word of what he was saying got back to the elder Selman, who was angered by what he considered Hardin's insults to his son. Beulah left town, but that didn't smooth over the hard feelings between Hardin and the Selmans.

All his life, John Wesley Hardin had been quick to perceive an insult, quicker still to settle a problem with gunplay. That was about to catch up to him at last.

—————•◆•—————

HARDIN rattled the dice in his hand and got ready to throw them out on the bar. Probably, he had forgotten already about an argument he'd had earlier in the day with John Selman. Selman still had a burr under his saddle about the things Hardin had said about his son. He had even wanted to shoot it out with Hardin, who hadn't been armed at the time. During the evening, Selman had wandered in and out of the Acme several times. Hardin had noticed him, but not really paid that much attention. As it usually was these days, Hardin's attention was fixed more on his drinking and gambling. He was throwing dice with a local grocer, Henry S. Brown.

Hardin leaned an elbow on the bar and rolled the bones, then slapped his hand lightly on the hardwood when he saw what numbers had come up. "Brown, you've got four sixes to beat," he said with a grin.

A gun crashed as soon as the words left Hardin's mouth. Unseen by him, John Selman, Sr., had come back into the saloon with a gun in his hand and fired as he strode up behind Hardin. The bullet slammed into the back of Hardin's head on the right side, behind the ear, angled through the brain, and came out beside his left eye. As Hardin fell, already dead or dying, Selman shot him twice more, once through the right arm and once in the right side of the chest. Hardin's gunman's luck finally had run out.

Selman was arrested and put on trial for killing Hardin. Controversy broke out over whether Selman had fired the fatal shot from behind Hardin or in front of him, an argument that still rages in some circles today. What is certain is that Selman was acquitted by a jury. Prosecutors intended to retry him, but before they could do that, a drunken Selman tried to pull a gun on Deputy U.S. Marshal George Scarborough. That was Selman's fatal mistake, because Scarborough ventilated him four times in the space of a few seconds. Selman died later that day in an El Paso hospital.

Hardin was buried in El Paso. Eventually, through the efforts of his children, the autobiography he had written in his last year was published, under the title *The Life of John Wesley Hardin, as Written by Himself.* The book rationalized and defended the multitude of killings Hardin carried out, but remains in print because of the details it provides about his life that are unavailable elsewhere. Officially, he is credited with killing forty-four men, but the actual number could be higher or lower than that. One thing is certain, however.

From Abilene to El Paso, John Wesley Hardin was the deadliest gunfighter to ever strap on a Colt.

5

BEN THOMPSON AND THE VAUDEVILLE AMBUSH

The two men were drunk; anybody could see that. They swayed slightly as they walked down the streets of San Antonio. Or maybe they weren't three sheets to the wind after all. Despite their apparent inebriation, both men snapped to instant alertness at the least suspicious sound or movement in the night around them. They had been drinking, right enough, and were on their way to do more, but later on, witnesses would never agree on whether or not Ben Thompson and King Fisher actually were drunk.

That was not the last question on which witnesses to the events of this night would disagree.

It was March 11, 1884, and these two men, two of the most feared gun-throwers in the whole Southwest, were on their way to the Vaudeville Variety Theatre and Gambling Saloon—and a date with destiny.

BEN Thompson was a Canadian by birth, like Bat Masterson, who was his friend in later life. Born in Nova Scotia in 1843 to English parents, Ben lived there until he was nine years old, when the family moved to Austin, Texas, which would be Ben's home for most of the rest of his life. His father had been a member of the Royal Navy, and had acquired quite a drinking habit while sailing the seven seas and protecting the interests of the British Empire. Ben and his younger brother Billy took to life in Texas, though they were both quick-tempered and involved in many fights with other boys as they were growing up.

Ben's father eventually deserted the family, leaving his wife to raise the boys and their two sisters. Through the generosity of a lawyer who befriended the family, Ben was able to attend a private school in Austin for two years. When he had to quit school and go to work to help support his family, the same lawyer helped him get a job as an apprentice printer with one of the local newspapers.

Ben was good at the printing trade, good enough so that after a year he was able to move to New Orleans and go to work for the *Picayune*, the leading paper in the Crescent City. It was while he was in New Orleans that controversy and violence first dogged Ben Thompson's trail. Most accounts of his life include a mention of a duel to the death between Ben and a young Frenchman, Emile de Tours, who supposedly earned Ben's enmity by insulting a young woman on a streetcar. Ben and de Tours were said to have fought to death with knives in a locked, darkened room, with Ben emerging the victor. In recent years doubts have risen about this story; some historians believe the duel never occurred. Whether it did or not, something prompted Ben Thompson to leave New Orleans in a hurry. A knife fight is as good a reason as any.

Back in Austin, Ben returned to work for the newspaper, and in his off hours he discovered that he was a good gambler, good enough to make as much money with the cards as he did at his regular job. He discovered as well that he was a fast, accurate shot when a sore loser accused him of cheating and grabbed for a gun. Ben drew first and killed him.

During this time, in the days before the Civil War, Texas still faced a threat from the Comanches and Kiowas, even in cities like Austin. When several children were carried off by a war party that raided into the city itself, Ben was a member of the group that went after them. His skill with a rifle helped considerably in the battle that was fought to recover the kidnapped children, all of whom were brought back safely to Austin.

When the war came, Ben joined the Confederate cavalry, but his first battle was with men in his own outfit. During a brawl he killed two fellow soldiers, and was thrown in the stockade at Fort Clark for it. The stockade was unable to hold him. He escaped, went elsewhere, and enlisted all over again. This time he saw action against the Yankees on several occasions.

While on leave, he returned to Austin and married Catherine Moore, a young woman he had been courting. They would remain married, though not always living together, for the rest of Thompson's eventful life.

After the war, Federal troops occupied Texas and a Reconstruction government ruled the state. Both Thompson brothers were thrown in jail over an old scrape in which a man had been killed. Ben escaped and went to Mexico to fight as a mercenary for the Emperor Maximilian. When the empire was overthrown and Maximilian was killed, Ben barely slipped out of the country in time to escape being executed. He returned to Texas, weak from a bout of yellow fever he'd suffered while in Vera Cruz.

His brother Billy was out of jail, but not for long. He was arrested for shooting a Yankee officer in Austin, and for good measure, or maybe to answer for some of those old fracases, Ben was thrown in jail, too. Both brothers were tried, convicted, and sentenced to ten years in the state penitentiary at Huntsville.

They served two years before being released by the new state government that finally had forced out the carpetbaggers and scalawags of Reconstruction.

By this time, thousands of Texas cattle were going up the trails to the railhead towns in Kansas. Ben, having operated several gambling houses in Austin, heard that Abilene, Kansas, was a wide-open town and decided to try his luck there. He had only a small stake when he reached Abilene, but in a single session at the poker tables he parlayed that into a much larger sum. Forming a partnership with Phil Coe, another Texas gambler Ben knew from Austin, he opened the Bull's Head Saloon . . . and that put Ben and Coe on a collision course with Abilene's new marshal, James Butler "Wild Bill" Hickok.

(For the full story on Ben Thompson and Phil Coe's troubles with Wild Bill Hickok, see "Wild Bill's Tragic Mistake," elsewhere in this volume.)

A buggy accident outside Kansas City in 1871 left Ben injured, along with his wife and their young son. It was while he was recuperating there along with the other members of his family that he heard the news of Phil Coe's death at the hands of Hickok. Ben was already giving some thought to leaving Abilene. The death of his friend and partner helped him make up his mind. He was finished in Abilene. When they were able to travel, the Thompson family returned to Austin, where Ben continued in the saloon business.

He had a natural restlessness to him, though, and by the summer of 1873 he had returned to Kansas, this time to open a saloon in Ellsworth with his brother. Ben and Billy were both heavy drinkers and had volatile tempers; they were even worse when they were together than when they were apart. They got into an argument with two other gamblers, and when those men pulled guns, Ben and Billy defended themselves. The problem was that the local sheriff, who had been trying to head off trouble, wound up being killed by a stray shot from Billy Thompson. Once again the time had come for Ben to get out of Kansas and head back to Texas, this time taking his brother with him.

For the next few years, Ben gambled and operated saloons around Texas, Colorado, and New Mexico. When a shooting war broke out between two rival railroads, the Santa Fe and the Denver & Rio Grande, as they competed to expand into Colorado's rich gold fields, Ben went to work as a gunman for the Santa Fe. It was during this time that he met and became friends with another fast gun, Bat Masterson. The Denver & Rio Grande finally prevailed over the Santa Fe in court, and Ben went back to Texas. His pay for the gun work he had done: $2,300—and a handful of diamonds.

Bat Masterson, who knew something about the subject of gunfighting, considered Ben Thompson to be the single most dangerous man with a gun in the history of the Old West. In later years, Masterson praised such luminaries as Wild Bill Hickok, Wyatt Earp, Luke Short, and Clay Allison for their skill with a pistol, but in Masterson's opinion, none of them could have defeated Ben Thompson in a man-to-man showdown.

In 1879, Ben did something that few if anyone who knew him would have expected of him: He ran for the office of Austin's city marshal. Why he decided to turn to law enforcement at this point in his life is a mystery. Given his restless personality and his fondness for a good time, it's possible he thought of it simply as a lark, one more exciting adventure in a lifetime of adventures. Ben lost the election, but two years later, he ran again, and this time he won.

No one could ever accuse Ben Thompson of doing things halfway. Now that he was on the right side of the law, he enforced it fully, fairly, and efficiently. The crime rate in Austin dropped significantly, and not a single murder was committed in the town while he served as marshal. Had he continued in office, eventually he might have put up a record as a lawman to equal or better that of Wyatt Earp, Bat Masterson, or Wild Bill Hickok.

Gambler, saloon owner, and gunman Ben Thompson, who always
dressed well and served for a time as chief of police in Austin, Texas.
There were those who said he was actually the fastest with a gun of
them all, despite the fact that he looked like a dude.

(Courtesy of Texas State Library and Archives Commission)

As it was, though, trouble and Ben Thompson never stayed
strangers for long, and that was true now as it always had been
before.

In the summer of 1882, friction developed between Ben and
Jack Harris, a gambler and the owner of the Vaudeville Variety
Theatre in San Antonio. Ben and Harris, as fellow members of
the gambling fraternity, had known each other for a long time and
had never liked each other. This dislike became open hostility
when the two men argued over the value of the diamonds Ben
had brought back with him from Colorado as part of his payment

from the Santa Fe Railroad. If Ben had stayed in Austin, the trouble might have blown over, but he liked to take frequent trips to San Antonio to drink and gamble, and one of the places he always went was the Vaudeville. Knowing that Ben might show up and would likely be looking for trouble if he did, Harris got into the habit of carrying a shotgun with him all the time.

He had the Greener with him, as usual, when Ben Thompson walked into the Vaudeville on the evening of July 11, 1882. Harris swung around, let out a stream of curses when he saw Ben, and lifted the shotgun to fire. Ben, who made it a policy in his gunfights to let the other man fire first so that he could claim self-defense later, couldn't afford that luxury on this night. Giving Harris a chance to blaze away at him with a shotgun would be fatal. So Ben drew and fired three times before Harris could pull the triggers of the scattergun. Harris went down, fatally wounded, even as the theater's band continued to play, drowning out the sound of the shots.

Ben was arrested and put on trial for murder, but given the bad blood between the two men and the fact that Harris had been armed with a shotgun, no self-respecting frontier jury was going to vote to convict. Ben was acquitted, and returned to Austin on the train to find that the word had been flashed on ahead of him. The train station was packed with well-wishers who threw a huge celebration for him. Ben had resigned as Austin's marshal after killing Harris, but the town that had once thought of him as nothing but a rowdy young troublemaker now loved him.

Unfortunately, Austin's affection for Ben Thompson soon grew strained. The business in his gambling house declined, and Ben began to drink even more. He took to roaming the streets at night when he was drunk and taking potshots at anything that struck his fancy as a good target, often the streetlights. His early experiences as a printer had left him with an abiding fascination for newspapers, and he often visited the composing room of the local paper. When he was in his cups, though, he liked to knock over the boxes of type and shoot up the presses. He caused a commotion in the Austin Theatre when he interrupted a performance to start shooting at the actor portraying the villain of the piece. His gun was loaded with blanks and the whole thing was a practical joke, but the members of the troupe who ran for cover and the terrified audience didn't know that until later. When he was summoned to appear in court on another matter, he rode into the courtroom on horseback and scandalized the judge. With all this and more going on, it's no wonder that the town turned against him.

One of Ben's few friends during this time was King Fisher, a gunfighter and rustler from South Texas. They went on drinking sprees together every time Fisher visited Ben in Austin. They must have made quite a pair: Ben, who was short, stocky, and mild-looking in conservative suits and hats, and King Fisher, swaggering and flamboyant, sporting two silver-plated, ivory-handled revolvers in fancy hand-tooled holsters. Fisher came to Austin in March of 1884 to see his friend, and when it came time for him to board the train that would carry him back to Laredo, he persuaded Ben to ride with him as far as San Antonio. They would stop there for the night, Fisher suggested, and do some more drinking and carousing. Ben agreed.

They disembarked from the train in San Antonio that evening and took in a play first of all, then headed for the Vaudeville Theatre to see the stage show and indulge in some drinking and gambling. Ben had not returned to the Vaudeville since killing Jack Harris nearly two years earlier. He had vowed, in fact, never to set foot in the place again. He'd let King Fisher convince him otherwise.

Harris's former partners, Billy Simms and Joe Foster, were running the Vaudeville now. Ben had been friends with Simms in the past, when Simms was a gambler in Austin, but they had had a falling-out. They weren't bitter enemies, but there was no love lost between them. There was the matter of Harris's killing to cause a grudge, too.

Ben must have boasted before leaving Austin that he and Fisher intended to visit the Vaudeville, because one of Foster's friends sent him a telegram warning him that Ben and King Fisher were on their way to San Antonio. When Ben and Fisher came into the place, Simms was there to greet them, but there was no sign of Foster. Simms escorted the two men to a table and sat down with them. A local policeman who moonlighted as a guard at the Vaudeville, Jacob Coy, drifted over and sat down with them. The atmosphere was jovial on the surface, but tense underneath. Simms seemed to be doing everything he could to defuse the situation and avoid trouble.

Ben asked where Joe Foster was and said he wanted to see him. Simms went to summon Foster. When Foster walked up to the table, Ben held out his hand, offering to shake and call a truce. He would even seal the agreement by buying a drink for Foster, he said. Foster not only refused the drink, but declined to shake hands as well, saying that he and Ben Thompson could never be friends. Angry at this insult, both Ben and King Fisher leaped to their feet.

And at this point, the story diverges, depending on who tells it. According to the testimony of Simms and Coy, Ben drew his gun and jammed the barrel in Foster's mouth, breaking his teeth. Coy claims to have lunged at Ben and grabbed the pistol's cylinder in an attempt to keep Ben from firing. Shots rang out anyway, and when the smoke cleared, Ben, King Fisher, and Joe Foster all lay on the floor. Ben and Fisher were dead, and Foster was mortally wounded. At the inquest, a coroner's jury ruled that Ben and Fisher had been killed by shots fired by Foster and Coy in self-defense.

However, eyewitnesses to the fray insisted that as soon as Foster insulted Ben, Foster and Simms and Coy stepped back hurriedly, as if they knew what was about to happen. Ben and

Fisher came to their feet, but never had a chance to pull their guns. Before they could, a volley of rifle fire came from above them and to the left, where one of the theater's curtained boxes was located. According to this version of the story, Ben and Fisher were ambushed by hired killers, cut down without even a slim chance to defend themselves.

When these eyewitnesses came forward with their story, the Austin newspapers pressured the San Antonio authorities to examine the bodies of Ben and Fisher again. This time, the evidence showed that both men had been shot from above with rifles, rather than at close range with pistols, as the coroner's jury had found. Despite this revelation, the law in San Antonio never conducted any further investigations, and no one was ever indicted for the killings.

The shadowy circumstances of his death did nothing to detract from the legend that grew up around Ben Thompson. Unlike some Old West figures who never really deserved their acclaim, Ben Thompson was the genuine article. Indian fighter, cavalryman, gambler, gunfighter, lawman . . . he seems to have done it all. In addition, unknown to most of Austin's citizens during his lifetime, he was also a philanthropist, providing food and clothing for many of the town's orphans. It's no wonder that after his death, Austin forgave Ben's many excesses and gave him the biggest funeral the town had ever seen.

A proper send-off for the Old West's deadliest gunfighter and one of its most colorful characters.

PART SIX

GUNFIGHTING
MISHAPS
AND
MISFORTUNES

*I never killed a man
who didn't need killing.*

—*Clay Allison*

PART SIX

GUNFIGHTING MISHAPS AND MISFORTUNES

THAT WASN'T
CLAY ALLISON

The so-called badman wasn't always in the wrong.
Often on the frontier, outright murder was classed
as self-defense, but sometimes that actually was the
case. Take what happened one Christmas season in Las Animas,
New Mexico Territory.

Clay Allison was born in Tennessee in 1841, and when the
Civil War began, he went off to fight the Yankees like many of the
other young men from his state. But the Confederate Army dis-
charged him after military doctors found that he was too emotion-
ally unstable for duty. The physicians blamed Clay's problems on
a head injury he received as a child, but such instability may have
been just his natural state.

After the war, Clay headed west, finding work as a cowboy on
the ranches in the Brazos River country of Texas. He went along
on some of the first cattle drives that saw vast herds of longhorns
going up the trail through Indian Territory to the railheads in
Kansas. Clay also was part of some drives that went west to New
Mexico Territory, and he found that he liked that part of the

country even better than Texas. He settled there in the 1870s, establishing his own ranch near Cimarron.

Despite the fact that his chosen career as a rancher was a respectable one—and he was successful at it, too—he soon gained a reputation as a violent, dangerous man, especially when he'd been drinking. Unable to hold his liquor, Clay pulled all sorts of outrageous stunts when he was under the influence. Wearing only boots and hat, he galloped his horse up and down the streets of more than one town, shooting out windows and lights. Summoned to court to answer for some of his antics, he rode his horse into the courtroom. He particularly delighted in shooting at the feet of Easterners who were unfortunate enough to cross his path, forcing them to dance a desperate jig in order to avoid the slugs. (In a bit of irony, the most serious gunshot wound Clay ever received was his own fault, when he shot himself in the foot during the confusion of a mule stampede.) Allison's other notorious actions including the vigilante lynching of a settler suspected of being a mass murderer, the destruction of a newspaper's printing press when the paper printed articles critical of him, and the killing of fellow shootist Chunk Colbert, who admittedly was trying to kill Clay at the time, thinking that to gun down the famous Clay Allison would increase his own reputation.

Given Clay Allison's history, it was natural enough that a lawman would be wary of trouble any time he saw Clay ride into town. That was certainly the case on December 21, 1876, when Sheriff John Spear saw Clay and his brother John enter Las Animas, a cowtown in New Mexico Territory on the plains east of Pueblo. As the day went on, a worried Spear listened to the reports coming in that the Allison brothers were boozing it up heavily in the town's saloons. Clay Allison was capricious, a troublemaker under the best of circumstances. Drunk, he was a case of dynamite waiting to explode.

Spear summoned his deputy, Charles Faber, who also served as the constable of Las Animas. The sheriff explained that Clay

Allison was in town and getting liquored up. That was bad enough in any case, but on this night, a dance was scheduled that would bring even more people than usual into Las Animas. Cowboys, farmers, everyone from miles around would head for town to attend the dance. With that many people around, the chances that the Allisons would cause trouble increased that much more.

Faber must have been of two minds when he heard about this. On the one hand, he was a lawman, charged with protecting the public good. On the other hand, he was also ambitious and had a thirst for some fame and notoriety of his own. Clay Allison was widely thought of as the fastest man with a gun in the entire territory. He was, in fact, known to be one of the fastest on the draw in the whole of the West, rivaled by only a handful of shootists and gunfighters. If Faber could make him back down, or even better, kill him in a duel . . .

Visions of fame must have been dancing in Charles Faber's head on that fateful day.

Evening arrived, and the celebration got under way. The local dance hall was packed with merrymakers. Clay and John Allison, well and truly snockered already, sauntered in to join the festivities. Not surprisingly, it wasn't long before complaints began to be heard. The Allison brothers were loud, profane, and worst of all, clumsy, their cowboy boots coming down hard on the toes of some of their fellow dancers. Word was sent to the sheriff's office, and John Spear dispatched Charles Faber to see what could be done to stop the Allisons from disturbing the dance.

By this time, Clay was drunk enough so that he began to indulge in one of his favorite pastimes: taking his clothes off in public. Not his gunbelt, though. He hadn't shed that vital accessory when Deputy Faber walked into the dance hall. John Allison was still wearing his gun, too. As soon as Faber saw that the Allisons were packing iron, he knew he had his opening. He called out to them, causing the music to fall silent. The other people on the dance floor began to back away, clearing a space around the Allisons in case lead was about to fly.

Faber demanded that Clay and John surrender their guns. Legally, he was on solid ground with this ultimatum, because a town ordinance stated that weapons would be checked upon attending a dance. But instead of losing his temper, Clay Allison just laughed and suggested that Faber look around the room. He and John weren't the only ones wearing guns, Clay pointed out, and that was undoubtedly true. Many of the other men in the room also were armed. If Faber intended to take his and John's gun, Clay asked in mocking tones, was he going to disarm everyone else at the dance, too?

Now Faber realized his mistake. By pointing out the lawman's double standard, Clay hadn't necessarily won the sympathy of the crowd—they were still too frightened of him for that—but he had succeeded in making Faber look foolish. Seething with anger, Faber withdrew from the dance hall, stepping back out into the chilly December night.

He wasn't through with Clay Allison, though. No gunslinger was going to make a fool of him. Faber must have decided that he needed to be better armed before confronting Clay a second time. He fetched a shotgun from the sheriff's office and headed back toward the dance hall, followed by Sheriff Spear and several bystanders who were sworn in hurriedly as special deputies.

Carrying the scattergun, Faber burst through the doors of the hall. Somebody yelled a warning, and once again, innocent bystanders headed for cover, this time diving out of the way to get as far from the Allisons as they possibly could. Spotting an armed cowboy, Faber swung the shotgun toward him and fired one barrel as the cowboy turned around and reached for his gun. The charge of buckshot slammed into the chest and shoulder of the victim.

But Deputy Faber had made one crucial error: He had mis-

A young Clay Allison, c. 1866, already a
dangerous man with a gun. Mentally
unstable, perhaps because of a head
injury as a child, he could be honest and
friendly or violent and lethal, as the
mood struck him.

(Courtesy of Big Bend Quarterly)

taken John Allison for his even more deadly brother Clay, who
was standing some yards away.

Seeing his brother's bloody body fall to the floor, Clay
instantly threw off the effects of his day-long drinking bout and
reached for his gun with the blinding speed that had made him
feared all through the Texas–New Mexico border country. He
triggered four times in a matter of split seconds, and although
only one of his bullets struck Faber, that was enough. The slug
tore into the deputy's chest and dropped him dead on the floor of
the dance hall. Unfortunately for John Allison, in dying Faber
pulled the trigger of the Greener's other barrel, and that load of
buckshot tore into John's body as well.

Sheriff Spear and the special deputies watched all this in horror from the doorway, and as Clay Allison turned toward them,
smoke curling from the barrel of his revolver and hatred blazing

in his eyes, they decided on following the old saying about dis-
cretion being the better part of valor and ran like hell.

Convinced that his brother was dying, Clay holstered his gun
and rushed over to Faber's body. Stooping, he grabbed the dead
deputy by the hair and dragged him across the floor, leaving a trail
of blood behind him. Cold-blooded killer Clay Allison may have
been on other occasions, but this night tears ran down his cheeks
as he lifted Faber so that John could see him.

"John, this is the son of a bitch who shot you," Clay said. "I
got him, all right. Everything's going to be all right. Don't you
fret."

Despite those words of encouragement, Clay clearly thought
that his brother was on the verge of death. Still, he bound up the
wounds as best he could, and soon John was loaded on a wagon
that headed as fast as possible for Fort Lyon, where the nearest
sawbones could be found. Clay sat beside John for the whole trip,
and surprisingly, John was still alive when they reached the fort.
The wounds he had suffered were serious, of course, but perhaps
not fatal after all.

Since Clay Allison was actually a fairly law-abiding man when
he wasn't drinking, he returned to Las Animas to stand trial for
killing Deputy Charles Faber. John Allison remained behind to
recuperate from his wound. His testimony was not needed.
Plenty of people—everyone in the dance hall, in fact—had witnessed the events of that violent night. Clay Allison had made no
threat against Deputy Faber. In fact, it could be argued that for
once, Clay had tried to turn aside trouble by pointing out to
Faber that he and John weren't the only ones in the place who
were violating the ordinance against carrying guns at a public
dance. And everyone had seen as well the way Faber burst into
the dance hall and fired the shotgun without warning. The jury
wasted no time in concluding that Clay had been justified in firing to save his own life and to avenge what seemed to be the murder of his brother. Clay was found not guilty.

John Allison recovered from his wounds. Clay continued his life as a rancher, but his behavior became even more erratic and violent. After masterminding the lynching of several more men he blamed for the murder of a popular preacher, he was forced to leave New Mexico and returned to Texas, where he worked as a drover and eventually settled down near Pecos. He met an untimely end in 1887, but not in a blaze of gunfire, as might have been expected. While taking a load of grain back to his ranch, he fell off the wagon he was driving and broke his neck. He is buried in Pecos, Texas, just down the street from the famous Orient Saloon.

While boastfully proud of his record as a gunman, Clay Allison also claimed that he never killed a man who didn't need killing. On that night in Las Animas, he might well have been right.

WILD BILL'S TRAGIC MISTAKE

If ever a town was ripe for trouble, it was Abilene, Kansas, on the evening of October 5, 1871. Several factors had come together to create a tinderbox of a situation. Abilene, like many another Kansas cowtown, had a love-hate relationship with the rambunctious cowboys who brought herds of longhorn cattle up the long trail from Texas to the railhead. Abilene's citizens loved the money that the cattle industry pumped into their economy, but they hated the rowdy Texans who were ready to blow off weeks' worth of steam when they hit town with their herds. By October, though, the trail-drive season was over. The last of the herds had been brought in for this year. Some Texas cowboys were still in town, but they would soon be leaving, along with most of the gamblers, saloon-keepers, and soiled doves who descended annually on Abilene to harvest the wages paid to the cowboys. For the winter months, at least, Abilene would be peaceful again.

But before that could come about, the Texans and those who made their livings from them would have one final blowout, a last hurrah that would rattle Abilene's hinges. It didn't help matters that October 5 was also the date of the Dickinson County Fair, which brought all the farmers within a day's ride into town. It rained earlier in the day, which kept attendance down somewhat at the fair and kept the celebrating Texans off the street at least part of the time, but that was too little, too late to keep trouble from breaking out. By evening, Abilene was packed, and mobs howled their way up and down the streets. The celebrants may have intended to just have a good time and didn't mean any real harm, but with that many people around and with emotions so high, something was bound to happen.

Inside the Alamo Saloon, the town marshal of Abilene waited for the lid to come off. When it did, he would deal with it, whatever trouble might come. He was something of a dandy, a handsome man with shoulder-length blond hair and a full mustache. He wore a flat-brimmed, flat-crowned hat, a frock coat, a silk shirt with ruffles and frills on the bosom, an equally fancy vest, checked trousers, and high-topped black boots. A red sash was tied around his waist. He carried two Colt Navy revolvers tucked in that sash, butts forward. His name was James Butler Hickok.

But everybody just called him Wild Bill.

WILD Bill Hickok was a famous man even before he took the job of town marshal in Abilene the previous April. The phrase "legend in his own time" might as well have been invented for him. He didn't start out that way, of course. He was born in Illinois in 1837. His parents supported the abolitionist cause, and even used their house as a stop on the Underground Railroad, helping runaway slaves reach sanctuary in Canada. With this early background, it's no surprise that their son James was ardently pro-Union during the Civil War.

Those times were still ahead of James Butler Hickok, of course. Before that, he worked at the Rock Creek stagecoach station in Nebraska, which was on land purchased by the stagecoach company from a man named Dave McCanles. Some say that Hickok took the job at the stage station so that he would have something to do while he recovered from being mauled by a grizzly bear—which he in turn killed with only a knife. Maybe there was some truth to that story; with Hickok, it's hard to be sure. What is certain is that Hickok and McCanles clashed over the affections of a woman, and when it came to a fight, Hickok shot the older man dead.

Later, after enlisting in the Army, Hickok served as a scout, spy, and sharpshooter. Later, many accounts circulated of his daring exploits against the Confederates during this period of his life, but again, it's difficult to know which stories are true and which are fiction. Trouble cropped up soon after the war when Hickok killed another man, Dave Tutt, in a gun duel over yet another woman. He was developing a reputation as a gunman and shootist. That reputation exploded with the publication of the February 1867 issue of *Harper's New Monthly Magazine*, which featured a long article by Colonel George Ward Nichols entitled "Wild Bill."

Nichols's article was a wildly exaggerated version of what happened at Rock Creek Station between Hickok and McCanles. Instead of a fight over a woman, Nichols's version of the story has Hickok defending the station from a large gang of outlaws led by McCanles, and credits Hickok personally with killing ten of the desperadoes. Shortly after that, Hickok began to show up as the hero of a series of totally fictional dime novels published under the imprint "Dewitt's Ten-Cent Romances," with titles such as *Wild Bill, the Indian Slayer* and *Wild Bill's First Trail*. Some readers surely recognized these stories as fiction, but many people believed them to be the gospel truth, just as they swallowed the equally fictional dime novel adventures of one of Hickok's acquaintances, William F. "Buffalo Bill" Cody.

While his history was being inflated and sensationalized,

Hickok was adding to the real thing. He served as a scout for General George Armstrong Custer's Seventh Cavalry, and was known personally to both the general and Mrs. Custer and remembered fondly by them. Custer was later quoted as saying that Hickok was his favorite scout.

Hickok first wore a lawman's star as a deputy U.S. marshal, then was acting sheriff of Ellis County, Kansas, where the wild cowtown Hays City was located. While he was in Hays City, proddy cowboys drew on him on two separate occasions. Hickok killed both of them. Also in the line of duty as a lawman, he killed a drunken, troublemaking cavalry trooper from the Seventh Cavalry, earning him the enmity of Tom Custer, the brother of Hickok's former commanding officer.

Deeming it better to leave Hays City than to stay and fight the U.S. Cavalry, Hickok wound up in Abilene in the spring of 1871. He was hired to be the town's second marshal. The first, Thomas "Bear River Tom" Smith, had cleaned up the rugged cowtown using little more than his fists, and was regarded somewhat as the savior of Abilene. But Smith was dead, having been killed the previous autumn by an ax-wielding homesteader who turned violent when Smith tried to serve court papers on him. The city fathers of Abilene had searched all through the winter for a suitable replacement, and now with summer coming on and thousands of Texas cowboys trailing up through Indian Territory with their herds, they were convinced they had found the right man in the famous Wild Bill Hickok.

Hickok was always one to take advantage of his own legend when it suited his purposes. He settled into the job as Abilene's marshal, spending most of his time in the Alamo Saloon. He had several deputies to take care of any trouble, but there wasn't much, because three times a day, like clockwork, Wild Bill emerged from the Alamo and strolled up and down the length of the street, resplendent in his finery, the sun glinting off the ivory handles of the Colts tucked behind his red sash. Just the regular sight of the famous shootist was enough to make even wild and woolly Texas cowboys think twice about starting any trouble.

One of Abilene's attractions was the Novelty Theater, where traveling shows played to audiences of enthusiastic cowboys. The theater owners found themselves in need of someone to keep order and keep the cowboys from bothering the female members of the acting troupes. Hickok's influence swung the job to an old friend of his from Army days, Mike Williams.

Not all the Texans who came up the trail were afraid of Hickok. Ben Thompson, a well-known gambler and gunman, arrived in Abilene and opened a saloon in partnership with another Texan, Phil Coe. Thompson was reputed to be just as fast on the draw as Hickok, if not faster, and most people suspected that sooner or later there would be a showdown between the two men. Thompson was rather pragmatic about the whole thing, though, and reportedly tried to enlist a young Texas firebrand, John Wesley Hardin, to brace Wild Bill and kill him. Hardin wasn't interested. He didn't mind killing, but he didn't want to do it just as a favor to somebody else, not even a fellow Texan like Ben Thompson.

Actually, there was more bad blood between Hickok and Phil Coe than there was between Hickok and Thompson. The saloon established by Thompson and Coe was called the Bull's Head, and the sign above the entrance to the place featured a painting of a bull, a painting that was anatomically correct, though hugely exaggerated. Naturally, the good citizens of Abilene were offended by the sign and considered it obscene. Marshal Hickok was instructed to do something about it.

When Hickok asked Coe and Thompson to either take down the sign or have the offending part painted over, they refused. So Hickok fetched a double-barreled shotgun, bought a gallon of paint, and came back with a workman to take care of the chore. He stood by, cradling the scattergun in his arms, while the worker painted over the sign. The poor painter must have been rather nervous as he tried to work, never knowing from one second to the next if he was going to find himself in a crossfire between Hickok and the Texans.

But nothing happened except that a gallon of paint got slapped on the offending sign. Trouble had been headed off again . . . so to speak.

The anticipated duel between Hickok and Ben Thompson never took place. Toward the end of summer, Thompson left Abilene and went to Kansas City to meet his wife. They returned from there to Texas, but a buggy accident along the way left both of them seriously injured.

Meanwhile, back in Abilene, a circus owned by an attractive widow named Agnes Thatcher Lake had come to town, and Wild Bill and Agnes developed a romantic interest in each other right away. Agnes wanted him to travel with her as the star of her circus, and would have married him, but Hickok was having none of that. He had been involved briefly with one of Bill Cody's Wild West extravaganzas, and wanted nothing more to do with such foolery. He and Agnes parted, for the time being.

Hickok had always had a fondness for less respectable women, anyway. He dallied for a time with Mattie Silks, the madam of Abilene's leading house of ill repute, and actually taught her how to make a fast draw and shoot a gun. From Mattie he transferred his attentions to one of the girls who worked for her, Jessie Hazel. Hickok knew, of course, how Jessie earned her living, but he decided that except professionally, she was off-limits to other men. So it infuriated him when she took up with his old enemy, Phil Coe. Once again, Hickok was ready to kill over a woman, and when he burst in on Coe and Jessie as they shared a drink one afternoon, it might have come to that if not for one fact: Coe was unarmed. He had the odd habit, for a gambler, of seldom if ever carrying a gun.

Wild Bill Hickok was a lot of things, but a murderer wasn't one of them. He couldn't shoot Coe in cold blood, and Coe, big-

The flamboyant James Butler "Wild Bill" Hickok, lawman, gunfighter, and gambler, and one of the Old West figures who truly lived up to his reputation. Bad eyesight led to him killing one of his own deputies while he was serving as the marshal of Abilene, Kansas, in 1871. Bad judgment put him with his back to the door in Mann's No. 10 Saloon in Deadwood, Dakota Territory, in 1876, where he was killed by Jack McCall.

(Courtesy of Denver Public Library, Western History Collection)

ger and stronger than Hickok, threw him out. This humiliation fanned the flames of hatred between the two men even higher.

Then came that day early in October, the day when the remaining cowboys would cut loose and hoo-raw the town one last time before heading back to Texas. Phil Coe planned to go with them. The Bull's Head was closed down for the winter. Jessie Hazel had gone to St. Louis, where Coe promised to come for her the next spring before returning to Abilene. As the rainy day slid into evening, Coe and the other Texans roamed the streets, grabbing any respectable citizen unlucky enough to cross their path, hoisting the unfortunate onto their shoulders, and carrying him into the nearest saloon, where he would be forced to buy a round of drinks before the mob would let him go. No doubt this activity was frightening for the men who were caught that way, but the Texans considered it harmless fun. They even accosted Hickok at one point, but they stopped short of trying to physically grab him and lift him to their shoulders. Playing along momentarily, Hickok told them to go to one of the saloons and have a round of drinks on him. The bartender could put the bill on Hickok's tab.

That offer was enough to send the mob storming off to take advantage of it. Hickok walked across the street to the Novelty Theater to speak to Mike Williams. He told his old friend to be sure and stay on that side of the street during the evening, in case he was needed to quell any trouble over there. The marshal no longer had any deputies, the town council having relieved them of their duties several weeks earlier, thinking they were no longer needed. Hickok returned to the Alamo to wait out the tumultuous evening.

One thing he didn't know was that Phil Coe had broken with his personal tradition on this night. Coe was carrying a gun for a change.

Inside the Alamo, Hickok sat at a table with his back to the wall. That was *his* habit, and it was one he never broke. He squinted slightly as he looked around him and blinked his eyes against the haze of tobacco smoke floating in the air. The noise from outside increased as the mob of Texans approached again.

The crack of a shot made Hickok come smoothly to his feet. The sound had come from the boardwalk right outside the Alamo. Men got out of his way as he strode toward the door. He stepped outside and found Phil Coe standing on the boardwalk, some eight feet away. Smoke still curled from the barrel of the revolver in Coe's hand.

Although he already knew the answer, Hickok asked who had fired the shot. Coe laughed and said, "I shot at a stray dog."

Hickok knew there was no dog. Coe had fired the shot to draw him out of the Alamo. Now, surrounded by his friends, Coe was going to force the long-delayed showdown between him and Hickok. No fool, Hickok might have tried to retreat in the face of such overwhelming odds, but Coe didn't give him the chance.

The Texan whipped up his gun and fired twice. The first bullet tugged at Hickok's coat; the second went between his legs and smacked into the planks of the boardwalk behind him.

With the blinding speed that had kept him alive this long, Hickok palmed both of the Colt Navy revolvers from behind the sash around his waist. He fired, sending two slugs into Coe's belly. While the shots were still echoing, Hickok heard the slap of boot leather on the walk behind him. He spun around, saw a figure coming toward him at a run, saw the gun in the man's hand. He triggered both Colts again. The man rushing at him fell dead with two bullets in his head. Hickok menaced the crowd of Texans around him, challenging them to come and get the rest of his bullets if they wanted them.

Nobody took him up on this offer. Instead, the stunned cowboys backed off, and Hickok walked over to the second man he had shot.

Only then, in the light that spilled through the windows of the Alamo, did Wild Bill Hickok see that he had just gunned down his friend, Mike Williams.

Shocked to the depths of his soul, Hickok picked up the body and carried it into the Alamo. Tears shone in his eyes as he gently laid Williams on one of the saloon's pool tables. Then he pulled up a chair and sat down. Long minutes ticked by in silence as Hickok sat there next to the body of his friend.

Then, in the grip of a terrible rage, he stood up and stalked out of the Alamo. He spent the next hour going up and down Texas Street, bursting into the saloons where the cowboys had congregated. In the roaring voice of a mad old bull, Hickok bellowed for them to clear out of Abilene, pronto. A couple of men argued with him. He pistol-whipped them to their knees. Everyone watching knew it could have been worse. The offenders had gotten off lightly. Hickok could have just as easily shot them.

Abilene emptied of cowboys. They jumped on their horses and lit a shuck for their trail camps, outside of town. Hickok was only one man and there were dozens of the Texans, but on this night, numbers didn't matter. The lights went out in Abilene. Its season of hell-raising was over.

Phil Coe lingered for several days before dying from the belly wounds. He was taken back to Texas and buried there. Mike Williams had already been laid to rest in Abilene. As for Wild Bill Hickok, the town council dismissed him from the post of marshal on December 12, 1871. He had served approximately eight months in the job, and during that time, Phil Coe and Mike Williams were the only men he killed.

The death of Mike Williams was a tragic mistake on Hickok's part, no doubt about it. But under the circumstances, it was certainly understandable. Hickok would make one more tragic mistake in his life.

Going against his longtime habit, he sat with his back to the door in Carl Mann's No. 10 Saloon, in Deadwood, Dakota Territory, on August 2, 1876, and played a game of poker. The hand he was holding when he was shot in the back of the head by Jack McCall: a pair of aces, a pair of eights, and a queen.

Known forever after as the Dead Man's Hand.

ROURKE'S BAD LUCK ROBBERY

As usual, winter on the plains of Kansas was cold and icy in January of 1878. In Kinsley, a small settlement northeast of Dodge City, the citizens were probably just trying to keep warm as much of the time as possible and not really expecting trouble. But they got it anyway one evening, as half a dozen or so strangers galloped up to the Santa Fe depot with guns on their hips and larceny in their hearts.

The gang of would-be train robbers was led by Mike Rourke, a tough hombre who had ridden the owlhoot trail for quite a while. This would not be the first holdup Rourke had ramrodded. This time, though, the outcome was fated to be different. In fact, things had started to go wrong already for Rourke and his gang, which included another experienced desperado named Dave Rudebaugh.

The outlaws' original plan called for them to hold up the eastbound train when it stopped for water at a tank several miles west of Kinsley. They had been in place, ready to leap out of hiding and take over the train, but as the locomotive approached the water tank, the engineer never slowed down. The train barreled on through, heading toward Kinsley. Unknown to Rourke, Rudebaugh, and the other outlaws, the train had run low on water ahead of schedule and had stopped to take on more in Dodge City.

After staring for a moment in disbelief and confusion at the eastbound train as it dwindled in the distance, the outlaws flung themselves onto their horses and fogged after it, intending to catch up and carry out their robbery while the train was stopped at Kinsley. When they thundered up to the station in the small settlement, no train was in sight. Thinking that they had beaten it there, they rushed into the depot, guns drawn.

Only one man was present in the railroad station, a young telegraph operator named Andrew Kinkade. Since they had gotten there before the train, Rourke must have figured this was a chance to grab even more loot. He leveled his pistol at Kinkade and demanded all the money that was on hand at the depot. The cool-headed Kinkade opened the cash drawer in the desk to show the outlaws that it was empty.

With his frustration surely growing, Rourke asked about the safe. That was locked, Kinkade explained, and he could not open it. The only key was in the possession of the station agent, who was down at the hotel asleep.

The outlaws must have looked at each other, wondering what to do next. While they were doing so, the shrill sound of a train's whistle floated in from the chilly night outside. Rourke and his gang had been expecting that, knowing that the eastbound would announce its arrival with the whistle before pulling into the station.

There was only one problem. The sound of the whistle came from the east, not the west.

The approach of a train from that direction meant that the eastbound train, the one that had been the original target of the outlaws, had already gone through Kinsley after all. They had just thought they'd beat it to the station. Now a westbound was about to pull in.

And even worse, there were passengers who intended to board that westbound train, because at that moment two men walked up onto the platform. Kinkade spotted them through the window and, ignoring the menacing guns of the owlhoots, let out a yell of warning.

Not wanting the men to get away and spread the alarm, the members of the gang charged out of the station to take them prisoner. The commotion provided enough of a distraction for Kinkade to be able to jerk free of Rourke's grip. The young telegraph operator lunged through the door onto the platform.

By this time, the westbound train had almost reached the station. The rumble of the engine filled the air. No one expected what Andrew Kinkade did next. With the iron horse rolling into the station like some lumbering behemoth, Kinkade flung himself off the platform into the air, right in front of the train.

The daring maneuver paid off. Kinkade sailed all the way across the tracks and landed on the ground beyond them as the train just missed him. The massive locomotive now provided cover for Kinkade as he rolled over and sprang to his feet. He cupped his hands around his mouth and shouted up to the engineer in the cab that the station was being robbed. Frantically, he signaled for the engineer to keep the train moving. To Kinkade's delight, the locomotive continued to roll on down the tracks.

But the next moment, Rourke, Rudebaugh, and the other outlaws got their only lucky break of the whole affair. The engineer hadn't seen Kinkade's daring leap in front of the train or heard his warning after all. Instead, the train's brakes were malfunctioning. The engineer finally got them to work, bringing the westbound to a halt about a hundred yards past the depot.

Rourke and the other desperadoes dashed after it, running

awkwardly in their high-heeled horseman's boots. Rourke and another man were quick enough to reach the locomotive while the engineer still didn't know what was going on. Throwing down on him, they ordered him to get the train rolling again. Rourke wanted the train out of town so that it could be robbed at the gang's leisure, without having to worry about armed townspeople taking a hand.

The engineer must have gulped when he stared down the barrels of the outlaws' guns, but he was quick-witted enough to tell Rourke that he couldn't move the locomotive yet. He had released the pressure from the boiler when he was pulling into the station, he said, and not enough steam had built back up yet. As it turns out, this statement wasn't true, but it was plausible enough to convince Rourke.

Meanwhile, two more members of the gang ran along the train to the express car to make the express-company messenger open the safe for looting. By this time, however, the messenger had figured out that something was wrong, and when the outlaws slid open the door, a shotgun blast erupted from inside the car. The messenger hadn't waited, but had fired as soon as he saw men with guns outside the car.

The buckshot slammed into one of the would-be robbers and threw him backward onto the ground. The other man turned tail and ran rather than face such a fate.

Up in the cab, Rourke and his companion heard the roar of the Greener. No doubt biting back curses, they leaped down and hurried along the train toward the express car. As soon as the outlaws were gone, the engineer put the lie to his statement about the engine not having enough steam. He shoved the throttle ahead and the train began to move. It clattered away past the startled outlaws.

Rourke and his men knew it was time to cut their losses. They leaped on their horses, even the wounded man, and galloped away into the night, just as they had raced up to the station a short time earlier. Practically everything that could go wrong with this would-be robbery had gone wrong.

The gang's troubles weren't over. Even though the attempted holdup had been a failure, the express company wasn't in the mood to let it pass unchallenged. The company turned to the newly elected sheriff of Ford County and asked him to go after the outlaws. The young lawman was eager to do so.

His name was Bat Masterson.

A former buffalo hunter who had served as a deputy in Dodge City, Masterson had won the election for sheriff by only three votes. (For more on Bat Masterson, see "Bat Masterson and the Battle of the Plaza" elsewhere in this volume.) Knowing that if he captured Rourke's gang people would be more likely to forget about the narrowness of his election victory, Bat collected a posse of tough, seasoned frontiersmen, all of whom were friends of his. Accompanied by Kinch Riley, who had been with him at the Battle of Adobe Walls in the Texas Panhandle, Prairie Dog Dave Morrow, and John Joshua Webb, the new sheriff set out on the trail of Mike Rourke and the rest of the robbers.

There were other posses out searching for the outlaws, but Bat Masterson knew the ground in this area probably better than anyone else in Kansas, having hunted buffalo over every foot of it. Guided by his instincts, Bat led his posse to Crooked Creek. Snow began to fall as they rode, and grew heavier as they camped at the creek on their first night out from Dodge City.

The next day the snowstorm became even worse, turning into a veritable blizzard as the lawmen rode through it along Crooked Creek. An early dusk found them at the mouth of the creek, where a cattle camp belonging to rancher Harry Lovell was located. Bat and his companions spent the night in the camp's crude cabin.

The storm was so bad by now that traveling in it was well nigh impossible. Bat suspected that the outlaws were in the vicinity and would have to seek shelter from the blizzard. If they knew of the cattle camp, which seemed likely, there was a good chance they would head for it in order to get out of the storm.

The next day, Bat's hunch paid off as two riders approached the cabin. Watching them through the swirling snow, Bat recognized them as Dave Rudebaugh and Edgar West. Rudebaugh had been identified as one of the train robbers, and it seemed likely that West was part of the gang, too. J. J. Webb, who wasn't known to the two owlhoots, volunteered to go out and pretend to be a chuck-line rider so that the outlaws wouldn't suspect there were lawmen waiting inside the cabin.

This decoy maneuver worked flawlessly. Laughing and joking about the blizzard, Webb led Rudebaugh and West to the cabin and let them go in first. As they stepped inside, Bat Masterson moved out from behind the door and ordered them to elevate. Seeing the pair of six-shooters in Bat's hands, Edgar West decided the best thing to do was cooperate. He reached for the sky. Dave Rudebaugh, on the other hand, was in no mood to be taken without a fight. His hand moved toward the gun on his hip.

That was when Webb eared back the hammer of the gun he had quietly drawn as he entered the cabin. The unmistakable sound of a revolver being cocked right behind his head convinced Rudebaugh that there was no point in resisting. He raised his hands, too.

The other deputies moved in and disarmed the outlaws, then snapped handcuffs on them.

The party had to wait out the storm in the cabin, but the next day they were able to start back to Dodge City to deliver their prisoners. Once that was done, Bat Masterson took up the trail of the remaining outlaws, but by now they had too much of a head start. Bat and his men were unable to catch up to them.

A couple of months later, though, two of the outlaws slipped into Dodge. Bat had identified them by now, and had his deputies and other townspeople on the lookout for the fugitives. When he received a tip that the two men had been in town, Bat gathered a posse consisting of his brother Jim, J. J. Webb, and the former sheriff, now deputy, Charley Bassett, and went after them. The lawmen caught up to the owlhoots just outside of Dodge City and arrested them without any gunplay. One man reached for his gun, just as Dave Rudebaugh had, but when it snagged in his pocket and he found himself surrounded, he decided on the better part of valor, again just as Rudebaugh had.

Mike Rourke, the leader of the gang, was still at large, and Bat Masterson still wanted to bring him to justice. Once, Bat and a posse rode hard to Lovell's camp on Crooked Creek after hearing that Rourke was there, but they just missed him.

Rourke didn't elude the law forever. Less than a year later, another outlaw betrayed Rourke to the authorities. He was captured, put on trial for the attempted holdup at Kinsley, and following his conviction was sentenced to ten years in prison.

Bat Masterson had tracked down and arrested four of the outlaws without firing a shot, and the affair was considered a spectacular success for him, one of the first of many during his long career as a lawman. But it all started with a series of unforeseeable blunders and pure bad luck that dogged Mike Rourke and his ill-fated gang, on a cold winter night in Kansas.

WICHITA'S NEW YEAR'S DAY GUNFIGHT

Cold air fogged the breath in front of the man who walked along Douglas Avenue, Wichita's main thoroughfare, on the evening of January 1, 1877. He was small in stature, with brown hair, but he moved with a confident assurance and quiet dignity that belied his size, limping slightly from an old wound that hadn't healed quite right. A city marshal's badge was pinned to his coat. This was the time of day when he made his rounds, even on a holiday such as this one. The saloons in Wichita never closed, and trouble could break out any time of the day or night. In its early days as a wide-open cowtown, signs were posted on all the main roads leading into the settlement. Those signs proclaimed *EVERYTHING GOES IN WICHITA*. In the years since then, the community had quieted down a little, due in no small part to the efforts of the man who strolled down Douglas Avenue this evening. But he kept a watchful eye out, anyway.

The marshal walked past Hope's Saloon. Though all the windows and doors were closed against the chilly air, muffled sounds of music and laughter could be heard coming from inside the establishment. Since everything seemed to be normal, the marshal turned down the alley beside Hope's and walked along it to the rear of the saloon. There was an outhouse back here, and the marshal figured it was as good a time as any to take care of some unofficial business.

He had just sat down when gunshots roared out, shattering the quiet of the peaceful night, and bullets began to slam through the outhouse door.

Only in Wichita. Everything went in Wichita. . . .

———◆———

IN 1871, entrepreneurs Bill Greiffenstein and Jim Meade founded Wichita for the express purpose of taking the cattle shipping trade away from Newton, where the railhead of the Atchison, Topeka & Santa Fe Railroad was located. For the past year, the trail herds that came up from Texas through Indian Territory had been heading for Newton. "Bloody Newton" it was sometimes called because of all the violence that took place there between the citizens and the drovers from Texas. Now, with the construction of the Wichita & Southwestern Railroad from Newton to the new townsite of Wichita, the herds would have a shorter distance to travel before they could be loaded on the cars that would carry them to the slaughterhouses in Chicago. The Wichita & Southwestern was an adjunct to the Santa Fe and had backers in common. In order to get Newton to agree to help fund the new line, a deal had been struck with the railroad executives and the county commissioners. Sedgwick County, which contained both Newton and Wichita, would be split in two. The northern part would become Hardy County, and Newton would be the county seat. Wichita would be the new county seat of Sedgwick County. Everyone hoped that the arrangement would prove to be lucrative for all involved.

In actuality, Wichita got the better end of the deal. The town grew by leaps and bounds, becoming not only the cattle shipping center of Kansas, but also the hub of the state's burgeoning wheat industry. With everything that was going on and with so many wild Texas cowboys pouring into town, the city fathers soon realized there was a need for at least a little law and order, despite Wichita's reputation as a wide-open town.

They turned to a man named Mike Meagher, and over the next five years, off and on, Meagher gave them more law and order than they had ever bargained for.

Born in County Cavan, Ireland, in 1843, Mike Meagher was the very opposite of the brawling, fiery-tempered Irishman so popular in myth, at least on the surface. Small and quiet-natured, Meagher possessed courage and an iron will, as well as a determination to step aside for no man. How he wound up in Kansas is unknown, but considering the great famines that swept Ireland in the 1840s, it seems a reasonable assumption that his family emigrated to the United States to escape the harsh conditions in their homeland. Meagher's brother John, sometimes assumed to be his twin because of the strong resemblance between them but actually two years younger, came to Kansas with him.

The city commissioners appointed Mike Meagher the marshal of Wichita in 1871, when the town was just getting a good foothold. His brother John served as his chief deputy. The next year, the position was made an elective one, and Meagher campaigned for the job. In the year since his appointment, however, the commissioners had turned on him to a certain extent because, in their eyes, he was doing his job too well. Enforcing the city ordinances, cracking down on gambling and graft, forcing the Texas cowboys to comply with the law that forbade them to carry guns . . . all these and similar things worried the men who ran Wichita. With such a hard-nosed lawman cracking down on things, the city's prosperity was threatened. Wichita had to remain wild and woolly in order to thrive. The city commissioners put up their own candidate for marshal who would obey their edicts and loosen up on the reins.

The citizens were having no part of that. Mike Meagher won

the first ever election for the job of city marshal in Wichita, Kansas.

The next year, Meagher lost the services of his brother as chief deputy when John was elected sheriff of Sedgwick County. The two lawmen still worked closely together, though, sometimes even riding together as they pursued outlaws. One particular gang of horse thieves led by a Texan named Bill Talbot was running roughshod over the county. The badge-toting Meagher brothers closed in on the gang one evening as they caroused in Rowdy Joe Lowe's saloon in Delano, a red-light district just outside the city limits of Wichita. The horse thieves put up a fight, but when Bill Talbot was fatally wounded by Mike Meagher, the rest of the bandits gave up. Talbot was the half brother of an even more notorious Texas badman, Jim Sherman, but Meagher was not the sort to worry about possible retribution or anything like that. He went ahead and did his job as he saw fit.

City marshals in Wichita served a term of one year. Mike Meagher was re-elected in 1873, but in 1874, with another candidate handpicked by the city commissioners running against him, he lost by a slight margin. Bill Smith took his place as Wichita's marshal. At the same time, former mayor Jim Hope, a wholesale liquor dealer and owner of one of Wichita's most prosperous saloons, was voted back into office. With Hope and Smith running things, the prospects looked rosy for their cronies on the city commission.

But once again, the plans of the commission backfired on them. Over the past three years with Mike Meagher enforcing the law, the city coffers had come to depend on the money that Meagher's arrests generated in convictions and fines. Of course, that was less than the city made from the cowboys, but it was a significant shortfall in the city's finances nonetheless. Bill Smith turned a blind eye to most violations of the city ordinances and seldom arrested anyone. No doubt he thought this was exactly what his bosses, both official and unofficial, wanted him to do.

Meanwhile, Mike Meagher had found work as a deputy United States marshal. His reputation as a solid, no-nonsense lawman worked in his favor in that job.

Mayor Hope tried to get rid of Marshal Smith in June of 1874, but the city commission overruled him. Smith was kept on, but the commission increased the licensing fees due from every business in the city as a way of making up some of the lost revenue. It was the city marshal's job to collect such fees. Smith asked the commission for more help, and as a result several more officers were hired and sworn in. One of them was a young man named Wyatt Earp. This job as a city policeman was the first in which Earp wore the badge of a lawman. Not the last, of course.

Even with the extra help, Smith did a poor job of enforcing the law in Wichita. A group of citizens formed a vigilance committee, and it was more successful at running outlaws and troublemakers out of town than Smith ever had been. When the time for an election came up again in 1875, Marsh Murdock, the editor of one of the local newspapers, the *Wichita Eagle*, convinced Mike Meagher to run against Smith again. Despite everything that had happened, the city commission backed Smith yet again, but his ineffectiveness and the way he had been made to look ridiculous in the eyes of the citizens were enough to turn the tide. Once more, the election was close, but this time Meagher came out on the winning end.

He gave up his job as a federal deputy and moved back into the city marshal's office. He fired several of the deputies and policemen who had worked for Smith, but not Wyatt Earp. As a matter of fact, Meagher suspected that Earp had been skimming money from the license fees and fines he was collecting in his official capacity, and planned to investigate that possibility. Before that could happen, Earp resigned and left Wichita, heading farther west to Dodge City, which was now the same sort of booming, dangerous place Wichita had been in its early days.

With Mike Meagher back in office and much of the cattle-shipping business having moved, Wichita settled down some over the next few years. It continued to be the center of the wheat-growing industry, with silos and granaries dotting the landscape around it. The relative peace was broken from time to time, however, and Meagher, who continued to win re-election each year, was there to handle trouble. At one point, still casting about for some way of making extra money, the city commission decided to increase the fines levied against Wichita's prostitutes if they were caught plying their trade on the street. This move angered the calico cats and their pimps, and even though Meagher had nothing to do with the ordinance other than enforcing it, much of the anger was directed at him.

One evening, as he walked through a beer garden operated by a German immigrant, Emil Warner, he encountered one of the pimps, a man named Jim Fisher. When Fisher saw Meagher, he leaped to his feet from the table where he had been sitting and started cursing the marshal. Fisher had guzzled down a considerable amount of Warner's suds during the evening, and Meagher no doubt saw that the pimp was drunk. He ignored Fisher and walked on, dignified as always, certainly not a man who would stoop to trading obscene insults with a whoremonger.

This was a rare occasion when Meagher made a mistake. Overcome by fury, Fisher jerked out a revolver and threw a bullet after Meagher. The slug caught the marshal in the hip, wounding him and spinning him around, but not knocking him off his feet. With his usual coolheadedness, Meagher drew his own gun and fired, ventilating Fisher. The pimp crashed to the floor, dead, one of only three men Mike Meagher killed during his career as a lawman.

The hip wound healed, but left Meagher with a limp. That didn't keep him from doing his job as marshal. As 1876 drew to a close, Wichita was a peaceful place for the most part.

But then, on the morning of January 1, 1877, a stagecoach driver with a history of troublemaking named Sylvester Powell stole a horse from one of the town's hitch rails.

Powell didn't even do a particularly good job of horse thievery. The animal's owner saw Powell taking the horse. When he hurried to confront the stage driver, Powell pulled a gun and brandished it at the man, warning him to get back and leave him alone. Unwilling to get shot over a horse, the man backed off—and went running to the law instead.

As always, Meagher didn't hesitate to do what was required of him. He went out and confronted Powell, who had the evidence of his crime with him. Meagher arrested him and marched him off to jail, intending to let him sit there until he came to trial. With that bit of business behind him, Meagher went on about his duties.

Unknown to him, as he was making his rounds that evening, the owner of the stage line that employed Powell showed up at the jail. The businessman had posted bail for Powell and demanded that he be released. Faced with official paperwork signed by a local judge, the jailer had no choice but to comply.

The motives of the stage line owner in bailing out Powell are unknown. Maybe he was just doing a favor for an employee. Perhaps he was trying to stir up trouble, since some of the businessmen in Wichita resented Meagher for his rigorous enforcement of the law. Regardless of why the man acted as he did, the results of his actions are well documented. Powell went from the hoosegow to one of Wichita's saloons and started varnishing his tonsils with bottled courage. When he was sufficiently liquored up, he went looking for Marshal Mike Meagher.

Powell must have seen Meagher walking down the street, and followed him through the alley beside Hope's Saloon. Otherwise he would not have known that the lawman was in the outhouse behind the saloon. As Powell approached, he drew his gun and started blasting away at the door of the outhouse, shooting through it.

After firing several times, Powell was sure he must have hit Meagher. Keeping the revolver trained on the outhouse door, he walked toward the little structure slowly and carefully. He was almost there when the door suddenly slammed open and Mike Meagher lunged out at him.

Meagher was hit, all right. One of Powell's slugs had bored through the muscles of his leg but missed the bone, so he was able to overcome the pain and burst out of the outhouse to confront his attacker. The shock of seeing Meagher coming at him made Powell's finger clench involuntarily on the trigger. His gun exploded again, and this time the bullet went through Meagher's hand. Not his gun hand, though, to Powell's misfortune.

Meagher snapped a shot at the bushwhacker, missing with it. Powell turned and ran. The injured marshal could only hobble after him, hindered now not only by his old limp, but by the new leg wound as well. Powell ran back up the alley and turned down Douglas Avenue. No doubt the courage given to him by the whiskey he'd consumed had evaporated by now. He probably wished he had never gone after Meagher, and could only hope that the marshal was too badly hurt to catch up to him. As he passed Hill's Drug Store, Powell slowed to a walk. People were on the street, despite the fact that it was a holiday, and maybe Powell didn't want to call any more attention to himself.

That was when, from behind him, Meagher called his name.

Powell turned and started to lift his gun. Meagher had drawn a bead on him already, and pressed the trigger before Powell had the chance to get off another shot. The bullet drilled Powell through the heart, killing him instantly. He slumped to the ground.

Mike Meagher limped toward the man he had just killed. Blood welled from the wounds in his leg and hand. What would come to be known as the New Year's Day Gunfight was over.

———◆◆———

MEAGHER recovered from his wounds, but his days as a lawman were drawing to a close. He and his wife left Wichita and moved to Caldwell, Kansas, where he ran a saloon and ultimately was elected mayor. It was while he was serving in that position that fate caught up to him, in the person of an outlaw with a grudge against him.

Jim Sherman, also known as Jim Talbot, was the half brother of the horse thief Bill Talbot, whom Meagher had killed years earlier. Sherman had waited all this time for a chance to wreak his vengeance and settle the score for his half brother. On December 17, 1881, Sherman and half-a-dozen outlaw cronies rode into Caldwell and starting shooting up the main street. Their purpose was to draw out Meagher. Sherman figured that the former marshal would rush out to help quell the disturbance. He was right. Hearing the shots, Meagher hurried out of his saloon, intending to go to the aid of Caldwell's marshal. Instead he ran into a rifle bullet that cut him down. He died on the boardwalk in front of Caldwell's Opera House, a victim of Jim Sherman's thirst for revenge.

Sherman and the rest of the gang blasted their way out of town, losing only one man in the process. Sometime later, Sherman was arrested and brought back to Caldwell to stand trial for the slaying of Mike Meagher. Most of the witnesses had died or moved on in the meantime, however, and Sherman was acquitted. He moved to California and lived there until 1926, when he was killed under mysterious circumstances. Some old-timers theorized that John Meagher, Mike's brother, had waited a long time to take some vengeance of his own, but the truth was never known.

Though a better lawman than many better-known figures from the Old West, Mike Meagher's chief claim to fame is still the New Year's Day Gunfight, a good example of what a wild place Wichita was in its heyday, when a man couldn't even visit the outhouse in peace.

5

MILLER AND FRAZER, FIGHTING AGAIN

oyah, Texas, wasn't much of a settlement in the 1890s, not much more than a wide place in the trail, really. But this rangeland community approximately twenty miles southwest of Pecos boasted several saloons, and to the thirsty cowboys who worked on the ranches in the area, that was all that mattered. Toyah was a favorite watering hole of the punchers, so naturally gamblers, soiled doves, and all the other typical denizens of the Old West congregated there, too.

On a September day in 1896, a tall, lean man in a black hat and black frock coat walked along the street in Toyah toward one of the saloons. He had a shotgun tucked under his arm, but other than the weapon, he had a mild appearance and might almost have been taken for a minister. In fact, some people knew him as Deacon Jim, not because he was actually a deacon, but because of the way he looked and because he had a habit of attending church services.

He was not on his way to church today.

Moving purposefully, he went to the entrance of one of the

saloons and lifted the shotgun. The saloon had the usual batwing doors. Deacon Jim thrust the twin barrels of the shotgun over the batwings and peered inside, probably squinting a little as his eyes adjusted to the relative dimness inside the saloon. He spotted his quarry sitting at a table, a hand of cards laid out on the felt in front of him.

Deacon Jim didn't hesitate. He pressed both triggers of the shotgun. The weapon roared deafeningly as it recoiled against the shoulder of the man who wielded it.

This time, the fight was going to have a different outcome.

————◆◆◆————

THE trouble all started in Pecos, the county seat of Reeves County, which had been founded in 1881 when the tracks of the Texas & Pacific Railroad reached the area. Within a few years Pecos had gone from a single-tank water stop to a bustling community that served as the supply point for ranches all across vast, sprawling West Texas. With the growth of Pecos came the need for law and order. Bud Frazer was one of the first sheriffs to serve in Reeves County. He was a tough man who brooked no nonsense and enforced the law competently.

Reeves County was huge, though (and still is), and no one man could cover all of it, so Frazer hired several deputies to assist him. One of them who signed on with the sheriff's office in 1891 was a man from Arkansas named Jim Miller.

Miller was born in Van Buren, Arkansas, not far from the Ozark Mountains, in 1861. He was a quiet, unassuming young man who spoke little of his past, and for good reason. His peaceful exterior concealed a man who, in modern-day terms, would be called a sociopath, a man without feelings who could kill in the blink of an eye and never feel any remorse. Westerners who came to know him well enough to see past his pious facade said he was just no good, a pure hydrophobic skunk. But you would never know it to look at him. He dressed well, in a sober black hat and

A saloon in Pecos, Texas, was the scene of this faro game in the 1880s, in which the
notorious man-killer Deacon Jim Miller takes part. Miller, wearing a white hat, is
seated at the table in an unusual pose for a gunman: He doesn't have his back against
the wall.

(Courtesy of Denver Public Library, Western History Collection)

a black frock coat that was buttoned up nearly to his chin no matter what the season, even in the blazing heat of a Texas summer.

Later, it was said by some that Miller had murdered his own
grandparents when he was only eight years old. His first documented killing was that of his brother-in-law when Miller was
twenty-two. Already, Miller's weapon of choice was a shotgun.
He was put on trial in Arkansas for blasting his brother-in-law into
eternity and found guilty, but the conviction was overturned by
an appeals court and Miller moved on to Texas before the prosecution could make up its mind whether or not to try the case
again. When he reached Pecos, he found Sheriff Bud Frazer in
need of deputies and applied for one of the jobs. Frazer, who
probably wished later that he had done some checking into
Miller's background, swore him in and gave him a badge.

Most folks in Pecos liked Jim Miller at first. He was polite, soft-spoken, didn't booze it up in the saloons or dip snuff. He attended church faithfully and seemed to love belting out the hymns with the rest of the congregation. Handsome in a way, with dark hair and sweeping mustaches, he must have been looked on with favor by some of the mothers in town with spinster daughters.

It was a young woman named Sallie Clements who caught Miller's attention, though. He married her and started up a ranch while continuing to serve as a deputy sheriff. It was about this time that people began to wonder about Miller. No one could quite figure out where the money and the livestock he used to establish his ranch had come from. But some of the cattlemen in the area had been hit recently by rustlers, and suspicion soon fell on Miller and his new wife's family, most of whom were gunquick and had dubious reputations.

The question of whether or not Miller had turned cattle thief has never been settled. The Clements family, despite their failings, seem to have been honest and probably came in for an undue share of the blame. But the suspicion surrounding Miller served to drive a wedge into Pecos's population. Some of the citizens still believed in and supported Miller; others were of the opinion that no matter how civilized he seemed to be, he was nothing but a crook.

No matter what Sheriff Bud Frazer thought about it, he had to look into the situation. Miller was one of his deputies, after all, and he couldn't allow that cloud of suspicion to hang over Miller's head. Frazer's investigation satisfied him that Miller was not involved with the rustling in the area, but the damage had already been done. Miller resented Frazer's actions, and Frazer didn't like the way Miller had made the sheriff's office look bad.

Still, when Frazer had to leave Pecos for a while on business, he put Miller in charge. That proved to be another mistake.

Miller looked the other way whenever there was any lawbreaking. That was just about the end of any sympathy Miller had from the townspeople.

Rumors began to be whispered around Pecos that Miller was plotting to have Frazer killed when the sheriff returned. Friends of Frazer got the word to him in El Paso and warned him of the scheme. Miller's plan called for two of his outlaw friends to be on the platform at the Texas & Pacific station when the train carrying Frazer pulled in. The gunmen would pretend to have an argument and start blasting away at each other, missing their shots, of course . . . except for a "stray" bullet that would fell Frazer, so that his murder would look like an accident.

The plan might have worked if Frazer had not been warned. But when the train hissed to a stop in Pecos, Frazer wasn't alone when he stepped onto the platform. He had two tough-looking hombres with him, one of whom was the well-known Texas Ranger Captain John Hughes. Miller's henchmen took one look at the setup and decided that they wanted no part of it. They sidled away while Frazer spotted Miller, strode over to him, and placed him under arrest on a charge of conspiracy to commit murder.

No one was willing to testify against Miller, and the rumors that had gone around about his plan weren't sufficient evidence to convict him. He was acquitted at a trial in El Paso and returned to Pecos, no longer a deputy sheriff, of course, but still a thorn in Bud Frazer's side.

Miller bought a hotel in Pecos and seemed to be living the life of an honest citizen. Frazer didn't believe that for a second. He had a grudge against Miller that wouldn't go away, and it was made worse by the fact that some of the townspeople talked behind his back about the whole affair. The feeling in Pecos was that Miller had put one over on Frazer by being found not guilty at the trial. Frazer's resentment and anger toward Miller grew so strong that he couldn't stand it anymore. Despite having no legal justification for doing so, Frazer took his gun and went looking for Miller.

They met on the street, and with no warning, Frazer opened fire. His first shot hit Miller in the chest, but somehow, it seemed to have no effect. Frazer fired again, drilling Miller's right arm. That was Miller's gun arm, so to defend himself, he had to reach awkwardly across his body and draw his gun with his left hand. Unlike some gunmen who were equally deadly with either hand, Miller wasn't very good with his left. His first shot plowed up the dirt of the street at Frazer's feet. He squeezed off another, and it went wide of the mark and winged Joe Kraus, a local storekeeper who had the bad luck to be in the wrong place at the wrong time.

While Miller was throwing lead around wildly, Frazer continued to fire. His slugs smacked into the breast of Miller's frock coat, but did no damage. Frazer's final shot tore into Miller's abdomen and doubled him over, dropping him in the street. A shaken Frazer holstered his gun and walked away, thinking that the fight was over.

In a way it was, because Miller was out of action on this day, but in a way it was just beginning. . . .

Bystanders picked up Miller's crumpled, bloody form and carried him inside the lobby of his hotel. A local doctor was summoned, and when the sawbones peeled back the lapels of the frock coat to get at Miller's wounds, the men surrounding him frowned in surprise at what was revealed. They knew now why Miller had always worn that coat, no matter what the weather.

An iron breastplate was inside it. That was why Frazer's shots had bounced harmlessly off Miller's chest.

Though the wound to Miller's belly was a serious one, he survived and began a slow recuperation. While he was recovering from the injury, the election for sheriff came up. The whole debacle with Miller had made Frazer look bad, and the fact that he had opened fire on Miller without warning couldn't have helped his cause, either. Frazer lost the election and left Pecos, moving to New Mexico. Miller got some satisfaction out of that, telling his friends that he had run Frazer out of town. One of these days, Miller declared, he would settle the score between him and Frazer once and for all.

Months passed. Miller was back on his feet and still living in Pecos when Frazer rode into town on the day after Christmas in 1894. Frazer still had business interests in Pecos and had returned to look after them. He had been in touch with friends who had told him of Miller's boasts, and Frazer had no doubt that Miller would try to kill him if they ran into each other. So, when Frazer spotted Miller as he was walking along the street, he acted first, just as he had on the previous occasion. He hauled his six-shooter from its holster and commenced shooting.

In an odd coincidence, Frazer's first bullet ripped through Miller's right arm. Miller had to use his left hand to draw his gun and return Frazer's fire. He was no more ambidextrous now than he had been six months earlier, and once again his bullets flew wildly around the street, missing their target by a considerable margin. Frazer shot Miller in the leg, but failed to knock him off his feet. Then Frazer closed in, ready to finish the fight and end the feud between him and Miller at last. He fired three shots—

Right at Miller's chest.

Incredibly, no one had ever told Frazer the reason Miller survived their first shoot-out. Frazer's eyes must have widened in horror and surprise when the three shots to Miller's chest had no effect. It was as if Miller were invulnerable to Frazer's bullets. The former sheriff backed away, gaping, then turned and ran. Miller, unable to shoot accurately with his left hand and hurting from the two wounds he had sustained, let his enemy go.

Now it was Miller's turn to bring in the law. Plenty of witnesses had seen Frazer fire the first shot, so Miller brought charges against Frazer, who had to stand trial in El Paso for the attempted murder. Despite the evidence, the jury was unable to reach a verdict, so the case had to be retried. It was moved to Colorado City, and the jury there found Frazer not guilty. Miller's reputation must have hurt his case, because the facts of the incident seemed to be on his side.

The hostilities continued to simmer as Miller recovered from these latest wounds. Frazer drifted around West Texas and New Mexico. His once-promising career as a lawman was over, and he probably blamed Jim Miller because his life was in a shambles. He took to drinking and gambling, and it was a common occurrence to find him in a saloon.

It was in a saloon in the small town of Toyah that Miller found him on September 13, 1896. There's no way of knowing whether Miller had been looking for Frazer, or simply happened to be in Toyah and saw Frazer go into the saloon. Whatever the case may be, Miller seized this opportunity. He carried his shotgun down the street and stopped in the saloon's doorway, aiming over the batwings. Twice before, Frazer had opened fire on Miller without warning. Now Miller returned the favor, blasting the double load of buckshot into Frazer, blowing him backward out of his chair and scattering the cards on the table. Frazer had no hidden armor to protect him. He hit the floor as dead as could be.

Deacon Jim Miller turned and walked away.

Later, he was arrested and tried for killing Bud Frazer. The trial took place in Eastland, Texas, and in another of the strange similarities about the blood feud between these two men, the first jury was unable to reach a verdict, just as the jury had been in Frazer's trial for attempted murder. And yet again, a second trial produced the same result: Miller was acquitted just as Frazer had been.

Jim Miller went on to a long career as a bushwhacker and hired killer, and was considered one of the most cold-blooded killers in the West. He was even suspected by some of having been hired to murder Pat Garrett, the New Mexico lawman who killed Billy the Kid. No doubt Miller was every bit as deadly as his reputation.

But his luck ran out when he was hired to ambush and kill a man in Oklahoma Territory in 1909. He carried out the murder, but the men who hired him were caught by the authorities. They put the law on Miller's trail, and he was arrested soon after in Fort Worth. He was taken to Oklahoma to stand trial, but didn't seem overly concerned about the outcome. He probably felt that there was no reason to worry. He had been tried for murder before and had always walked out of the courtroom a free man.

The only problem was that this time the case never came to trial. A mob stormed the jail where Miller and the men who had hired him were being held. They took the four prisoners out of their cells and dragged them into a nearby barn. Ropes were thrown over the rafters and nooses placed around the necks of the four men. One by one, with Miller saved for last, they were hauled off their feet and strangled.

Not even a whole suit of armor would have saved Deacon Jim Miller from that fate.

BULLET TO BULLET

I t's difficult to pin down when the Old West truly ended. Many consider the beginning of the twentieth century to be the finale of the Old West, but many famous robberies and shoot-outs occurred after this. Even after the first decade of the twentieth century, in many places in the West the only reliable transportation was still four-footed, and men still had to go armed in case of trouble because the nearest law could be half a day's ride away—or more.

Still, by all reasonable expectations, by 1917 the area around the city of Wharton in southeast Texas could have been considered civilized. The Old West, the Wild West, should have been long gone by then.

Just goes to show how appearances can be deceiving and assumptions are not always met.

Named after the Wharton brothers, who fought in the Texas Revolution, the town served as the seat of Wharton County and the headquarters for the cattle industry in the area, which had been built up after the Civil War largely by legendary cattleman

Abel Head "Shanghai" Pierce. Not long after the turn of the century, sulfur deposits were discovered in the eastern part of the county, and this caused it to grow and become even more prosperous.

Naturally the town needed a marshal. In 1917, that post was filled by W. W. Pitman. Unassuming and small in stature, Pitman preferred to head off trouble rather than letting it get ahead of him, but he had plenty of nerve, as he proved on the night of September 15.

Francisco Lopez was an unsavory character who had a bad reputation around Wharton. Suspected of several robberies, he also liked to drink, and when he had poured too much tequila down his throat he had a habit of turning violent. On this night he went on a real bender and proceeded to roam around town taking random potshots at anything that moved. The townspeople scurried for cover as the bullets flew. Glass crashed as Lopez shot out windows in buildings and the windshields of flivvers parked along the street. No one had been hurt yet, but it was only a matter of time before that happened . . . unless someone could put a stop to Lopez's rampage.

As town marshal, that job fell to W. W. Pitman.

This close to the Gulf Coast, even in late summer the night air was probably hot and muggy. Sweat may well have popped out on Pitman's forehead as he walked down the street looking for Lopez. Chances are he was able to follow the commotion until he found the troublemaker. A crowd formed and began to trail after Pitman, eager to witness the confrontation between the marshal and the badman who seemed to fancy himself a throwback to the wilder and woollier days of the Old West.

Pitman likely cast worried glances over his shoulder at the bystanders. These were the citizens of his town, the people whose protection he was charged with. He didn't want any of them getting hurt, but that was exactly what was liable to happen if Lopez resisted arrest. Of course, Pitman couldn't allow him to continue shooting up the town, either. That was bound to lead to injury for some innocent person, too.

Pitman spotted Lopez in Wharton's main street. Even though the suspected outlaw and gunman had been drinking, he seemed steady on his feet. At the moment, his pistol was holstered on his hip, but he might slap leather and start blazing away again at any moment, without warning. Still, Pitman saw this as his chance, an opportunity to take Lopez into custody without any gunplay or anyone getting hurt.

With the same cool, collected demeanor he always displayed, Pitman walked up to Lopez and greeted him. Then he said that he was placing Lopez under arrest for disturbing the peace and asked him to come along quietly. Lopez was in no mood to honor that request. With a mocking laugh, he stepped back and reached for his gun.

Lopez was considerably faster on the draw than Pitman. The badman's gun came up while the marshal was still pulling his weapon from its holster. Colt flame bloomed in the night as Lopez triggered once, then again. The very thing Pitman had worried about was coming true. The slugs sang past his head, flying on by to menace the crowd of onlookers. Pitman had to end this, end it in a hurry.

He brought his gun up and fired just as Lopez pulled the trigger for the third time.

Witnesses said the two shots sounded so close together there was no way to tell them apart. The next instant Lopez let out a yell of pain as his revolver went spinning out of his hand. It fell at his feet, and as Lopez stared down at the weapon in amazement, Pitman moved in and took him into custody, handcuffing him and leading him away to the jail.

It was only later, when Pitman came back for Lopez's gun, that he discovered what had really happened. Shooting the gun out of his opponent's hand would have been rare enough, a virtual miracle shot. What had happened in Wharton on this night went beyond even that. Pitman's shot hadn't hit Lopez in the hand; except for some stinging in his fingers, the gunman was unharmed. Nor had the lawman's slug smashed the cylinder or the grip of Lopez's gun.

It had gone down the barrel instead.

What's more, the physical evidence showed that Pitman's first shot had beaten Lopez's third one. The two bullets had impacted just as the one fired from Lopez's gun left the cylinder and entered the barrel. The weapon was deformed, the barrel bulging out where the bullets had struck each other and mushroomed. Though it came at the very tail end of the Old West era, Pitman's shot was perhaps the most amazing ever made in any gunfight.

Of course, considerable luck was involved, too, but that luck never would have had the chance to come into play if not for the cool nerves and steady hand of Marshal W. W. Pitman, the lawman who proved that for one night, at least, the Old West still lived in Wharton, Texas.

BIBLIOGRAPHY

LUKE SHORT'S WHITE ELEPHANT SHOOT-OUT

Cox, William R. "Luke Short." *True West*, September/October 1961

Cunningham, Eugene. "Courtright the Longhaired." *True West*, June 1957

Fairly, Bill. "Tales from Where the West Begins: Feud Reached Climax in 1887." *Fort Worth Star-Telegram*, Nov. 13, 1996

Pirtle, Caleb. *Fort Worth: The Civilized West.* Tulsa: Continental Heritage Press, Inc., 1980

Rosa, Joseph G. *Age of the Gunfighter.* Norman: University of Oklahoma Press, 1995

Selcer, Richard F. *Hell's Half Acre.* Fort Worth: Texas Christian University Press, 1991

Trachtman, Paul. *The Gunfighters.* Alexandria: Time-Life Books, 1974

END OF AN EARP

Drago, Harry Sinclair. *The Legend Makers.* New York: Dodd, Mead, 1975

Horan, James D. *The Authentic Wild West: The Lawmen.* New York. Crown Publishers, 1980

Murray, Virgil. "Warren Baxter Earp." *Wild West*, August 1998

Rabinowitz, Harold. *Black Hats and White Hats: Heroes and Villains of the West.* New York: Metro Books, 1996

Tefertiller, Casey. *Wyatt Earp: The Life Behind the Legend*. New York: John Wiley & Sons, 1997

Trachtman, Paul. *The Gunfighters*. Alexandria: Time-Life Books, 1974

Turner, Alford E., ed. *The Earps Talk*. College Station: Creative Publishing Company, 1980

Waters, Frank. *The Earp Brothers of Tombstone*. Lincoln: University of Nebraska Press, 1976

DOC'S LAST GUNFIGHT

Horan, James D. *The Authentic Wild West: The Lawmen*. New York: Crown Publishers, 1980

Johnson, Dorothy M. *Western Badmen*. New York: Dodd, Mead, 1970

Metz, Leon Claire. *The Shooters*. New York: Berkley Books, 1996

Rabinowitz, Harold. *Black Hats and White Hats: Heroes and Villains of the West*. New York: Metro Books, 1996

Trachtman, Paul. *The Gunfighters*. Alexandria: Time-Life Books, 1974

Wallace, Robert. *The Miners*. Alexandria: Time-Life Books, 1976

THE LONG BRANCH SALOON'S SPECTACULAR FRAY

Carter, Samuel, III. *Cowboy Capital of the World: The Saga of Dodge City*. Garden City: Doubleday, 1973

Patterson, Richard. *Historical Atlas of the Outlaw West*. Boulder: Johnson Books, 1985

Rosa, Joseph G. *Age of the Gunfighter*. Norman: University of Oklahoma Press, 1995

Vestal, Stanley. *Dodge City, Queen of Cowtowns*. New York: Harper, 1952

SHOOT-OUT AT THE TUTTLE DANCE HALL

Drago, Harry Sinclair. *The Legend Makers*. New York: Dodd, Mead, 1975

Patterson, Richard. *Historical Atlas of the Outlaw West*. Boulder: Johnson Books, 1985

Rosa, Joseph G. *Age of the Gunfighter*. Norman: University of Oklahoma Press, 1995

Trachtman, Paul. *The Gunfighters*. Alexandria: Time-Life Books, 1974

LEVY, THE UNDERRATED GUNFIGHTER

Patterson, Richard. *Historical Atlas of the Outlaw West*. Boulder: Johnson Books, 1985

Secrest, William B. "Jim Levy: Top-notch Gunfighter." *True West*, July/August, 1978

Thrapp, Dan L. *Encyclopedia of Frontier Biography*, Vol. II. Lincoln: University of Nebraska Press, 1988

Wolle, Muriel Sibell. *The Bonanza Trail: Ghost Towns and Mining Camps of the West*. Chicago: Sage Books, 1953

THE CAPTURE OF "BLACKFACE CHARLEY" BRYANT

Breihan, Carl W. *Outlaws of the Old West*. New York: Bonanza Books, 1957

Drago, Harry Sinclair. *Outlaws on Horseback*. New York: Bramhall House, 1964

———. *Road Agents and Train Robbers*. New York: Dodd, Mead, 1973

Johnson, Dorothy M. *Western Badmen*. New York: Dodd, Mead, 1970

Raine, William MacLeod. *Famous Sheriffs and Western Outlaws*. New York: Doubleday, 1929

BATTLE FOR THE COUNTY SEAT

Arnold, Anna E. *A History of Kansas*. Topeka: State of Kansas, 1920

Cain, Del. *Lawmen of the Old West*. Plano: Republic of Texas Press, 2000

Horan, James D. *The Authentic Wild West: The Lawmen*. New York: Crown, 1980

Miller, Floyd. *Bill Tilghman: Marshal of the Last Frontier*. Garden City: Doubleday, 1968

Rabinowitz, Harold. *Black Hats and White Hats*. New York: Metro Books, 1996

Rosa, Joseph G. *Age of the Gunfighter*. Norman: University of Oklahoma Press, 1995

Thrapp, Dan L. *Encyclopedia of Frontier Biography*, Vol. III. Lincoln: University of Nebraska Press, 1988

THE LAST DALTON RAID

Breihan, Carl W. *Outlaws of the Old West*. New York: Bonanza Books, 1957

Bruns, Roger A. *The Bandit Kings*. New York: Crown, 1995

Drago, Harry Sinclair. *Outlaws on Horseback*. New York: Bramhall House, 1964

———. *Road Agents and Train Robbers*. New York: Dodd, Mead, 1973

Horan, James D. *The Authentic Wild West: The Outlaws*. New York: Crown, 1977

Johnson, Dorothy M. *Western Badmen*. New York: Dodd, Mead, 1970

Metz, Leon Claire. *The Shooters*. New York: Berkley Books, 1996

Rabinowitz, Harold. *Black Hats and White Hats*. New York: Metro Books, 1996

Rosa, Joseph G. *Age of the Gunfighter*. Norman: University of Oklahoma Press, 1995

BAT MASTERSON AND THE BATTLE OF THE PLAZA

Carter, Samuel, III. *Cowboy Capital of the World: The Saga of Dodge City*. Garden City: Doubleday, 1973

DeArment, Robert K. *Bat Masterson: The Man and the Legend*. Norman: University of Oklahoma Press, 1979

Drago, Harry Sinclair. *The Legend Makers*. New York: Dodd, Mead, 1975

Horan, James D. *The Authentic Wild West: The Lawmen*. New York: Crown Publishers, 1980

Rabinowitz, Harold. *Black Hats and White Hats: Heroes and Villains of the West*. New York: Metro Books, 1996

Trachtman, Paul. *The Gunfighters*. Alexandria: Time-Life Books, 1974

Vestal, Stanley. *Dodge City, Queen of Cowtowns*. New York: Harper, 1952

THE YOUNGER BROTHERS–PINKERTONS SHOOT-OUT

Breihan, Carl W. *Outlaws of the Old West*. New York: Bonanza Books, 1957

———. *Younger Brothers*. San Antonio: The Naylor Company, 1961

Bruns, Roger A. *The Bandit Kings*. New York: Crown, 1995

Drago, Harry Sinclair. *Outlaws on Horseback*. New York: Bramhall House, 1964

———. *Road Agents and Train Robbers*. New York: Dodd, Mead, 1973

Horan, James D. *The Authentic Wild West: The Outlaws*. New York: Crown, 1977

Johnson, Dorothy M. *Western Badmen*. New York: Dodd, Mead, 1970

Metz, Leon Claire. *The Shooters*. New York: Berkley Books, 1996

THE SAM BASS GANG'S LUCK RUNS OUT

Bruns, Roger A. *The Bandit Kings*. New York: Crown Publishers, 1995

Frontier Times. "Outlaws: Sam Bass," http://www.frontiertimes.com/outlaws/bass.html

Handbook of Texas Online, "Sam Bass," http://www.tsha.utexas.edu/handbook/online/articles/view/BB/fbaab.html

Hendricks, George. *The Badman of the West*. San Antonio: The Naylor Company, 1970

Horan, James D. *The Authentic Wild West: The Outlaws*. New York: Crown Publishers, 1977

Johnson, Dorothy M. *Western Badmen*. New York: Dodd, Mead, 1970

Robinson, Charles M., III. *The Men Who Wear the Star: The Story of the Texas Rangers*. New York: Random House, 2000

Unknown, "The Story of Sam Bass," http://www.ci.round-rock.tx.us/planning/rrcollection/mainstreet/sambass/

DIABLO CANYON TRACKDOWN

Drago, Harry Sinclair. *The Legend Makers*. New York: Dodd, Mead, 1975

Patterson, Richard. *Historical Atlas of the Outlaw West*. Boulder: Johnson Books, 1985

Rosa, Joseph G. *Age of the Gunfighter*. Norman: University of Oklahoma Press, 1995

Thrapp, Dan L. *Encyclopedia of Frontier Biography*, Vol. II. Lincoln: University of Nebraska Press, 1988

Trachtman, Paul. *The Gunfighters*. Alexandria: Time-Life Books, 1974

CALIFORNIA'S MOST WANTED OUTLAW

Horan, James D. *The Authentic Wild West: The Outlaws*. New York: Crown, 1977

Patterson, Richard. *Historical Atlas of the Outlaw West*. Boulder: Johnson Books, 1985

Unknown, "Berton Mills Tibbet," http://www.ci.bakersfield.ca.us/police/Chiefs/Berton_Mills_Tibbet.htm

Unknown, "Packard, Thomas J. & Tibbet, William E.," http://www.camemorial.org/htmprev/packard.htm

Unknown, "Porterville Celebrating 100th Birthday," *Visalia Times-Delta*, http://www.visaliatimesdelta.com/communities/sesquicentennial/200207713/292948.html

Unknown, "Thomas Jefferson Packard," http://www.ci.bakersfield.ca.us/police/Chiefs/Thomas_Jefferson_Packard.htm

GUNFIGHT AT STONE CORRAL

Bruns, Roger A. *The Bandit Kings*. New York: Crown Publishers, 1995

Patterson, Richard. *Historical Atlas of the Outlaw West*. Boulder: Johnson Books, 1985

Smith, Wallace. *Prodigal Sons.* Boston: Christopher Publishing House, 1951

THE DOOLIN BUNCH VS. THE U.S. MARSHALS
Breihan, Carl W. *Outlaws of the Old West.* New York: Bonanza Books, 1957
Bruns, Roger A. *The Bandit Kings.* New York: Crown Publishers, 1995
Drago, Harry Sinclair. *Outlaws on Horseback.* New York: Bramhall House, 1964
Horan, James D. *The Authentic Wild West: The Outlaws.* New York: Crown, 1977
Johnson, Dorothy M. *Western Badmen.* New York: Dodd, Mead, 1970
Kerr, William Ray. "In Defense of Ingalls, Oklahoma." *True West,* October 1964
Miller, Floyd. *Bill Tilghman: Marshal of the Last Frontier.* Garden City: Doubleday, 1968
Raine, William MacLeod. *Famous Sheriffs and Western Outlaws.* New York: Doubleday, 1929
Terrell, Ron. "Heck Thomas," *Guns and the Gunfighters.* New York: Bonanza Books, 1982
———. "The Dalton-Doolin Gang," *Guns and the Gunfighters.* New York: Bonanza Books, 1982

BUNGLED BANK ROBBERY
Lyttle, R. G. "The Meeker Bank Robbery October 13, 1896." *The Rio Blanco Historical Society,* May 1965
Patterson, Richard. *Historical Atlas of the Outlaw West.* Boulder: Johnson Books, 1985

THE CAPTURE OF "BLACK JACK" KETCHUM
Bruns, Roger A. *The Bandit Kings.* New York: Crown Publishers, 1995
Hovey, Walter C. "Black Jack Ketchum Tried to Give Me a Break!" *True West,* March/April 1972
Metz, Leon Claire. *The Shooters.* New York: Berkley Books, 1996
Patterson, Richard. *Historical Atlas of the Outlaw West.* Boulder: Johnson Books, 1985
Romero, Trancito. "I Saw Black Jack Hanged." *True West,* September/October 1958
Unknown, "Tom 'Black Jack' Ketchum," http://www.geocities.com/folsom_museum/ketchum.html

THE BANK-ROBBIN'EST OUTLAW IN AMERICA

Adelsbach, Lee. "Henry Starr: Thumbs Up and Stand Ready!" *Guns and the Gunfighters*. New York: Bonanza Books, 1982

Bruns, Roger A. *The Bandit Kings*. New York: Crown Publishers, 1995

Drago, Harry Sinclair. *Outlaws on Horseback*. New York: Bramhall House, 1964

Johnson, Dorothy M. *Western Badmen*. New York: Dodd, Mead, 1970

Shirley, Glenn. *Henry Starr: Last of the Real Badmen*. New York: David McKay, 1965

Young, Richard, and Dockery Young, Judy, eds. *Outlaw Tales*, Little Rock: August House, 1992

EXPRESS COMPANY FRAUD

Anderson, H. Allen. "McGee, Thomas T." *The Handbook of Texas Online*, http://www.tsha.utexas.edu/handbook/online/articles/view/MM/fmcbz.html

Patterson, Richard. *Historical Atlas of the Outlaw West*. Boulder: Johnson Books, 1985

Stanley, F. (Stanley F. Crocchiola). *Rodeo Town (Canadian, Texas)*. Denver: World Press, 1953

THE MAN WHO KILLED THE MAN WHO KILLED JESSE JAMES

Cloud, Jim. "Dead: The Man Who Killed the Man Who Killed Jesse James," http://www.theoldwestwebride.com/txt1A/edkelly.html

Horan, James D. *The Authentic Wild West: The Outlaws*. New York: Crown Publishers, 1977

Johnson, Dorothy M. *Western Badmen*. New York: Dodd, Mead, 1970

Terrell, Ron. "The James/Younger Gang," *Guns and the Gunfighters*. New York: Bonanza Books, 1982

Unknown, "Bob Ford: Dirty Little Coward," http://ri.essortment.com/bobfordjesse_rzfk.htm

MAKE SURE YOUR MAN IS DEAD!

Boren, Kerry Ross. "Jack Slade's Grave Located," *Frontier Times*, April/May 1976

Johnson, Dorothy M. *Western Badmen*. New York: Dodd, Mead, 1970

Patterson, Richard. *Historical Atlas of the Outlaw West*. Boulder: Johnson Books, 1985

Rosa, Joseph G. *Age of the Gunfighter*. Norman: University of Oklahoma Press, 1995

Thrapp, Dan L. *Encyclopedia of Frontier Biography*, Vol. III. Lincoln: University of Nebraska Press, 1988

PAT GARRETT'S MYSTERIOUS DEATH
Drago, Harry Sinclair. *The Legend Makers*. New York: Dodd, Mead, 1975
Hurst, James W. "The Death of Pat Garrett," http://www.southern newmexico.com/snm/garrett.html
Metz, Leon Claire. *The Shooters*. New York: Berkley Books, 1996
Patterson, Richard. *Historical Atlas of the Outlaw West*. Boulder: Johnson Books, 1985
Rabinowitz, Harold. *Black Hats and White Hats: Heroes and Villains of the West*. New York: Metro Books, 1996

THE END OF THE NOTORIOUS JOHN WESLEY HARDIN
Carter, Harlon. "John Henry Selman." *Guns and the Gunfighters*. New York: Bonanza Books, 1982
Hardin, John Wesley. *The Life of John Wesley Hardin, as Written by Himself*. Norman: University of Oklahoma Press, 1961
Horan, James D. *The Authentic Wild West: The Gunfighters*. New York: Crown, 1976
Johnson, Dorothy M. *Western Badmen*. New York: Dodd, Mead, 1970
Lachuk, John. "John Wesley Hardin." *Guns and the Gunfighters*. New York: Bonanza Books, 1982
Marcello, Patricia Cronin, and Hart, Louis. "Did Gunfighters Hickok and Hardin Have a Showdown in Abilene?" *Wild West*, April 1998
Metz, Leon. *John Wesley Hardin: Dark Angel of Texas*. Norman: University of Oklahoma Press, 1996
Rabinowitz, Harold. *Black Hats and White Hats: Heroes and Villains of the West*. New York: Metro Books, 1996
Raine, William MacLeod. *Famous Sheriffs and Western Outlaws*. New York: Doubleday, 1929
Robinson, Charles M., III. *The Men Who Wear the Star: The Story of the Texas Rangers*. New York: Random House, 2000
Trachtman, Paul. *The Gunfighters*. Alexandria: Time-Life Books, 1974

BEN THOMPSON AND THE VAUDEVILLE AMBUSH
Breihan, Carl W. *Outlaws of the Old West*. New York: Bonanza Books, 1957
Drago, Harry Sinclair. *The Legend Makers*. New York: Dodd, Mead, 1975
Horan, James D. *The Authentic Wild West: The Gunfighters*. New York: Crown, 1976

Johnson, Dorothy M. *Western Badmen*. New York: Dodd, Mead, 1970

Metz, Leon Claire. *The Shooters*. New York: Berkley Books, 1996

Rosa, Joseph G. *Age of the Gunfighter*. Norman: University of Oklahoma Press, 1995

Streeter, Floyd B. *Ben Thompson: Man with a Gun*. New York: Frederick Fell, 1957

Trachtman, Paul. *The Gunfighters*. Alexandria: Time-Life Books, 1974

THAT WASN'T CLAY ALLISON

Hendricks, George. *The Badman of the West*. San Antonio: The Naylor Company, 1970

McLoughlin, Denis. *Wild & Woolly: An Encyclopedia of the Old West*. Garden City: Doubleday, 1975

Rabinowitz, Harold. *Black Hats and White Hats: Heroes and Villains of the West*. New York, Metro Books, 1996

Stanley, F. (Stanley F. Crocchiola). *Clay Allison*. Denver: World Press, 1956

Trachtman, Paul. *The Gunfighters*. Alexandria: Time-Life Books, 1974

WILD BILL'S TRAGIC MISTAKE

Adare, Sierra. "Interview: Joseph G. Rosa." *Wild West*, April 1998

Drago, Harry Sinclair. *The Legend Makers*. New York: Dodd, Mead, 1975

Dunham, Jim. "James Butler Hickok: Prince of Pistoleers," *Guns and the Gunfighters*. New York: Bonanza Books, 1982

Hart, Louis. "Wild Bill Hickok Had a Way with Six-Shooters." *Wild West*, April 2000

Horan, James D. *The Authentic Wild West: The Gunfighters*. New York: Crown, 1976

Marcello, Patricia Cronin, and Hart, Louis. "Did Gunfighters Hickok and Hardin Have a Showdown in Abilene?" *Wild West*, April 1998

O'Conner, Richard. *Wild Bill Hickok*. Garden City: Doubleday, 1959

Rabinowitz, Harold. *Black Hats and White Hats: Heroes and Villains of the West*. New York, Metro Books, 1996

Raine, William MacLeod. *Famous Sheriffs and Western Outlaws*. New York: Doubleday, 1929

Rosa, Joseph G. *They Called Him Wild Bill: The Life and Adventures of James Butler Hickok*. Norman: University of Oklahoma Press, 1974

———. *Wild Bill Hickok: The Man and His Myth*. Lawrence: University Press of Kansas, 1996

Trachtman, Paul. *The Gunfighters*. Alexandria: Time-Life Books, 1974

Young, Richard, and Young, Judy Dockery, eds. *Outlaw Tales*. Little Rock: August House, 1992

ROURKE'S BAD LUCK ROBBERY

Carter, Samuel, III. *Cowboy Capital of the World: The Saga of Dodge City*. Garden City: Doubleday, 1973

DeArment, Robert K. *Bat Masterson: The Man and the Legend*. Norman: University of Oklahoma Press, 1979

Horan, James D. *The Authentic Wild West: The Lawmen*. New York: Crown Publishers, 1980

Rabinowitz, Harold. *Black Hats and White Hats: Heroes and Villains of the West*. New York: Metro Books, 1996

Thrapp, Dan L. *Encyclopedia of Frontier Biography*, Vol. II. Lincoln: University of Nebraska Press, 1988

Trachtman, Paul. *The Gunfighters*. Alexandria: Time-Life Books, 1974

Vestal, Stanley. *Dodge City, Queen of Cowtowns*. New York: Harper, 1952

WICHITA'S NEW YEAR'S DAY GUNFIGHT

Drago, Harry Sinclair. *The Legend Makers*. New York: Dodd, Mead, 1975

Patterson, Richard. *Historical Atlas of the Outlaw West*. Boulder: Johnson Books, 1985

Thrapp, Dan L. *Encyclopedia of Frontier Biography*, Vol. II. Lincoln: University of Nebraska Press, 1988

MILLER AND FRAZER, FIGHTING AGAIN

Metz, Leon Claire. *The Shooters*. New York: Berkley Books, 1996

Patterson, Richard. *Historical Atlas of the Outlaw West*. Boulder: Johnson Books, 1985

Pool, William C. *A Historical Atlas of Texas*. Austin: Encino Press, 1975

Trachtman, Paul. *The Gunfighters*. Alexandria: Time-Life Books, 1974

BULLET TO BULLET

Anonymous. *The "Five States" Guide to Texas*. Dallas: Five States of Texas, Inc., 1963

Patterson, Richard. *Historical Atlas of the Outlaw West*. Boulder: Johnson Books, 1985

Pool, William C. *A Historical Atlas of Texas*. Austin: Encino Press, 1975

Thrapp, Dan L. *Encyclopedia of Frontier Biography*. Vol. III. Lincoln: University of Nebraska Press, 1988

ABOUT THE AUTHOR

James Reasoner is the author of the Spur Award–nominated novels *Cossack Three Ponies* and *Under Outlaw Flags*, both published by Berkley Books, as well as the *Civil War Battles* series and *The Last Good War*, a series of novels about World War II. A professional writer for more than twenty-five years, he has written everything from mysteries to science fiction and fantasy. As a lifelong Texan, he has a deep and abiding interest in the West and its history. He lives in a small town with his wife Livia, also known as the award-winning mystery and Western novelist L. J. Washburn, and their two daughters.

Draw! is Reasoner's first work of nonfiction.